E… …NALS

2

3

Educating Professionals
Practice Learning in Health and Social Care

Edited by

MARK DOEL
Sheffield Hallam University, UK

and

STEVEN M. SHARDLOW
University of Salford, UK

ASHGATE

Published by
Ashgate Publishing Limited
Wey Court East
Union Road
Farnham ·
Surrey GU9 7PT
England

Ashgate Publishing Company
Suite 420
101 Cherry Street
Burlington, VT 05401-4405
USA

www.ashgate.com

British Library Cataloguing in Publication Data
Educating professionals : practice learning in health and
    social care
    1. Medicine - Study and teaching 2. Experiential learning -
    Case studies 3. Medical personnel - Training of
    4. Interprofessional relations
    I. Doel, Mark II. Shardlow, Steven, 1952-
    610.7'155

Library of Congress Cataloging-in-Publication Data
Educating professionals : practice learning in health and social care / [edited] by
Mark Doel and Steven M. Shardlow.
        p. ; cm.
    Includes bibliographical references and index.
    ISBN 978-0-7546-4810-9 (hardback) -- ISBN 978-0-7546-4811-6 (pbk.)
    1. Medical education. 2. Social work education. I. Doel, Mark. II. Shardlow,
Steven, 1952-
    [DNLM: 1. Education, Professional--methods. 2. Health Care Sector. 3.
Community Health Services. 4. Internship, Nonmedical--methods. 5. Learning. 6.
Social Work. W 18 E24495 2009]

    R737.E286 2009
    610.71'1--dc22

                                                                        2008054353

ISBN 978-0-7546-4810-9 (Hardback)
ISBN 978-0-7546-4811-6 (Paperback)
ISBN 978-0-7546-9063-4 (E-book)

Mixed Sources
Product group from well-managed
forests and other controlled sources
www.fsc.org Cert no. SGS-COC-2482
© 1996 Forest Stewardship Council
FSC

Printed and bound in Great Britain by
TJ International Ltd, Padstow, Cornwall

Contents

List of figures

List of tables

About the contributors

Auldeen Alsop, BA, MPhil, EdD, DipCOT, FCOT, is Professor of Occupational Therapy at Sheffield Hallam University. She also currently holds an Adjunct Professorship at the University of Alberta, Canada. Her career in occupational therapy has spanned over 27 years, with experience in practice, management, education and research. She has worked with the College of Occupational Therapists in many capacities and is currently chairing the Learning and Development Board of the College. As a result, she holds a seat on the Council of the British Association and College of Occupational Therapists. Auldeen has published widely on topics such as practice education, continuing professional development and work-based learning. In 2006 she was awarded a Fellowship of the College of Occupational Therapists for her contribution to the profession.

Shelagh Brumfitt, MPhil, PhD, CertMRCSLT (Hons), RegHPC, is a Professor in Speech and Language Therapy Education at the University of Sheffield where she was the Programme Director for the BMedSci (Speech) from 1992 to 2003. She has a long-standing interest in approaches to professional education. From 1997 to 1999 she was Chair of the Academic Board of the Royal College of Speech and Language Therapists and was awarded the Honours of the Royal College of Speech and Language Therapists in 2006. In 2007 she was awarded a University of Sheffield Senate Award for Sustained Excellence in Teaching and Learning. Her clinical research interests focus on the psychosocial effects of communication impairments.

Val Collington, DipNursing, MSc, PhD, MTD, RM, RN, is the Head of School of Midwifery in the Faculty of Health and Social Care Sciences, Kingston University/St George's, University of London. She is experienced in planning, implementing and evaluating midwifery education programmes at undergraduate and postgraduate levels. As the Nursing and Midwifery Council Lead Midwife for Education her role includes taking responsibility for students' learning in both the academic and practice contexts. She has held senior education management/leadership posts over the past ten years, including a current position as Associate Dean within a multi-professional faculty. Her research interests are in reflection in midwifery education and practice, and learning from experience.

Mark Doel, MA (Oxon), PhD, CQSW, DipAppSocStud, is Research Professor of Social Work in the Centre for Health and Social Care at Sheffield Hallam University. He has almost 20 years' experience as a social work practitioner and practice teacher working in community-based settings in England and the US. He is co-editor of *Groupwork* journal and an elected member of the international Association for the Advancement of Social Work with Groups. His research interests focus on practice methods (especially groupwork and task-centred practices), practice education, international comparative social work and evaluative research, particularly service user and carer involvement. His publications include 13 books, several in foreign translation.

Beryl Gillespie, BA (Hons), MSc, GradDipPhys, MCSP, RegHPC, is an Honorary Lecturer in physiotherapy at the School of Allied Health Professions, Faculty of Health, University of East Anglia. She is a member of the Chartered Society of Physiotherapy with a special interest in clinical education and health and social care management. Previously an NHS and private sector physiotherapy manager, she now works as Head of Older People's Services for a registered social landlord in Cambridgeshire.

Cheryl Gray, BSc, PGCert (Aphasia), PGCert (MedEd), MRCSLT, RegHPC, is Practice Learning Director in the Department of Human Communication Sciences at the University of Sheffield, where she has worked since 1995 organizing and developing the practice learning components of the pre-registration speech and language therapy courses. Prior to moving into the higher education sector she worked for 11 years in NHS settings with roles in practice and management. Her academic interests are professional education and practice learning.

Fran Jones, BA (Hons) Nurse Education, MA, SCPHN, DNCert, RN, FHEA, is Principal Lecturer for Work-Based and Employer-Led Learning in the School of Health and Social Sciences at the University of Bolton, where she has worked since 1994 developing and delivering the specialist community nursing programmes, in particular Health Visiting (now Specialist Community Public Health Nursing). Prior to entering the education profession she worked for 16 years as a health visitor. Her other developments have been in the educational provision of non-medical prescribing, continuing professional development programmes and new foundation and master's degrees, with the 'Delivering the Workforce' initiative for Greater Manchester. Current academic interests are public health and her newly defined role in work-based practice.

John Keady, PhD, RMN, RNT, is Professor of Older People's Mental Health Nursing, a joint appointment between the University of Manchester and the Greater Manchester West Mental Health NHS Foundation Trust. John trained as a Registered Mental Nurse at Warley Hospital, Brentwood, Essex, between 1983 and 1986, before moving to North Wales and working as a Community Mental Health Nurse in a community dementia team. From this time he has maintained an active research, publication and teaching profile in dementia care. John is founding and co-editor of *Dementia: The International Journal of Social Research and Practice* and the first edition of this quarterly Sage journal was published in February 2002.

Kate Leonard, BA, MSW, CQSW, AASW, PT, CLTHE, is Course Director for the Practice Education Programme (Nursing and Social Work) at London South Bank University. She also teaches for the Post-Graduate Certificates in Higher Education and Medical Education. She is a qualified social worker and has extensive experience of supervising staff and students. Until recently she also worked part-time as a Children's Guardian. She works as a freelance mentor, coach, work-based assessor, trainer and consultant in health and social care. She has written about the development of interprofessional practice education courses, the use of direct observation as a method of assessment and has recently co-authored a book entitled *Leadership and Management in Social Care*.

Joyce Lishman, MA (Oxon), PhD, DipSW (Ed), is Professor and Head of School of Applied Social Studies, The Robert Gordon University, Aberdeen. She is the General Editor of the 'Research Highlights in Social Work' series and has a particular interest in evaluation, research and evidence-based practice and how they are utilized in social work practice. Her most recent publications are *The Handbook for Practice Learning in Social Work and Care* and *Communication in Social Work*.

Deborah G. Murdoch-Eaton, MBBS, MD, FRCPCH, NTF, is Professor of Medical Education at the University of Leeds and an honorary consultant neuro-paediatrician at Leeds Teaching Hospitals Trust and Primary Care Trust. She graduated from St Mary's Hospital Medical School, University of London. After initial paediatric training in London at Great Ormond Street and Hammersmith Hospitals, she moved to Leeds, intending to pursue a career in academic neonatal neurology. Instead, her interest in undergraduate education was sparked, resulting in the creation of a new Senior Lecturer post within the evolving Medical Education Unit in Leeds, combined with a Consultant post to develop a regional rehabilitation service for children after acquired brain injury. She was awarded a personal Chair in 2002, and a National Teaching Fellowship in 2004. Her research interests include the development of lifelong learning/generic skills, enhancing individuality and excellence and mechanisms for effective feedback. From 2004 she has been undertaking consultancy and development work in a number of medical schools in developing countries.

Barbara Richardson, MSc, PhD, DipTP, FCSP, is Reader in Physiotherapy at the School of Allied Health Professions, Faculty of Health, University of East Anglia. She is a Fellow of the Chartered Society of Physiotherapy, Foreign Adjunct Professor of Physiotherapy at the Karolinska Institute, Stockholm, Sweden, and associate editor-in-chief of *Advances in Physiotherapy*. Her research interests are in education and professional development, in particular in the development of professional knowledge, situated learning, professional socialization and work in interprofessional teams. She has published many papers on these topics and is co-author of *Developing Practice Knowledge for Health Professions* (Elsevier, 2004).

Trudie E. Roberts, BSc, MBChB, PhD, FRCP, NTF, is Professor of Medical Education, Head of the School of Medicine, and Director of the Medical Education Unit, University of Leeds. She graduated from Manchester with a degree in medicine and a BSc in anatomy. After early medical training in Manchester and her research in Manchester and the Karolinska Institute in Sweden she was appointed as Senior Lecturer in Transplant Immunology at the University of Manchester. In 2000 she was appointed Professor of Medical Education and Director of the Medical Education Unit at the University of Leeds. Her main research interests are assessment of competence development of expertise and professionalism. She examines for the GMC and is a GMC visitor for medical school undergraduate courses and a PMETB collaborator. She sits on the executive committees of the Association for the Study of Medical Education and the Association of Medical Education in Europe. In 2005 she became the Director of the Centre for Excellence in Learning and Teaching focused on Assessment and Learning in Practice Settings which involves five higher education institutions. In 2005 she was awarded a National Teaching Fellowship. In January 2006 she took up the role of Head of the School of Medicine in Leeds.

Sandra M. Rowan, MA, DipCOT, is Deputy Director and Access and Progression Coordinator at the North East Higher Skills Network. Since qualifying as an occupational therapist she has worked in a wide range of clinical settings, gaining experience in all aspects of practice including management and education. Sandra worked for five years as Senior Lecturer/Professional Practice Coordinator for the Occupational Therapy programmes at York St John University, going on to join the education team at NHS North East. Her current role in the North East Higher Skills Network is concerned with developing access and progression opportunities into and through higher education. She has worked extensively on the European

Occupational Therapy Tuning Project and continues to be a member of the British Association of Occupational Therapists. Her academic interests are in work-based learning, interprofessional learning and continuing professional development at all levels.

Steven M. Shardlow, MA(Oxon), MSc (Oxon), PhD, CQSW, AASW, RSW, FHEA, is Foundation holder of the Chair of Social Work at the University of Salford, UK, where until recently he was Director of the Institute for Health and Social Care Research. He has held academic appointments in Norway, Italy, is currently visiting Chair Professor at Hong Kong Polytechnic University, and in the UK he is director of a Social Work masters professional qualification programme. He is founding editor-in-chief of the *Journal of Social Work*. Previously Chairperson of The Association of Teachers of Social Work Education (ATSWE-UK) and UK representative on the Executive Committee of the European Association of Schools of Social Work (EASSW), he has worked as a social work practitioner and manager. He is a registered social worker in England and has worked extensively in international social work, through research, consultancy and development work. Current research interests are in the following areas: evidence-based policy and practice, particularly in respect of social work with children and families and older people; welfare and social capital; applied professional ethics; comparative research in social work; professional knowledge and education. He has published widely in these fields, including 15 books, and his work has been translated into several languages.

Jenny Spouse, MSc, PhD, DipNursing (London), CertEd, CertTeaching in Higher Education, SCM, RGNT, RCNT, RN, was until recently the Associate Dean for Practice Education at St Bartholomew School of Nursing and Midwifery, City University, London. In this role she had responsibility for pre-registration nursing and midwifery students' clinical practice placements across central and east London. A nurse and qualified midwife, Jenny worked in cardio-thoracic surgical units and intensive care units in Canada, Australia and the Yemen, before rejoining the NHS and subsequently becoming an academic. She was a link lecturer throughout her academic career and a member of the Nursing and Midwifery Board of two NHS acute hospital foundation trusts as well as member of an NHS foundation trust board. Over many years she was external examiner to pre- and post-qualification programmes, including master's level and teacher preparation courses. She was a visitor for the Nursing and Midwifery Council and is Lay Chair of the Accreditation Board for the National Institute of Medical Herbalists. She is a research supervisor for health care students at the Open University. She is on the editorial board of two leading health care journals and has published and edited several books and journal articles on professional education and mentorship as they relate to professional development in practice settings.

Rachel Thompson, BA (Hons), RGN, RMN, is the National Practice Development Lead for Admiral Nursing, as supported by the charity 'for dementia'. As a nurse she has worked for 20 years across a range of settings, specializing in the care of people with dementia and their families. Rachel has acted as Chair for the Higher Education for Dementia Network (HEDN), a national network of lecturers involved in the delivery of dementia education, since 2004. She has co-authored and published a number of articles on the provision of dementia education for health and social care professionals.

Jenny Weinstein, BPhil (Social Work), MSc (Interprofessional Health and Welfare), CTL, HE, is Director of Interprofessional Projects at London South Bank University. Before becoming an academic in 2004, her career spanned practice, training and management roles in local authorities, leading for the Social Work Education Council on practice learning/interprofessional education and involving senior management in the voluntary sector. Jenny is a member of the editorial board of the *Journal for Interprofessional Care* and has written a number of publications on interprofessional working and learning, social work education and, more recently, mental health. Current research/publication projects are service user involvement in mental health and evaluation of joint qualification programmes.

Foreword

Government asserts, regulatory bodies require and professional associations expect courses leading to health and social care qualifications in the United Kingdom (UK) to include interprofessional learning. Universities respond in partnership with employing agencies which contribute shared learning opportunities to enhance understanding and improve collaboration between professions.

But work-based learning for each profession has its own culture, customs and conventions which can compound endeavours by teachers and practice educators to devise and deliver shared practice between two, let alone several, professions. This book makes their task less daunting. It offers a model for work-based learning which holds the promise to reconcile competing perceptions and expectations, informed by descriptors to facilitate comparison between nine of the health and social care professions most often included, enlivened by frequent visits with students to residents in 'Derby Street'.

The model focuses on learning in community settings where relationships between professions may be more flexible than in hospitals and opportunities greater for learning that transcends professional boundaries. That equates with the rationale for interprofessional learning conceived in the UK and other countries during the 1960s in response to complexities of need and ambiguities in professional relationships in newly created primary and community care services. Woe betide us if we neglect also to provide interprofessional learning in hospitals in view of reports attributing the abuse of long-stay patients and the untoward death of babies following heart surgery to lapses in collaboration, but the case is compelling for all entrants to the health and social care professions, regardless of the settings in which they may work later, to have at least one experience of work-based learning in a community. Only then may they discover what it means to respond to people on their own territory and their own terms, to mobilize restorative resources in families and neighbourhoods, to work with professions beyond institutional walls and to follow the patient's journey from community to hospital and back.

This book is an authoritative and indispensable source wherever teachers, practice educators and their managers recognize that need. More support than ever is available to help them design and deliver effective professional and interprofessional teaching and learning in the classroom and the workplace. Thanks to finance from the Higher Education Funding

Council for England (HEFCE), the following are possible: three of the subject centres of the Higher Education Academy commission interprofessional projects, disseminate papers and arrange workshops; many of the Centres of Excellence in Teaching and Learning (CETLs) focus on health, including ALPS (Assessment and Learning in Practice Settings) which strives to improve work-based learning within and across professional boundaries (www.alps-cetl.ac.uk); while findings from the PIPE project (Promoting Interprofessional Education) explain the role of facilitator (Howkins and Bray, 2008). Thanks to the Department of Health, four leading-edge sites for interprofessional education were piloted, three of which focused on work-based learning (Barr, 2007). Thanks to the Economic and Social Research Council (ESRC), four other English universities are mounting a rolling programme of workshops to synthesize theoretical perspectives for interprofessional learning and practice (shean@bournemouth.ac.uk).

Thanks above all to Mark, Steven and their fellow scribes, we have a timely and much-needed text to complement these other resources, packed with information about professions and their education systems, and pregnant with implications for new and better professional and interprofessional work-based learning, responsive to the needs of students and, through them, the individuals, families and communities whom they serve.

Hugh Barr
President
The UK Centre for the Advancement of Interprofessional Education
Emeritus Professor of Interprofessional Education
University of Westminster
September 2008

Core text recommendations

Barr, H. (ed.) (2007), *Piloting Interprofessional Education: Four English case studies* (London: Higher Education Academy: Health Sciences and Practice). Available at: www.health.heacademy.ac.uk.
Howkins, E., and Bray, J. (2008), *Preparing for Interprofessional Teaching: Theory and practice* (Oxford: Radcliffe Medical Press).

Preface

Before the reader visits the body of the book we would like to highlight some key issues.

- Our central focus is on the education of professionals at the pre-qualifying and pre-registration level – the people we know as 'students'. However, in each of the profession-specific chapters, authors also briefly consider issues concerning continuing professional development (continuing education) for qualified practitioners and the training that can be expected for practice educators themselves. In the final chapter Leonard and Weinstein focus on these issues in the context of interprofessional practice.
- In recent years, in England and Wales, there has been a realignment of some services into children's services (for example, with education and children's social work combining), mental health services and adults' services. This has a critical impact on practice education; whereas most academic components of training programmes remain generic, the opportunities for practice learning in agencies are now considerably specialist. These tensions are reflected in this book, but the full implications of these organizational changes on the practice education of professionals are yet to be realized and await a future text.
- The book has an unapologetic emphasis on practice education in community settings. 'Derby Street', the community with which the reader will become familiar, highlights the role of the community not just as the backcloth for students' learning but as an active and key player in the education of new professionals. Though we understand the community to have a particular and special role to play in the education of practitioners, we do not mean to diminish the importance of clinical and institutional settings for practice learning; indeed, interprofessional practice and learning is just as important an ingredient of good practice in these settings as it is in the community.
- We have reflected on the role of Derby Street (described in Chapter 2) as a kind of independent editor for all of us, editors and contributors. Coming from the same professional background, it has been important for the editors to take care not to privilege that profession (social work) and Derby Street has helped this.
- The countries of the UK are moving in increasingly varied directions as the full effects of devolution are felt. The contributions to the book

are cited within the UK and mostly in England (one chapter, on social work, is set in the context of Scotland). Even so, the messages in this book have implications that are relevant outside these shores and Derby Street could be located in many places.

- The nine professions which are represented in the book are intended to be indicative rather than representative; not only are there other professions in the health and social care family, but there are also many others with whom health and social care practitioners work – especially in the fields of education, youth and community, and the law. Exploration of practice education in these other fields falls outside our scope and awaits a further volume. The chapters that tell of the individual professions (Chapters 3–11) are ordered solely alphabetically so readers may wish to read them in their personally preferred order.

Mark Doel and Steven M. Shardlow
Sheffield and Salford 2009

List of acronyms

ACE	Accreditation of Clinical Educators Scheme
ALPS	Assessment and Learning in Practice Settings
AMEE	Association for Medical Education in Europe
APPLE	Accreditation of Practice Placement Educators Scheme
ASME	Association for the Study of Medical Education
CATS	Credit Accumulation Transfer Scheme
CCETSW	Central Council for Education and Training of Social Workers (*no longer in existence*)
CCT	Certificate of Completion of Training
CDE	Curriculum for Dementia Education
CETHV	Council for Education and Training of Health Visitors (*no longer in existence*)
CETSW	Council for Education and Training of Social Workers (*no longer in existence*)
CFP	Common Foundation Programme
CMHN	community mental health nurse
CMHT	community mental health team
CoD	Council of Deans
COT	College of Occupational Therapists
COTEC	College of Occupational Therapists in European Countries
CPD	continuing professional development
CPHVA	Community Practitioners and Health Visitors Association
CPN	community psychiatric nurse
CSIP	Care Services Improvement Partnership
CSP	Chartered Society of Physiotherapy
DoH	Department of Health (UK government department)
DipSW	Diploma in Social Work (*no longer in existence*)
DOPS	directly observed procedural skills
EBL	enquiry-based learning (*see also PBL*)
EEC	European Economic Community
ENB	English National Board for Nursing, Midwifery and Health Visiting
ENOTHE	European Network of Occupational Therapists in Europe

EU	European Union
EWTD	European Work Time Directive
GCSE	General Certificate of Secondary Education
GDP	gross domestic product
GMC	General Medical Council
GNC	General Nursing Council
GP	general practitioner
GSCC	General Social Care Council
HEA	higher education academy
HEDN	Higher Education for Dementia Network
HEFCE	Higher Education Funding Council (England)
HEI	higher education institution (university or college) *(see also IHE)*
HPC	Health Professions Council
ICM	International Confederation of Midwives
IFSW	International Federation of Social Workers
IHE	institute of higher education (university or college) *(see also HEI)*
IP	interprofessional
IPE	interprofessional education
JPTI	Joint Practice Teaching Initiative
KSF	*Knowledge and Skills Framework*
LEEP	Learning for Ethical and Effective Practice project
MBBS	Bachelor of Surgery
MBChB	Bachelor of Medicine
MDT	multi-disciplinary team
Medev	Medicine, Dentistry and Veterinary Medicine Subject Centre
MEU	medical education units
Mini-CEX	mini-clinical evaluation encounter
MMC	Modernising Medical Careers
MPET	Multi-Professional Education and Training levy
NHS	National Health Service
NICE	National Institute for Clinical Excellence
NMC	Nursing and Midwifery Council

OSCE	objective structured clinical examination
OT	occupational therapist
PBL	problem-based learning *(also practice-based learning)*
PCT	primary care trust
PE	placement educators
PIPE	Promotion of Interprofessional Education project
PMETB	Postgraduate Medical Education and Training Board
PREP	post-registration education and practice
QAA	Quality Assurance Agency
RAE	research assessment exercise
RCM	Royal College of Midwives
RCN	Royal College of Nursing
RCP	Royal College of Physicians
RCSLT	Royal College of Speech and Language Therapists
RLO	reusable learning object
RPL	recognition of prior learning
SCIE	Social Care Institute for Excellence
SCPHN	Specialist Community Public Health Nursing
SCQF	Scottish Credit and Qualification Framework
SETs	Standards of Education and Training (HPC)
SHA	strategic health authority
SHO	Senior House Officer
SIESWE	Scottish Institute for Excellence in Social Work Education
SIFT	service increment for teaching
SiSWE	Standards in Social Work Education
SLT	speech and language therapy
SSCs	student-selected components
SSSC	Scottish Social Services Council
TESCs	Ten Essential Shared Capabilities
UKCC	United Kingdom Central Council for Nursing, Midwifery and Health Visiting *(changed to NMC in 2002)*
WFOT	World Federation of Occupational Therapists
WTE	whole-time equivalent

Glossary

This brief glossary of key terms used in the book provides a brief overview of their meaning. Several of the professions in the book use different terms for similar ideas or concepts – although precisely how similar is a matter of debate. No detailed mapping of terms for each profession has been attempted.

Accreditation: every programme of study leading to a professional award must also seek accreditation as a recognized programme of study from the appropriate regulatory body which has designated power to act on such matters. Such powers are usually conferred by statute.

Care (primary; secondary; social): primary care is a term used for the first point of consultation, where decisions are made about referral to secondary care specialists. Social care is the general term for care designed to support people in their communities, such as social work, home care and day centres.

Clinical educator: an HPC registered (physio)therapist with a responsibility for the management of student placements in clinical practice. Increasingly renamed as a practice educator (PE).

Competences (capabilities; criteria for knowledge and performance; descriptors; key capabilities; standards for proficiency, learning outcomes, proficiencies, assessment criteria): these terms are used to describe the content of the student's curriculum in terms of practical abilities; there might be very specific indicators which specify what students will need to be able to do in order to demonstrate individual competences. There is some criticism of 'competence approaches' that they can concentrate too closely on fine detail and lose sight of the larger picture.

Declaration of Good Character and Good Health (fit for practice, fit for award, fit for purpose): a declaration signed by a duly authorized member of a university at the end of a programme signifying to the professional body that the student upon qualification is an appropriate person to enter the profession and to be licensed to seek employment (nursing). Students must also be deemed to be 'fit for practice', and each profession will have procedures to identify those students who are not fit for practice for whatever reason. Similar considerations apply to students that are not fit to receive an award.

Elective: a part of the programme (module, unit or period) of learning that a student can choose.

Field of practice: used especially in nurse training to identify a specialty such as mental health nursing.

Foundation year: the first year of professional practice (doctors).

Lecturer/practitioners (joint appointments): where a clinician or practitioner shares roles with academic staff; there are many different models.

Newly qualified professional (preceptorship; probationary period): usually refers to the first year of practice following qualification.

Placement (blocks; clinical placements; placement provision; practice learning experience/opportunity; practice setting/site): these are all terms for the period of time that is spent learning about professional practice in work settings. Sometimes the student is there for whole blocks of time (five days a week); sometimes the week is split between study in the academy and practice learning in the agency (concurrent).

Placement coordinator: member of HEI faculty responsible for allocating placements, auditing placement process and sourcing new placements.

Placement director: member of faculty with responsibility for quality of placement process, parity of student experience and commonality of practice between the university and placement providers.

Placement provider: an area of clinical practice offering placements for students, such as an NHS trust, PCT or school.

Portfolio: the detailed record of work undertaken that students must keep to identify continuing professional development.

Practice educator (fieldwork teacher; lecturer practitioner; link worker; mentor; practice teacher; [off-site] practice assessor; [on-site] practice supervisor; singleton practice teachers): there are many terms for the person who supports the student in identifying relevant learning opportunities and teaching about the profession. There is some controversy about 'practice assessor' being a restricted term that refers to only one of the many functions (assessment) of this role, and the term 'practice educator' is becoming more widely used. Some practice educators are on-site and some off-site.

Practice learning (fieldwork; clinical practice; practice curriculum): the general term for the student's learning about professional practice. 'Practice learning' is not synonymous with agency-based learning, because students also learn about practice in the academy (for example, in skills workshops), though it is commonly identified with the learning that happens whilst on placements.

Preceptorship: the provision of support and guidance that enables newly registered practitioners to make the transition from student to accountable practitioner.

Primary visit: the first visit made by a health visitor following the birth of a baby.

Professional programme (access courses; cadet schemes; entry routes; Tuning [Bologna] programme; distance/Foundation/in-service/part-time/ service/work-based learning): the general term for the whole course of study which takes place across the academy and agency and is usually organized as a partnership between the two. This can take place at many different academic levels and for different lengths of time.

Registration (pre-registration; post-registration; proficient for registration): after students have successfully qualified they are required to register with their respective professional council. To be 'proficient for registration' a practitioner must have reached the standards of competence prescribed by the profession.

Services (community support; for profit; independent; local authority; private practice; public sector; statutory; voluntary): the health and social services are often described by the way they are funded. In health care the differences are largely public or private. Social care has a variety of sectors: the public or statutory sector which are services provided by local or central government; the voluntary sector, which comprises national or local organizations with charitable status; and private or independent agencies which are in business to make a profit.

Supernumerary: a member of staff additional to the normal or required complement.

Tutor (personal tutor; placement tutor): usually university lecturers who provide individual support to a student. Sometimes this is organized so that the student's pastoral needs are provided by a different tutor from the person who provides support for their practice learning. In some programmes the student will have the same placement tutor throughout and in others the tutor will depend on the placement setting.

Visiting tutor: a member of an HEI faculty with responsibility to visit students on placement, liaise with the PE and student, and monitor the on-going placement on behalf of the HEI.

Part I

Introduction

1 Health and social care: a complex context for professional education

Steven M. Shardlow and Mark Doel

Challenges and changes

Each of the professions represented in this book is faced with the challenge of educating professionals to work in the health and social care sector of a modern economically developed society – a highly complex task conducted in an ever-changing economic, social and political climate. In the UK, the annual spend on health care was £109 billion in 2006, some 8.3 per cent of gross domestic product (GDP);[1] actual expenditure on health care has been rising steadily since 2002. In 2006–07, £20.1 billion was spent by local authorities[2] on social care. Although the spend on social care has increased by 70 per cent in real terms since 1997, the total amount spent on social as opposed to health care is significantly less. Whether these levels of expenditure are sufficient, in total or in this particular ratio, to meet needs is a moot point, and indeed a political question. It is widely accepted that there is increasing demand for a range of services as our technological capabilities advance, some of which are very expensive to deliver; there is also a growing expectation that high-quality services can be provided as more 'consumerist' ageing cohorts in the population are less willing to accept levels of service provided to previous generations (the prime example being the 'baby-boomer generation' who are now entering the ranks of the retired). These tensions, singularly and cumulatively, increase the pressure on the government to provide more funding for health and social care provision and on the various professions included in this book to meet perceived levels of increasing need. There is

---

[1] Source of statistical information is the Office of National Statistics.
[2] Source is the Information Centre (Government Statistical Service); these figures relate to England and not the UK as a whole.

3

no easy and straightforward approach to the determination, that commands universal acceptance, of what would be a reasonable level of funding on health and social care. However, a good indicator is the comparative amount spent by other similar countries. In this respect, the UK spent less than 8 per cent of GDP on health expenditure in 2001;[3] in the EU15 only Spain, Finland, Ireland and Luxembourg spent a smaller proportion of GDP. Irrespective of the absolute or comparative levels of expenditure there are a series of pressures that have a tendency to increase demand for health and social care. For example, in the EU15 in 2003, some 4 per cent of the population were over 80, traditionally heavy users of health and social care, and by 2018 this figure will have risen by 50 per cent (European Commission, 2003).

Writing in 2009, the past ten years or so have seen a period of very rapid change in the political and organizational context in which health and social care are delivered within the UK, including the following: regulation by performance targets; introduction of national standards; the break-up and reconfiguration of existing organizational structures in health and social care; the growth of private and not-for-profit sectors; the changing nature of professional roles (role shift and the development of overlapping role boundaries); and an increased emphasis on inter-agency and multi-professional working. These factors present a challenging social and economic context for the delivery of health and social welfare.

The central concern of this book is to explore how a representative sample of health and social care professions (mental health nursing; medicine; health visiting; midwifery; nursing; occupational therapy; social work; physiotherapy; and speech and language therapy) educate new entrants to the profession through direct engagement with patients and service users in community or clinical settings – the very heart and soul of professional education. This education cannot just be a preparation for today's challenges, as specified above; it must also prepare these new entrants for professional practice in a changing world. Moreover, in focusing on these professions, it should not be forgotten that many who work in this sector, especially in social care, often have little or no training (Social Care Workforce Research Unit, 2003).

Education for health and social care

All of the professions have to answer many questions about how to provide practice-based learning in clinical or community contexts. One of the most

---

[3]   The latest year for which full EU figures are available, according to National Statistics Online, is the year up to July 2008.

intriguing questions is easily measured; that of what proportion of the student's learning experiences should be spent in the classroom and what proportion should be provided in the community or clinic. Several of the professions have adopted a 50 per cent allocation of practice-based learning across the curriculum (see Appendix 1). This begs the question: why that particular amount? Is it because of the nature of the curriculum (in other words, are there pedagogic reasons?); is it a matter of convenience; or is it perhaps a political move to resolve competing stakeholder wishes? Whatever the answers to these questions there is a difference across the professions in the way that the amount of time spent on placement is measured: in some professions it is precisely measured in hours and in others it is days (again, see Appendix 1); but then how long is a day? Then the more difficult questions follow about what to do with that time.

Whatever the way this time is used, there is likely to be an implicit, occasionally explicit, tension between the higher education institution (HEI) and the agency providing the placement or learning opportunity. The tension is hard-wired: one body, the HEI, has a primary duty to educate; the other, the agency, has a primary duty to provide care and services to the public. The structures and protocols used to regulate this tension have much to tell us about the nature and quality of learning based in the clinic or community that is provided as part of a professional qualification course in health and social care. Yet it would be a mistake to see this as solely a two-way relationship. In all of the professions included in this book, that relationship is mediated through a third party, the regulatory body for the profession. The reader may wish to contrast the ways in which this tripartite relationship is presented across the different professions.

In addition, there are a range of stakeholders, some with more power and influence than others, with an interest in determining the scope and depth of knowledge and level of applied skill required of each profession. The constituencies from which these stakeholders are drawn are similar from one profession to another (such as government, either directly or via arm's-length governmental agency, accrediting or validating body; professional association; employers; patients, services users and carers and the lay public; also, some professions have academic and professional colleges), but the distribution of influence to shape required levels of basic competence and performance are different across the professions. At the heart of stakeholder involvement lies a very fundamental debate about the nature, role and function of professional activity in modern society and the degree of accountability by external bodies to which professions should be subject; put conversely, the extent and degree of autonomy that professions should enjoy. In respect of the professions represented in this book the nature of stakeholder involvement in setting knowledge, skills and values requirements is highly nuanced. In particular, does the professional body enjoy freedom to set the learning outcomes or do government and employers have the determining say; and what of the power of other stakeholders? To give one example: in health visiting, commissioners, employers and the HEI exercise strong control over the curriculum though close partnership working (Chapter 5). Readers may wish to make their own judgements about the range of similarity and difference between the professions, and why such differences exist. The fundamental question remains: what does the professional need to know and who determines the extent of required knowledge?

Educational theory and research about professional learning

How to term the subject matter of this book is in itself quite a conundrum! The health and social care professions use a variety of terminologies to refer to the type of learning and site of learning (off-campus learning in the workplace). Adopting the preferred terminology of any particular profession might appear to privilege that profession unfairly; hence, our use of the more neutral term 'workplace learning'. According to the study of learning in smaller companies in Scotland conducted by Seagraves et al. (1996),[4] there are three different types of learning that occur in the workplace:

- learning for work (can be delivered anywhere and refers to any learning that is broadly vocational)
- learning at work (formal training and development delivered through the employer)
- learning through work (applying learning acquired elsewhere to a particular role at work and knowledge and learning that are obtained through the process of work) (adapted from Seagraves et al., 1996, p. 15).

In the context of this book, the term 'workplace learning' is used as an 'umbrella of convenience' that shelters *all* shapes and sizes of learning that occur in the workplace. It is helpful to have a neutral, all-embracing term such as 'workplace learning' when the need arises to refer to the various ways in which the different professions in the book refer to the learning that takes place when students engage in a period of structured learning, in the workplace, as part of required learning leading to a professional qualification in their chosen domain. Conceptualizations about the nature, form and structure of this type of workplace learning are not necessarily shared by

---

[4]   We are indebted to Fran Jones for bringing this report to our attention.

the professions represented in this book, nor are the names attributed to the various actors in the process the same. Inevitably, as a reader, the temptation is to assume similarity, particularly where the professions represented form a cognate professional grouping in health and social care. To assist the reader with the process of developing an understanding across each of the professions, we have compiled a brief glossary in which the reader will discover, amongst other things, that the most usual term for the type of work-based learning under discussion in this book is 'practice learning' or 'fieldwork', closely followed by 'clinical practice'. For this example, the glossary entry reads:

> **Practice learning** (fieldwork; clinical practice; practice curriculum): the general term for the student's learning about professional practice. 'Practice learning' is not synonymous with agency-based learning, because students also learn about practice in the academy (for example, in skills workshops), though it is commonly identified with the learning that happens whilst on placements.

In the opening pages of a report to the higher education authority concerned, Nixon et al. assert boldly:

> Workplace learning can be distinguished from other forms of education and training in that it is essentially a form of research, where established knowledge combines with new information gained from reflection and analysis of workplace practice to generate new knowledge (Nixon et al., 2006, p. 13).

The workplace is, then, no mere site for the application of existing knowledge but rather an opportunity for the individual to forge new knowledge and understandings through the dynamic interchange of existing knowledge with new experience. In this sense, professions and trades as distinct as potters, pilots and plumbers are united in a learning experience that is structurally similar at a meta-level. The professions represented in this book have incorporated a formalized approach to workplace learning as part of the educational experience that leads to professional qualification. How this has been done and how conceptualized varies from profession to profession.

Workplace learning draws upon a range of theories of learning. There is no consensus among the authors of this book about the theories embedded within the variants of workplace learning or, indeed, about the canon of theorists whose work has been seminal in its influence. Nonetheless, many of the chapters (for example, midwifery, physiotherapy, health visiting and speech and language therapy) draw explicitly and significantly upon Schön (1987; 1994), whose work, referred to by all professions in the book, has been highly influential in understanding the nature of professional learning, in particular his conceptualization of the nature of professional learning achieved through a reflexive process. In other chapters (for example, that about nursing) the idea of reflective learning is prominent but is linked to a secondary author known within a particular discipline, although by no means all of the authors in the book address the notion of learning through a reflexive process. The less accessible work of experimental psychologist Kolb, upon whom Schön drew, is less frequently mentioned by authors within the book although it is often used in social work. One approach to pedagogy, problem-based learning (PBL), is mentioned in several chapters (including those on medicine, occupational therapy, physiotherapy, and speech and language therapy). It is certainly used by other disciplines in the book and as a preferred pedagogy may be used in specific institutions or departments (see, for example, Chapter 11 on speech and language therapy). However, as Murdoch-Eaton and Roberts comment in Chapter 4, there is no unequivocal evidence to demonstrate that this pedagogic approach produces better outcomes than does any other.

Recently, the Department of Health (2006b) published *Our Health, Our Say, Our Care: New directions for community services*, which, as the title powerfully suggests, outlined a policy approach to ensure that services both meet the needs of people who use or receive them and that they are centrally involved in planning, delivery and evaluation of the quality of health care. The involvement of citizens, be they termed patients, carers or service users, is central to the future provision of health and social care across the UK. In the chapters that follow, readers may be able to determine the impact that this policy is having on the delivery of services and, more particularly, how this approach is feeding into the education that students receive as part of workplace learning. What role for the patient or service user as educator? For example, some professions make use of 'expert patients' or patients who simulate illness (medicine) or electro-mechanical manikins (nursing). Speech and language therapy students are assessed according to their judgements about virtual patients, while occupational therapy students (as with most professions in the book) have their assessment based upon an observation of their clinical practice with a patient. Moreover, in midwifery, service users are involved in both curriculum development and in teaching. Furthermore, in social work there is a very strong emphasis to involve service users in all aspects of the educational process; for example, it is required in student selection (GSCC, 2003).

The notion that learners progress through a series of learning stages from 'novice to expert'[5] (from the initiate to the experienced and exceptionally competent), is found widely in health and social care – hardly surprisingly

---

[5]   This is the core of the title of Benner's (2001) book, *From Novice to Expert: Excellence and power in clinical nursing practice*.

as it seems as if this notion, whatever its intellectual merit, is intuitively plausible. It is rather less clear what the nature of the precise difference between the various stages might be in terms of observable behaviour. It may be expected that the experienced practitioner would demonstrate greater success rates in achieving change; act with greater fluency in an interdisciplinary context; draw upon a wider range of knowledge than the initiate; and engender greater confidence in others. In health care, the primary example of this approach is found in the work of Benner (2001), who applied the Dreyfus and Dreyfus (1980) model of skill acquisition to nursing; the approach is also found in social work in the work of Reynolds (1942; 1965). Possibly these 'novice to expert' models provide a conceptualization of progress toward becoming a reflexive clinician or practitioner.

No doubt the professions represented in this book have much to learn from each other about the ways in which they enable students to learn about professional practice during placements in clinical or service delivery settings. All of the professions subscribe to the importance of the notion of evidence-based practice; that is, that clinical or professional interventions should be conducted according to the application of the best available evidence. This should also be true in the approach taken to the delivery of professional and clinical education. How much rigorous pedagogic research has been conducted into the outcomes of placements in professional settings as part of a programme of professional education? The intuitive answers – 'not much' and 'not enough' – are probably correct. One place to look for that evidence is the Cochrane Collaboration and the Campbell Collaboration, the premier organizations that conduct systematic reviews in health, social welfare and education. The Cochrane Collaboration lists no reviews on professional learning and just one systematic review on continuing professional development, a cognate domain to the subject matter of this book. This should not lead to despair! There is some evidence out there about what does and does not work. For example, Spector (2006), on behalf of the National Council of State Boards of Nursing (in the US), has published an 'evolving systematic review' of outcomes in nursing education. This systematic review concluded, amongst other comments:

> Five studies provided evidence that clinical experiences improve students' abilities to think critically when caring for patients, though there were no studies found that investigated specific numbers of clinical hours. Likewise, there were no studies that evaluated those programs that do not have, or have very limited, clinical experiences. Two studies found that reflective practice was a very important strategy for teaching nursing students to critically think (Spector, 2006).

Whether this is helpful to educators in health and social welfare depends in part on the strength of the evidence on which these conclusions are based. This requires a very detailed reading of the paper; each reader would have to be persuaded about the strength of evidence available. Let us consider a more generalizable case, that of problem-based learning. As long ago as 1993, Vernon and Blake conducted a detailed study of the effectiveness of problem-based learning in medical education, drawing on empirical studies published between 1970 and 1992. They concluded that problem-based learning was generally found to be superior to other forms of pedagogy in respect of 'affective outcomes and academic performance' (Vernon and Blake, 1993). So why have we not accepted these conclusions and adopted this approach universally? Quite simply because there is no universal acceptance of this or similar evidence. For example, the conclusions were challenged immediately by Wolf (1993) on methodological grounds. The same has been true of similar subsequent reviews. It is extraordinarily difficult to obtain evidence that is convincing beyond reasonable doubt in the field of pedagogy – there are just too many variables.

If the notions of reflexive learning and problem-based learning have currency within a significant number of professions represented within the book, is it to be expected that they would have developed similar approaches to the pedagogy of the workplace? That must be for you, the reader, to judge. Inevitably, in reviewing the approaches of the professions and seeking similarities one is always drawn to the unique, the different and the unusual. In the chapter on medicine, mention is made of 'spiral learning', in which the learner returns to the same topic or theme – each time deepening their knowledge. This is an interesting approach, given that the technology of learning frequently appears to assume that competency is demonstrable through a *single performance of a given task*.

Reading the book

Readers may approach this book with an interest in becoming a clinician or practitioner, may already be professionally qualified, or perhaps have a general interest in the way that professionals are educated for clinical and professional practice. Whatever the nature of your interest, the book has been designed to provide you with a text that presents a high degree of organizational and thematic unity. For this reason we have developed a prescriptive structure for each chapter, so that all the chapters will read as part of the same 'family'. The pattern for Chapters 3 to 11, each of which presents a specific profession, is as follows:

- Overview: An introduction to the general pattern of education and training.
- Recent developments: A very brief history documenting any trends and changes in training for the profession in question over the last decade or so.
- Models of teaching and learning: A discussion of particular approaches and understanding of different theoretical models of teaching and learning professional practice.
- The teacher in the practice or clinical setting: How is this role viewed within the profession and how is the role supported; what training do practitioners have to undergo before they can undertake this role?
- Content and structure of the student's learning: How is the content of the student's learning organized in the clinical or practice setting and what is the extent of prescription? Is there, for example, a 'practice curriculum'? Do students' experiences of practice learning vary considerably or are they standardized?
- Methods: What methods are typically used to facilitate the student's learning?
- Assessment: How is the student's ability assessed and what happens to students whose practice is considered to be 'failing' or 'marginal'? Is the practitioner who assesses the student's learning the same person who teaches and supervises? If not, how are the relations between these people managed?
- Continuing professional development: A commentary on the place of continuing professional development in the profession under consideration.
- Current debates: Current debates and issues in education and training for the profession in question and the impact this is having on the practice learning. For example, how are service users, patients and carers involved in the training, if at all?
- Future developments: Brief speculation from each contributor about the likely future for education and training in their particular profession: a preview of any forthcoming or likely changes in the pattern of practice learning.
- Core text recommendations: Pointers to core texts for readers to discover more about the teaching and learning of professional practice on placements in work settings in each of the particular professions.

In addition to this common structure, the book uses the device of an illustrative community in which the professions work; there is then the opportunity for each of the professions to refer to the same residents in this community across chapters. This virtual community was first used in an earlier book by the editors and appeared in *Modern Social Work Practice* (Doel and Shardlow, 2005); an expanded version of this simulated community is described fully in Chapter 2. Further details about this community and the linked books can be found at: www.shu.ac.uk/chscr/mswp.html. From time to time the community evolves and expands to provide a learning resource, along with a series of online exercises.

Three further devices are employed to enable cross-profession comparisons (see appendices for details).

- Appendix 1: Comparative information about the education of health and social care professionals
  This provides comparative information at a glance about the professions included in this book, with information such as the length of the professional award, approximate number of students, the total number of days a student is expected to spend in learning in clinical or professional practice settings, and so on.
- Appendix 2: Student supervision and teaching models
  Four models of learning are outlined: these provide a taxonomy of different models of learning. This taxonomy was first developed in respect of social work by Shardlow and Doel (1996). This conceptualization is not necessarily used by professions included in the book but it provides a reference point for the characterization and categorization of models of learning. If a similar characterization is not used then authors were encouraged to detail how practice learning of their particular profession could be typified.
- Appendix 3: Teaching and learning techniques
  A taxonomy of different methods and techniques for teaching and learning is not a simple thing to produce. Here, a characterization and grouping of pedagogic approaches and techniques has been constructed using four categories: experiential; written word; graphic and hardware (using an original idea by Catherine Sawdon). A list of different structural arrangements is included. As with Appendix 2, this characterization and categorization is designed to encourage comparability across the professions.

As mentioned previously, a glossary lists key terms used in the book. A wide range of terminology is used from chapter to chapter, some of which is specific to a particular profession, some shared, and (perhaps most confusing) some which are 'false friends' that appear to be the same across disciplines but are nuanced according to their professional domain. For example, '**Practice educator** (fieldwork teacher; lecturer practitioner; link worker; mentor; practice teacher; [off-site] practice assessor; [on-site] practice supervisor; singleton practice teachers)' are terms used to describe roles of people who teach students whilst the student is placed in a field/clinical/practice setting.

Communication across each of the professional domains is made that much more difficult without a shared vocabulary or conceptual map that governs the world of off-campus learning for health and social care professionals.

Other chapters (Chapters 1, 2 and 12) do not use this structure.

- Chapter 1 (the current chapter), written by the editors, is designed to provide a context for the book and to introduce the reader to organizational structure and devices employed in the book that have been designed to make the material as accessible as possible. In this chapter we provide a descriptive overview, with no intention of promoting any particular perspective on practice education.
- Chapter 2 is also written by the editors. This chapter presents our views concerning the importance of 'community' as a setting for practice learning. It also introduces and describes fully the illustrative community in which the practice examples of professional learning have been set. This simulation provides further contextual unity to the material presented in the other chapters in the book and enhances opportunities to compare the approaches of the different professionals as they learn.
- Chapter 12, the concluding chapter written by Leonard and Weinstein, focuses not upon a single profession but rather upon interprofessional learning. At the heart of health and social care professional practice in the community is the ability of the diverse professions to be able to work together, for which they also need to learn together. There is a requirement for many professions in the book to be educated for part of their course with other health care professionals. As the final chapter, this helps to bring the preceding chapters together.

We should not assume that the construction of professional education is, or will be, the same across each of the four countries within the UK – England, Northern Ireland, Scotland and Wales. Health and social care is partially but not fully devolved, so care must be exercised in making judgements about what is the situation in one country or what applies to the whole of the UK. For example, as John Keady and Rachel Thompson point out in Chapter 3, nursing is an all-graduate profession in Wales and Northern Ireland but not in Scotland and England. Joyce Lishman's contribution on social work (Chapter 10) is specifically set in the Scottish context and there are very significant differences between social work in Scotland and in other countries in the UK: a prominent feature of Scottish social work is that social work with offenders, probation, is still regarded as part of the domain of social work. In England there is a separate qualification. These factors clearly have an impact on the content of professional learning in the workplace.

The book is not a truly comparative study in the sense that identical data, themes and issues have been rigorously addressed by each author for each profession. Rather, the book makes a juxtaposition of the key issues that the authors deem to be the most important issues from within the perspective of their own professions. This allows the reader not only to be able to infer comparisons and contrasts between professions but also to appreciate something of how they are seen by those who are professionally qualified in a particular profession. It must be remembered that the contributors to this volume are writing in their own name; as such they provide an individual, if insider's, view of the profession in question. It is not intended to regard this view as the definitive one on professional education in that profession; however, these are insightful views provided by insiders.

We hope that you, the reader, both enjoy and learn from this book.

2 The community as a site for learning practice

Mark Doel and Steven M. Shardlow

There is a consensus across all the professions in health and social care that students' professional education should include practical experience of work with service users and patients. As we will see in the forthcoming chapters, the amount and nature of that practical experience varies from profession to profession. It is difficult to conceive of successful preparation for professional practice that is located solely in the classroom, as this site provides relatively limited opportunities to practise the application of skills and for skill development in real-life situations with actual patients or service users. This approach – live experience in the community or clinic – is fundamental to professionals and occupations that comprise practical or people skills along with intellectual ability: it is a model of learning that goes well beyond health and social care, and can be seen in the training for teachers, lawyers, architects and many others. The overviews of each of the professions in this book provide a graphic representation of the emphasis placed on this practical learning in the workplace, and it is the memories of these placements that students are most likely to take with them into their years of practice (Marsh and Triseliotis, 1996).

In order to develop their understanding and know-how, there is a wide variety of placement settings available to students. Much health and social care is delivered through institutions such as hospitals or care homes. There is a continuing debate about the extent to which health and social care should be based in the community or provided through large specialized institutions. At the time of writing there is an ideological preference at government level for community-based care. Though there is a case for a book that deals with learning in institutional settings, we have chosen to site this book in the context of professional learning that occurs within the community. There are three reasons for this: first, this site for learning is ideologically preferred; second, within the community the various professionals are not so constrained by organizational protocols and requirements and therefore must develop interprofessional working patterns based on negotiation and understandings of each other's role and with the community itself; third, and most importantly, the community is the site where the recipients of the health and social services live. Hence, community-based practice learning provides the opportunity to gain the fullest and deepest understanding of the reality of patients' and service users' lives. In this chapter we will explore in more detail the idea and potential of the community as a site for learning practice. We will introduce readers to the Green Hill community and, in particular, to the residents of one of its streets, Derby Street, whose layout is shown in Figure 2.1. This community provides the illustrations for the students' practice learning in all of the chapters that follow.

The Green Hill community

In *Modern Social Work Practice* (2005), Doel and Shardlow describe a community as the site for a series of possible professional interventions, focusing on the learning that students might gain from these experiences. The site was located in a street in a fictional estate, Derby Street in the Green Hill flats, an urban development that could be found in most cities and towns.

Green Hill flats provide the illustrative site for the many professions in this book. The reader will be able to engage with a variety of people in different circumstances and to see these situations from different professional points of view. What might the different professions contribute to the situations briefly described in each of the households in the Green Hill flats? What kind of learning would students from different professions derive from involvement in these households? How might they work together to provide a coherent and integrated service alongside the residents of Derby Street?

The Green Hill flats were built as public housing in the 1960s to provide decent housing for people then living in slums. However, many of these 'streets in the sky' acquired a bad reputation, partly because of the subsequent housing policies of the local authority, which used to concentrate people with considerable disadvantages and problems in certain blocks. Even so, many of the Green Hill residents are loyal to the estate, have lived there for two and even three generations and want to develop the sense of community. It has an active tenants' association and there is a popular pub, the Green Hill Arms, on Dover Street, another ground-floor street.

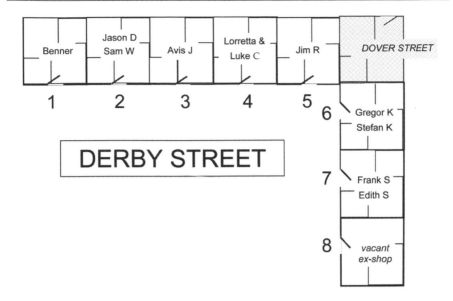

Figure 2.1   Location of the Derby Street residents

A modest walk away there is a school that serves the local community; this school (Uppergreen) houses the Tiny Tots Day Nursery, which provides nursery access to children as young as six months and up to three years of age. The school has a children's centre which provides health and social care as well as education for mothers and children of the local community. Some of the younger residents of Derby Street attend the day nursery and the school.

There is also a hospital (Eastern Hope) that serves the community; however, this hospital is two bus rides away from Derby Street. There is a rehabilitation unit attached to Eastern Hope Hospital for people following head injury or other neurological damage caused by trauma. Most of the patients are people who have experienced a road traffic accident or a sports injury, but some have also suffered episodes of bleeding into the brain, causing brain damage. The age range of the patients is wide, with many people in their teens and twenties. People coming to the unit have recovered from the acute stage of the trauma and from any surgical interventions. The aim of the unit is to teach patients how to 'redesign' their lives, so they can function independently.

Security doors, CCTV and intercoms have all been put in place and, for some time now, the council has had a policy of mixed habitation, so that families, young couples and older people live side by side.

Derby Street is one of the ground-floor streets in Green Hill flats. It consists of eight flats (Figure 2.1).

At Number 1 is **Zoë Benner**, a single parent who was in public care for much of her childhood, but is now reconciled with her mother, who lives on another street in Green Hill flats. Zoë has a 14-year-old son (**Jackson**), a 12-year-old daughter (**Kylie**), a 3½-year-old son (**Billy**) and a baby daughter (**Kara**) aged 11 months. Jackson was cautioned for shoplifting earlier in the year, and has just been arrested on a charge of criminal damage. Kylie has not been to school for several weeks. She has few friends and is reluctant to leave the family's flat. Kylie has been referred for help with her bed-wetting problem. Billy is having communication problems. Kara is Zoë's daughter by another man who is attempting to gain custody of her. Kara has asthma and seems to suffer from unspecified allergies. Zoë has another child, **Tilly**, a 7-year-old girl currently with foster carers on the other side of the city. **Nicky**, a pregnant relative of Zoë, is staying with her temporarily.

At Number 2 live **Jason Dean** and his partner **Sam Weiner**. Jason, a 28-year-old, has a previous drug-related charge and has just completed a rehabilitation programme. Jason is unemployed, but volunteers at a local drop-in centre for homeless people. Sam is 46 years old and is on long-term disability benefit, experiencing occasional periods of severe depression when he is treated by the community mental health team. He has in the past had several hospitalizations under the Mental Health Act (1983). When well, Sam is a leading light in the tenants' association for the block of flats.

Avis Jenkins lives at Number 3. She is 84 years old and her only son lives in another city, although he has regular contact with the local community mental health team for older people as he is worried about his mother's ability to look after herself and about her vulnerability. Jason Dean gives her quite a bit of support, calling in and helping her with cups of tea and the like. Mrs Jenkins has home care twice a week. Charging policies for home care services have changed recently and Mrs Jenkins is finding it difficult to cope financially. Her memory is deteriorating and she is a regular member of a group called Memory Joggers, a new service based at the local Day Centre which is run by a Community Mental Health Nurse, a social worker and a psychologist. Avis has lived in the area all her life and worked on the local newspaper until she retired.

Number 4 houses a young couple, **Lorretta and Luke Carter**. They both work in low-paid jobs, but put enough aside to run an old second-hand van. Luke also plays in a band, which sometimes comes to Number 4 to practise. The band play gigs most weeks and about once a month at the Green Hill Arms pub.

Jim Rafferty lives at Number 5. He used to work in the steel industry in quite a well-paid job, until he retired. He is now 72 years old and was widowed three years ago. Over the last five years he has gradually been losing his sight through macular degeneration. His daughter lives a short bus ride away. Jim has written to the council to complain about the noise from Number 4.

In Number 6 two Kurdish brothers from Iraq have recently been housed after successfully seeking asylum. They are trained as engineers. They are currently unemployed but are actively seeking work and are in regular touch with a local Kurdish support group. **Gregor Kiyani** has good English, though **Stefan Kiyani** is more faltering. They get on well with the others on the street and have gone out of their way to say hello and invite people round. However, they have recently been very distressed by an incident in which dog faeces were posted through their letter box.

Frank and Edith Sunderland live in Number 7. They are both 75 years old. A month ago, Frank suffered a stroke and he has been in acute care in a stroke unit at the city hospital. His difficulties include dysphagia and aphasia but it is planned for him to return home soon. Frank and Edith were leading lights in the (unsuccessful) campaign to keep the shop open at Number 8. They say they have still not given up. Edith has developed diabetes in the last year and also wears a hearing aid.

Number 8 used to be a small corner shop, but it closed four months ago and is currently boarded up, despite a local campaign led by the Sunderlands. The nearest shop is now a supermarket across a busy dual carriageway.

Derby Street and a number of other streets on the north side of Green Hill flats have an infestation of cockroaches. Green Hill flats was owned by the local council (public housing) but has recently been sold for redevelopment by a not-for-profit housing association. Tenants will be involved in decisions about the coming changes, which will result in some tenants moving from the block whilst extensive refurbishments are made.

Table 2.1 shows the residents of Derby Street in the context of this book, enabling the reader to cross-refer to the various chapters involved.

Table 2.1   Where to read about the Derby Street residents

Chapter:	3	4	5	6	7	8	9	10	11	12
#1 Benner family		x	x	x			x	x	x	x
#2 Jason and Sam		x				x		x		x
#3 Avis Jenkins	x	x					x	x		x
#4 Lorretta and Luke							x			
#5 Jim Rafferty		x				x				
#6 Kiyani brothers										
#7 Sunderlands							x		x	x
Tenants' association			x					x		
Green Hill Arms			x							
Playgroups					x					
Rehabilitation unit					x					
Neighbourhood watch									x	
Community as a whole								x		

Ch. 3   Community mental health nurse
Ch. 4   Doctor
Ch. 5   Health visitor
Ch. 6   Midwife
Ch. 7   Nurse
Ch. 8   Occupational therapist
Ch. 9   Physiotherapist
Ch. 10 Social worker
Ch. 11 Speech and language therapist
Ch. 12 Interprofessional education

The concept of community

The idea of 'community' is by no means new. However, according to Gusfield (1975), the term has been used in two main ways. First, it can refer to the residents of an identifiable geographical area, most usually a part of a city, town, village or grouping of villages. Here, the notion of a geographical unity is key. Second, the notion conveys a sense of unity, something about the nature of relationships between a socially identifiable grouping; 'the black community', 'the social work community', and so on, are clearly not tied to a physical turf. 'Community' is, then, a fluid term, not easy to define and one that has had its meaning extended by notions such as 'communities of practice' (Wenger et al., 2002).

What is central to the idea of community is the feeling of belonging and, for a geographical community, this is rooted in location. Although the notion of belonging generally conveys positive associations, we should note that it might not necessarily be so; the difference between a community of practice and a local community is that there is a definite choice to be a member of the former, whereas the latter is conferred on its members. Indeed, some members of the Green Hill community might, at best, feel ambivalent about belonging to it. In this sense, community is not unlike family; it is there, like it or not, capable of providing support and nuisance at the same time.

Why the community is important as a site for learning

The particular professional spectacles that each practitioner brings to an encounter are difficult to remove, no matter how loud the mantra 'Listen to the service user'. The professional title – for example, as occupational therapist or community nurse – already begins to define the role and the employer is likely to have increasingly prescribed definitions of what it considers to be eligibility for its services. So, the paradox is that, whilst government policy requires professionals to put down their metaphorical clipboards and listen to the people in front of them, local practices and procedures oblige them to retrieve the clipboard and follow tightly drawn assessment schedules. Of all the professions, social workers have traditionally had the widest brief, but the disaggregation into specialist services means that they, too, are likely to enter the service users' homes with very particular spectacles – child protection, mental health, and so on – rather than with 'eyes wide open'.

In these circumstances it is proper to ask who is working with the *person-in-the-community*? When we read about the households in Derby Street, it becomes evident that they are interconnected. The services might define these residents as 'someone with a speech and language problem' or 'a man with mental health problems', but this reflects only one reality, and probably not the way this community of households sees itself. Some neighbours provide support for one another and, yes, a degree of nuisance too. They are all affected by what is happening in the neighbourhood, such as the move from council to housing association ownership, the recent closure of the corner shop and the cockroach infestation. The factors that affect the health and well-being of the people in this estate are a complex mix of personal, physical and psychological forces, the immediate social and environmental context and the wider political influences and impact of social policies. The balance of these factors will vary from person to person and from community to community. However, it is not difficult to see how the closure of the corner shop could actually be the single most important concern for

Mr and Mrs Sunderland, the elderly couple at Number 7, despite all of their health difficulties. Apart from the fact that the nearest store is now across a busy dual carriageway, probably beyond their reach and therefore increasing their sense of dependency, they might also be despondent about the failure of their campaign.

Medicine has traditionally focused on a highly clinical professional education but there have been radical changes to the curriculum. For example, in one of the relatively newly established postgraduate medical training courses in England, the first semester is devoted to learning about the relationship between poverty, disadvantage and health, with students required to visit the local estates to interview users of the health service about their experiences of it. These approaches in medical education would have been unheard of a few years ago, so prospects for community approaches to professional practice might seem remote in some fields now, but experience tells us that things can change quickly.

One of the main policy drivers in recent years has been social inclusion. Of course, inclusion must be a part of all professionals' practice but as yet there is no profession of 'social inclusion worker'. Putting this in concrete terms and relating it to Derby Street, whose job is it, for example, to help integrate the Kiyani brothers into the community? Who has those professional skills and who is employed to do that? This could fall to a locality-based social worker working in concert with the community, but social workers now focus on specialties, none of which is likely to include this kind of work. The police might, or might not, be investigating the posting of dog dirt through the Kiyanis' letter box but who is working with the consequences of this – not just for the brothers, but for the community at large? The community is likely to be speculating whether this act has been committed by outsiders or someone from within the community. The anxiety, distress and distrust that this kind of incident has on the broader community should not be neglected.

Despite these major community concerns and the impact they are having on individuals, all of the students walking through the pages of this book are likely to be learning a very individualized practice, with the attendant dangers of segmentation. Of course, each profession has its particular skills and focus, and this is both a strength and a weakness. It is also an inevitability; clearly, it is not the responsibility of the general practitioner to work to re-open the corner shop. However, there is an imbalance between the focus on particular parts of the individual's existence and the broader context of their lives, and the balance needs to be redressed. Fortunately, there are some ways forward, as we shall see later in the chapter.

In this book we have used an illustrative community, Derby Street, to draw together all of the examples of learning. Hence, students from the various different professions in the book are to be found working with the various residents of the Derby Street community. The simulation of a community is both a device to bring added unity to the book (as each separate chapter uses it as a reference point) and an encouragement to question how the various professions might interact. Practice educators can use Derby Street to help students' learning and understanding.

Community strengths

We have made a case that the notion of community is a reality for its residents and that this reality therefore needs to be reflected in the professional response. In addition to this, the community is an important site for practice learning because it highlights not just the source of collective problems, but also communal strengths and the potential for mutual action. The campaign to keep the corner shop open might have failed in its main objective, but we can guess at some of the secondary benefits that could have resulted – the galvanizing of the community into action, bringing people together for a common purpose which might also be directed towards the problem of the infestation. We also learn of some bilateral acts of support (for example, Jason Dean for Avis Jenkins) and other community-oriented activities such as Jason's volunteering work.

The notion of social capital is enjoying a revival though it was first coined in 1916 and explained in this way:

> The individual is helpless socially, if left to himself [*sic*] … If he comes into contact with his neighbour, and they with other neighbours, there will be an accumulation of social capital, which may immediately satisfy his social needs and which may bear a social potentiality sufficient to the substantial improvement of living conditions in the whole community. The community as a whole will benefit by the cooperation of all its parts, while the individual will find in his associations the advantages of the help, the sympathy, and the fellowship of his neighbours (Hanifan, 1916, cited by Putnam, 2000).

More recently, the development of the notion of social capital has been strongly associated with ideas drawn from two sociologists, Bourdieu (1985) and Coleman (1988), and a policy analyst, Putnam (1993), whose book *Bowling Alone* (Putnam, 2000) has become a standard text in this field. The relatively recent definition provided by the World Bank provides an excellent working summary of the notion of social capital.

> Social capital refers to the institutions, relationships, and norms that shape the quality and quantity of a society's social interactions … Social capital is not just

the sum of the institutions which underpin a society – it is the glue that holds them together (World Bank, 1999).

The Derby Street community will have a particular characteristic pattern of social relationships and social interactions. The level of social capital embedded within the community could, if desired, be measured through a series of proxies. To some extent the actions of the various professions represented in this book will have an impact on the reservoir of social capital in this community, either by accident or by design.

Social capital is not a straightforwardly benign construct. Negative consequences have also been identified, such as the exclusion of outsiders, excessive claims on group members and restrictions on individual freedom (Portes, 1998). So, like the notion of community itself, we should not accept the notion of social capital uncritically. However, the community is a reality for the people experiencing it, even if its boundaries are uncertain and permeable; and if the community has the potential to create problems, it also has the resources to work with them.

Clinical settings play their part, of course, in helping students to develop their professional skills, but in these settings it is more likely that the focus is very specific to what is *wrong* in the person's life. The community setting is one where practitioners can see people in their broader context and become familiar with their strengths and potential resources. 'Treatments' in clinical settings might stumble in the transfer to the community setting (and then be called 'non-compliance') because the clinical environment is not the one in which people live their lives. Students learning their practice in the community have an opportunity not just to explore and understand the relationship between individual problems and social problems, but also to grasp how the community can be part of the solution.

So, lifting our eyes above the individuals and seeing them in the context of their communities helps us to see the strengths as well as the problems in their lives.

The professional community

Just as the individuals in Derby Street have threads that connect them to a local community, so the professionals who service that community also have connecting threads. As we will see in the final chapter, there are increasing opportunities for interprofessional learning, with students from different professions learning together in class-based groups and also in shared placements. Some of the students in this book will be experiencing collective learning with students from other professions (see Chapter 12).

This helps students and practitioners to coordinate their work and to ensure that their efforts are concerted.

Learning about other professions is the first step. The next is to achieve active collaboration with the community, perhaps with professionals and residents working together in a lay/professional community forum which focuses on wider concerns, all of which have an impact on the ability of professions to work effectively with individuals. This kind of community forum must include practitioners beyond health and social care – for example, local teachers, community police officers, youth inclusion workers, environmental health officers, community workers and benefits advice workers, perhaps some volunteer workers, all of whom have a perspective on the community and a concern for its well-being.

The Green Hill scenario can be used with a variety of students from health and social care professions (and others) to understand how different professions can work together and in partnership with the wider community.

Students as a force for change in the community

So far we have viewed the community as a context for students to gain a better understanding of the people they are working with and to understand how the community might have resources that can contribute to the work. The next step is to consider how students might engage with the community in a more active way. This resonates with developments in our understanding of the purpose of practice education, which increasingly sees students as active participants in their learning with potentially more active roles in developing services (Doel et al., 2007).

We have examples of students supporting services that would not survive without their presence (for instance, the refugee services described by Underhill et al., 2002, and Butler, 2005). These examples demonstrate how students, by engaging with communities, can act as a force for change (Dent and Tourville, 2002; Muzumdar and Atthar, 2002). They can provide services to communities without being exploitative or experiencing exploitation. Sometimes the communities are geographical, as in Derby Street; at other times the communities are based around a group of people facing a common challenge, such as refugee communities.

The range of practice placements is broadening to encompass community organizations led by service users (Doel et al., 2007). These offer students the opportunity to learn and work alongside service users on project-related work which helps students to see people as providers as well as users of community services. We need more research to understand the impact of these experiences but the hope is that the students provide a resource to the service user organization and that they, in turn, incorporate a community orientation into their subsequent practice.

In Derby Street, students could be involved in working with the tenants' association towards meeting some of the association's aims. Some of these are of direct relevance to the wider community's physical and mental well-being. Depending on the length of the placement and the skills, experience and confidence of the students, there is much scope for groupwork with the Green Hill estate. We know of at least one group in the neighbourhood – the Memory Joggers group which Avis visits. A midwifery student and health visitor student might together facilitate a sexual health group; a social work student and occupational therapy student could co-lead a group for teenage parents; a physiotherapy student and a community nurse student could run groups for well-being in the community.

Students can also be involved in helping communities with specific, focused projects that might require gathering data and other kinds of information, perhaps to make a case to present to a council committee or a charity for funding. If professionals are truly to embed their practice in the reality of local communities they must find ways to engage with local political processes without, of course, providing any partisan support or direction. Students bring additional time, most often enthusiasm and some new skills, all of which can be a great asset to the community. The time-limited nature of placements can be a benefit in helping to structure any plan and provide built-in deadlines. As we will see in the chapters ahead, students also need support and supervision in order to make sure that their efforts are focused and appropriately managed. However, we should not underestimate the support students can derive from one another where they are jointly placed in twos, threes or even greater numbers, and the credibility that peer advice and support carries.

Other influences on the students' learning

We have considered the significance of the community as a context for the student's learning and the often untapped potential of both the community and the student. There are, of course, a number of other external influences on the student's learning, in particular the nature of the organization in which the student is placed. The size and structure of the various agencies, services and organizations that serve the Derby Street community would make for very different experiences for the students learning their practices in this street. In particular, how is professional practice (and, therefore, learning) influenced by the fact that an agency is statutory, voluntary, independent or service user-led? What percentage of their time might students expect to be in direct contact with people in the community compared to time spent in the office, clinic, unit or wherever their office base is? How near or far from Derby Street is the base from which they operate?

Moving from Derby Street as our example, what kinds of difference to the student experience would a placement in a rural community provide (Pugh, 2000)? The challenge of providing group-based services is especially strong in rural areas, where adequate transport is frequently a problem. Students, themselves, might experience these challenges at first hand, with relatively large distances between the people with whom they work and increased travel times and costs between home and placement.

Community is, therefore, one of many variables in the quality of the student's practical experience; one of the most significant, undoubtedly, and with huge potential for learning and change.

Part II

The professions

3 The community mental health nurse

John Keady and Rachel Thompson

Overview

Within the UK, community mental health nurses (CMHNs) are Registered Nurses (Mental Health) who specialize in the assessment, treatment, care and support of people of all ages with mental health conditions (and their families) who are living at home (Hannigan and Coffey, 2003). CMHNs usually operate from a primary or secondary care base and they form an integral part of a multi-disciplinary community mental health team (CMHT). As a profession, CMHNs have a relatively long history within the National Health Service (NHS), one that stretches back to the late 1950s/early 1960s when psychiatric nursing began to view a life outside of the asylums and question the moral imperative of institutional provision for the 'mentally ill' (Simmons and Brooker, 1986; White, 1999a; Nolan, 2003). One specialist area of CMHN practice is in working with people with dementia and their families (for illustrations, see Keady et al., 2003; also Keady et al., 2007) and it is this focus that forms the substance of this chapter.

In a landmark paper, Greene (1968) spelt out the early role attributes of a psychiatric nurse working in the community with people with dementia. In this paper, the author suggested that conducting physical care tasks, such as bathing the person with dementia in their own home and attending to their personal care needs, were just as important as supporting families through regular visits and acting as a 'broker' to the provision of other community support services (see also: Towell, 1975; White, 1999b; Keady and Adams, 2001). By the beginning of the 1980s the Royal College of Physicians (1981) affirmed the value of CMHNs working within CMHTs for older people and provided an outline of their role, namely to: support relatives; advise on medication; and help settle and monitor disturbed patients in their own homes (p. 158). Indeed,

31

by the mid-1980s, Simmons and Brooker (1986) reported that when CMHNs specialized with a client group it tended to be 'with elderly mentally ill people' (p. 46), a population that included those with dementia. Whilst the primacy of this focus has now been superseded by CMHNs working with people with complex and enduring needs (such as working-age adults with schizophrenia), CMHN practice with people with dementia and their families is still embraced by the mental health profession and seen as a legitimate career choice (DoH, 2006c; Scottish Executive, 2006b). As an example of recent role development, the role of the Admiral Nurse is described below.

Role of the Admiral Nurse

All Admiral Nurses are Registered Nurses (Mental Health), most with previous experience of practising as a CMHN. The Admiral Nurse role started in the 1990s, derived from the work of the charity 'for dementia' (formerly the Dementia Relief Trust) to address the needs of carers for people with dementia living in the community. There are, at present, over 60 Admiral Nurses working in the UK, in areas such as London, the South East, the West Midlands, the North West of England, North Wales and North Lincolnshire. Admiral Nursing encompasses a variety of posts that enhance the core nursing role, including Admiral Nurse Consultant, Lecturer Practitioner and Research Practitioner. Many of the Admiral Nurse teams are located within NHS secondary mental health services and integrated health and social care trusts. However, each team works collaboratively with a range of local service providers including primary care, tertiary care, social care and voluntary and independent providers. This is a way of working that reflects the complex nature of dementia and the experiences of individuals and families.

The alignment of mental health nursing to people with dementia has its roots within the asylum-based system of care that operated within the UK from 1845 and where older people gradually made up a significant percentage of the asylum population – although reports show that staff–patient ratios on the 'psychogeriatric wards' were by far the most deficient in the asylum, operating at '1 staff member to 20 older residents' (Nolan, 2003, p. 8). In the twentieth century the mental health attendant roles morphed into those of the asylum nurses and by the 1920s into those of mental nurses, where education, training and a form of professional regulation through a written examination was conducted. This examination was facilitated through the Royal Medico-Psychological Association who, at the time, had sole authority for accrediting mental nurses. As the twentieth century progressed, mental nursing was subsumed under the larger 'family' of nursing (whilst retaining its distinct focus and separate place on the Nursing Register) and the professional regulation baton would eventually be handed over to the General Nursing Council, the United Kingdom Central Council for Nursing, Midwifery and Health Visiting (UKCC) and, in 2002, to the Nursing and Midwifery Council (NMC) where it currently resides. On the homepage of its website, the NMC defines its role as 'safeguard[ing] the health and well-being of the public by continually regulating, reviewing and promoting nursing and midwifery standards' (see http://www.nmc-uk.org/).

Overall patterns of training

Under the reconfiguration of nurse education put forward in the mid-1980s through the Project 2000 initiative (UKCC, 1986), and accepted at the end of the 1980s by the UK government, nurse education was relocated from education centres within the grounds of district general hospitals or, in the case of mental health nursing, from the grounds of the Victorian asylums (which was the training experience of both authors), and assimilated into more centralized colleges of nursing where their programmes were validated by local universities. From the early to mid-1990s these colleges were then fully merged into higher education institutions (HEIs), predominantly universities. By and large, this meant that from the 1990s onwards students of nursing followed a university-based three-year programme of study, although there was still a requirement that at least 40 per cent of time should be spent in practice. Macleod Clark et al. (1997, p. 247) listed the aspirations of Project 2000 as:

> ... a full-scale re-orientation of nurse training, based in institutions of further or higher education, with 'nursing students' supernumerary to service requirements, and their time in clinical settings better supervised and more directly linked to course-based learning. Educational placements would take place in both institutional and community settings, with a curriculum which was more health- (as opposed to disease-) related and with a new emphasis on people as members of a wider society.

Initially, Project 2000 had an 18-month Common Foundation Programme where students from all branches of nursing (adult, child, mental health and learning disability) studied together, with exposure to all branches being included during this time. From 1999, in response to the recommendations of two key documents, *Making a Difference* (DoH, 1999) and *Fitness for*

Practice (UKCC, 1999b), which sought to refocus pre-registration nursing programmes on an outcomes-based competency framework developed by HEIs in close collaboration with service providers, the Common Foundation Programme was reduced to one year and re-badged as a Foundation Programme or Foundation Year with subsequent branch programmes being extended accordingly to two years. When applying for most pre-registration nursing admission, prospective students are expected to nominate a chosen branch at the point of application to the university. The requirement for exposure to other branches during the Foundation Year remained. For pre-registration nursing students, mental health nursing is defined below.

Definition of mental health nursing

Mental health nurses care for people experiencing mental distress, which may have a variety of causative factors. The focus of mental health nursing is the establishment of a relationship with service users and carers to help bring about an understanding of how they might cope with their experience, thus maximizing their potential for recovery. Mental health nurses use a well-developed and evidence-based repertoire of interpersonal, psychosocial and other skills that are underpinned by an empathetic attitude towards the service user and the contexts within which their distress has arisen. Mental health difficulties can occur at any age and service users may be cared for in a variety of settings, including the community and their own homes. They may require care for an acute episode or ongoing support for an enduring illness. Mental health nurses work as part of multi-disciplinary and multi-agency teams that seek to involve service users and their carers in all aspects of their care and treatment (NMC, 2004e, p. 24).

Typically, the academic year for all pre-registration nursing students is split into a number of semesters with a 50/50 balance of theory and practice over a three-year training period. Students are allocated a mentor in practice, a qualified nurse who has undertaken an approved programme for mentorship preparation. The role of the mentor is support the student in identifying relevant learning opportunities, assess practice-based outcomes and provide more general support. Clinical placements involve shift systems, which may include weekends and night duty, and nursing students are expected to work with their mentor for at least 40 per cent of the placement time. The NMC proficiencies for registration and qualification as a mental health nurse are set out in the document *Standards for Proficiency for Pre-Registration Nurse*

Table 3.1   **The standards of proficiency: the overarching principles of being able to practise as a nurse**

- Manage oneself, one's practice, and that of others, in accordance with the NMC Code of Professional Conduct: Standards for conduct, performance and ethics (the Code), recognising one's own abilities and limitations.
- Practise in accordance with an ethical and legal framework which ensures the primacy of patient and client interest and well-being and respects confidentiality.
- Practise in a fair and anti-discriminatory way, acknowledging the differences in beliefs and cultural practices of individuals or groups.
- Engage in, develop and disengage from therapeutic relationships through the use of appropriate communication and interpersonal skills.
- Create and utilize opportunities to promote the health and well-being of patients, clients and groups.
- Undertake and document a comprehensive, systematic and accurate nursing assessment of the physical, psychological, social and spiritual needs of patients, clients and communities.
- Formulate and document a plan of nursing care, where possible in partnership with patients, clients, their carers and family and friends, within a framework of informed consent.
- Based on the best available evidence, apply knowledge and an appropriate repertoire of skills indicative of safe nursing practice.
- Provide a rationale for the nursing care delivered which takes account of social, cultural, spiritual, legal, political and economic influences.
- Evaluate and document the outcomes of nursing and other interventions.
- Demonstrate sound clinical judgement across a range of differing professional and care delivery contexts.
- Contribute to public protection by creating and maintaining a safe environment of care through the use of quality assurance and risk management strategies.
- Demonstrate knowledge of effective interprofessional working practices which respect and utilize the contributions of members of the health and social care team.
- Delegate duties to others, as appropriate, ensuring that they are supervised and monitored.
- Demonstrate key skills.
- Demonstrate a commitment to the need for continuing professional development and personal supervision activities in order to enhance knowledge, skills, values and attitudes needed for safe and effective nursing practice.
- Enhance the professional development and safe practice of others through peer support, leadership, supervision and teaching.

Source: NMC, 2004e, p. 5.

Education (NMC, 2004e). Whilst lengthy, it is worth replicating the overall standards of proficiency (previously called competencies) spelt out in this report (NMC, 2004e, p. 5) required to practise as a first-level nurse, of whatever chosen branch; this information is displayed in Table 3.1.

Thus, through its central role in education and quality assurance, the NMC defines and safeguards the standards that ensure excellence in nursing and midwifery education. This work is also detailed in Part IV of the Nursing and Midwifery Order 2001 which relates specifically to the NMC's duty to establish standards and to keep them under review. The NMC also retains and updates a national list of approved programmes leading to pre-registration nursing qualifications (diploma to degree level), including those leading to the award of Registered Nurse (Sub-part 1 of the Nursing Register), with 'mental health' the designated 'field of practice', as well as specific programmes of study such as community specialist practice and, more recently, independent and supplementary nurse prescribing. Pre-registration nursing programmes in the UK range from undergraduate diploma to undergraduate degree awards (with the exception of Wales and Northern Ireland, nursing is not an all-graduate profession in the UK). The full list of awarding institutions and their programmes of study are open to public scrutiny and can be found at: http://www.nmc-uk.org.

At present, the mental health branch of pre-registration nurse training equips qualifying students to work in community settings, and that would include work with people with dementia and their families should this be a focus of interest. Whilst specialist post-qualifying courses on 'community specialist practice mental health nursing' are available in the UK, with successful completion of approved courses open to recording on the Nursing Register, it is not a mandatory qualification to practise as a CMHN. For the purpose of this chapter, therefore, it is the alignment of pre-registration mental health nurse training set out in *Making a Difference* (DoH, 1999) that we will use to capture and report upon the student learning experience, and in the Derby Street community illustration of Avis Jenkins and her neighbours.

Recent developments

Within mental health nursing, the last four years (2004–08) has seen the publication of three reports that have been influential in shaping community practice and nursing students' experience of the profession.

'Best Practice Competencies and Capabilities for Pre-Registration Mental Health Nurses in England'

This report (DoH, 2006e) was the product of the Chief Nursing Officer's review of mental health nursing in England entitled *From Values to Action* (DoH, 2006c). This report, similar to the mental health nursing review in

Table 3.2   The recovery approach in mental health care

The recovery approach is based around a number of principles that stress the importance of:

- working in partnership with service users (and/or carers) to identify realistic life goals and enabling achievement
- stressing the value of social inclusion
- stressing the need for professionals to be optimistic about the possibility of positive individual change.

Source: Adapted from DoH, 2006c, p. 17.

Scotland (Scottish Executive, 2006b), promoted the adoption of the 'recovery approach' (see Table 3.2) to all aspects of mental health care, including working with people with dementia and their families.

In contrast, the same report (DoH, 2006e) identified 'the core' (p. 1) competencies and capabilities, including knowledge and performance criteria, essential for mental health nurses at the point of registration in England. The report clearly endorsed the *Ten Essential Shared Capabilities* and the *NHS Knowledge and Skills Framework* (both briefly described below) whilst it was careful to avoid any conflict with the mandatory NMC proficiencies set out in the *Standards for Proficiency for Pre-Registration Nurse Education* (NMC, 2004e; and see Table 3.1).

Three overarching best practice competencies for pre-registration mental health nurses in England were listed in the report (DoH, 2006e) and are summarized below:

Best practice competencies for pre-registration mental health nurses

1. Putting values into practice
2. Improving outcomes for service users through the provision of:
    i.   communication
    ii. physical care
    iii. psychosocial care
    iv. risk and risk management
3. A positive, modern profession supported by:
    i.   multi-disciplinary and multi-agency working
    ii. personal and professional development (DoH, 2006e).

The notion of recovery underpinned these best practice competencies, and linked to each competency statement are knowledge criteria, performance criteria and the corresponding NMC Standards of Proficiency for Nursing.

'The Ten Essential Shared Capabilities: A framework for the whole of the mental health workforce'

Again, in this report (DoH, 2004c) it was made clear that the ten essential shared capabilities (TESCs) (DoH, 2004c) were not intended to replace the *NHS Knowledge and Skills Framework* (DoH, 2004b, and below) but, instead, were designed to be complementary to this document and to provide a 'mental health specific context' (p. 3) for education, training and continuing professional development. Primarily, the purpose of the TESCs was to signpost 'best practice' for all staff working in mental health and to act as a framework for pre- and post-qualifying training, education and practice. The needs of service users and carers were seen as central to the development and implementation of the TESCs and to influence education and training provision within the mental health field as outlined below:

The TESCs

1. Working in partnership
2. Respecting diversity
3. Practising ethically
4. Challenging inequality
5. Promoting recovery
6. Identifying people's needs and strengths
7. Providing user-centred care
8. Making a difference
9. Promoting safety and positive risk taking
10. Personal development and learning (DoH, 2004c).

Each of these ESCs is meant to be actively integrated in pre-registration mental health training and course curriculum.

'The NHS Knowledge and Skills Framework (NHS KSF) and the Development Review Process'

This is a weighty (over 260 pages) and comprehensive guide (DoH, 2004b) whose purpose is to define and describe the knowledge and skills which NHS staff need to apply in their work in order to deliver quality services. It is not possible to do the framework justice in the space available, but the primary purpose of the NHS KSF is 'essentially about lifelong learning' (p. 17) and should be freely available to all staff and used as guiding their 'next steps' on career opportunities and personal development plans. The six core dimensions of the NHS KSF are displayed below:

NHS KSF core dimensions

1. Communication
2. Personal and people development
3. Health, safety and security
4. Service improvement
5. Quality
6. Equality and diversity (DoH, 2004b).

Each dimension has a graded (between 1 and 4) level descriptor: a level 1 descriptor is about more 'simple' tasks whilst a level 4 descriptor relates to the most complex activities.

Models of teaching and learning

Traditionally, over a three-year diploma- or degree-level nursing course, pre-registration mental health nurses have been taught through a mixture of approaches, with the month and year of the 'intake' group (across all branches of nursing) being the common, binding feature of student nurse identity. During the Foundation Year, the students are exposed to a combination of structured learning in a classroom and/or lecture theatre environment and a variety of practice placements, with all nursing students in the 'intake' group being exposed to shared, learning experiences. Whilst there is an NMC requirement for all students to have some exposure to mental health in the Foundation Year the extent and nature of this exposure is highly variable. Students therefore may or may not specifically explore issues of mental health and old age and there are no educational standards set down by the NMC to say that this must be a core element of shared learning/teaching within this period of study (Pulsford et al., 2007).

Typically, a Foundation Year would prepare all nursing students to understand and function effectively in practice; for example, learning about communication, physiology, psychology, the philosophy and organization of care, the context of health and social care, nursing informatics and research, health development opportunities with a focus upon personal and clinical skills development, and so on. Assessment of progress is through successfully negotiating a series of formal examination papers, summative assignments linked to modules of study and the successful achievement of learning outcomes and demonstrable competencies in practice placements.

Successful completion of the Foundation Year enables the student to progress to their chosen branch of study. To take the first author's own organization as a case example (as at March 2008), in Years 2 and 3 of pre-

Table 3.3   **Example curriculum framework of the Bachelor of Nursing (Hons) Mental Health – Branch Years 2 and 3**

	Term 1	Term 2	Term 3
Year 2	Introduction to the Care of People with Common Mental Health Problems	Acute Care of Individuals with Mental Health Needs and their Families	Elective
	Pathology	Health Psychology and Behaviour Change	
	Pharmacology	Nursing Assessment	
Year 3	The Care of Individuals with Serious and Enduring Mental Health Problems in the Community	Care of Older People with Mental Health Needs	Management and Consolidation of Practice
	Dissertation		

Source: School of Nursing, Midwifery and Social Work, the University of Manchester. Reproduced with permission.

registration mental health nurse training at degree level, the Bachelor of Nursing (Hons) Mental Health award offered by the School of Nursing, Midwifery and Social Work at the University of Manchester – and leading on successful completion to Registration in Nursing (Mental Health) on the NMC Register – is divided into three terms, as shown in Table 3.3.

Evidence-based care forms an integral component of structured classroom teaching, with an emphasis placed upon the application, practice and theoretical underpinnings of therapeutic techniques, such as behavioural therapy, cognitive skills, psychosocial models of treatment and support, and so on. During the second year of the first author's programme (this may differ in other institutions), all mental health nursing students undertake an elective placement at the end of that year to broaden their nursing experience. For those mental health students who are interested in dementia care, for instance, it is at this elective point that a CMHN placement could be sought and the student exposed to the Derby Street case scenario outlined in the book (DoH, 2004b). Towards the end of the three-year programme, there is a final period of consolidation that allows each student to reflect on their experience and prepare themselves for their new role as a qualified nurse (see also http://www.nursing.manchester.ac.uk/undergraduate/dpsn/?code=00749&pg=2).

Student learning in community mental health practice in dementia care, therefore, takes place within a group setting, tutorials, individual practice mentoring in the clinical area (by an experienced, qualified mental health nurse suitably prepared to perform this role), and measurement of growth and development through pastoral support. As seen in Table 3.3, managerial experience is of most importance in the final year when students are being prepared for the transition to qualified nurse practitioner status in which they will abide by the NMC Code which sets out 'standards of conduct, performance and ethics for nurses and midwives' (NMC, 2007a). This important document outlines the Registered Nurses' duty of care to patients and clients, reinforces the stance that each nurse is accountable for his/her practice and states that each nurse must:

- Make the care of people your first concern, treating them as individuals and respecting their dignity
- Work with others to protect and promote the health and well-being of those in your care, their families and carers, and the wider community
- Provide a high standard of practice and care at all times
- Be open and honest, act with integrity and uphold the reputation of your profession (NMC, 2007a).

Whilst structured learning is an important dimension of student learning, it is by no means the only way of acquiring practice knowledge. During clinical placements mentorship by experienced mental health practitioners forms an integral part of the learning experience and may well be instrumental in helping to shape the student's choice of professional practice following registration. Within a dementia care setting, the knowledge chain framework suggested by Clarke et al. (2003) provides an important conceptual and theoretical link in developing a 'bottom-up' process of practice learning. According to these authors, there are three knowledge changes in operation. The first is 'knowledge for practice' that is derived from sources outside the practice environment (also referred to as 'distal' knowledge). The second is 'knowledge from practice'; that is, knowledge derived from a specific care environment, with this type of knowledge reflecting individual practice philosophies and care values. This second knowledge chain was also labelled as 'proximal' knowledge. The third link in the knowledge chain was that deriving from the service user(s) and was defined as arising from the person's own experiences of self-management and 'the acquisition of information from family, friends and lay sources of information' (Clarke et al., 2003, p. 23).

Practice knowledge may also be enhanced and supported through the use of reflective practice, in which students are encouraged to learn from their experience using structured reflection. Within health care education, reflection on experience is considered an essential tool in helping students make links between theory and practice (Jasper, 2003). As students begin to integrate evidenced-based knowledge and development of practice skills, the use of reflective practice is seen to facilitate critical analysis and judgement and subsequently lead to further development of practice knowledge. A number of frameworks may be utilized to support this process, including

Gibbs reflective cycle (1988), Johns's model for structured reflection (2004) and Borton's developmental framework (1970). Whilst Johns's model was derived from and has been widely adopted in nursing, its use is primarily focused on critical incidents and stays at the contemplative stage. In contrast Borton's framework asks the practitioner to reflect using three types of questions: 'What?', 'So what?' and 'Now what?'. The final stage leads practitioners to develop or change their practice as a consequence of reflection. According to Jasper (2003), 'it is a relatively simple model that is very suitable for novice practitioners but can be used at different levels as students become more adept at reflecting on their practice and more critically analytical.'

Thus, in Derby Street, student learning could be enhanced through a biographical and life-story approach to assessment and care work. Knowledge and learning should be seen as a two-way process with the interaction enriching the life of the student nurse – in this context we will call her **Jane** – as much as the visit is seen to be 'therapeutic' by **Avis**. By tapping into the biography of Avis and her lifelong knowledge of the area and connections through her role on the local newspaper, Jane will develop and demonstrate two main learning processes. The first of these is the conduct of a person-centred approach to practice, an essential value in dementia care, where it is the person and not the dementia that should lead all communication and interactive approaches (Kitwood, 1997; Brooker, 2006). The second is the communication approach which also shares the predictive power of single and double loop reflective learning models as demonstrated by Schön (1991), Wong et al. (1995) and Greenwood (1998), and which prepares Jane to reflect upon and build from the experience of her encounter(s) with Avis.

The use of structured reflection would also enhance Jane's learning through considering interactions that took place during her contact with Avis. The mentor would probably wish to see how Jane could be involved in the Memory Joggers group, which is co-led by a CMHN, and would provide a real-life opportunity for Jane to engage in groupwork, group dynamics and cognitive rehabilitation. This exposure would build upon Jane's theoretical and experiential knowledge of group activities, which are important parts of student learning and classroom teaching within the mental health branch. The fact that the Memory Joggers group is also held in the vicinity of the Green Hill flats would help raise Jane's awareness and appreciation of community care, in the broadest sense of the word. Finding interconnections and relationships that nurture and support older people with cognitive frailty living in the community are important roles for the CMHN and Jane's informal social contact with Avis's neighbours, **Jason Dean** and **Sam Weiner**, would introduce her to learning built from community knowledge.

To develop this a little further, using Borton's (1970) framework as an example, cue questions for Jane might include:

- *What* is Avis's main problem? *What* do we know about her previous coping/life that might be helpful? *What* is the main problem identified by her son? *What* role do her neighbours have in supporting her?
- *So what* does that teach us about working with/supporting Avis and her son? *So what* other knowledge can we bring to the situation?
- *Now what* do we need to do in order to support Avis with her needs, minimize risk and improve her current experience/quality of life?

The application of such a reflective framework could be seen to enhance Jane's learning in the practice environment.

The teacher in the practice setting

With the advent of Project 2000 and subsequent developments (DoH, 1999) and the 50/50 split between (university/HEI-based) education and practice, emphasis is placed on the practice component by supporting existing, qualified, practitioners to provide student mentoring in the clinical area. This arrangement demands partnership working between NHS providers and university lecturers responsible for the Foundation Year and branch programmes. Mentors are prepared by the way of an NMC-approved programme of study with assigned lecturers acting as a bridge and broker between the university and clinical setting. NHS trusts may also seek feedback on the quality of student learning in practice, collecting experiences from mentors about student placement and feeding general thoughts and lessons back to the link tutor, and/or the responsible pre-registration branch lead within the allocating School of Nursing, for example.

Generally, practice-based mentors undertake/seek the role of mentor out of a sense of professional responsibility and duty. Additional remuneration for undertaking this role is not a feature of the position although it may be one of the clinical standards that become part of an advanced nursing role. In 2006 the NMC published *Standards to Support Learning and Assessment in Practice: NMC standards for mentors, practice teachers and teachers.* As stated in the Foreword to this document, the standards take the form of a developmental framework and the outcomes for each role are identified as different stages within the framework (NMC, 2006b). For nursing (which includes mental health nursing and a focus on dementia care), the NMC (2006b, p. 9) agreed the following mandatory requirements for entry onto the register. These are:

- Students on NMC-approved pre-registration nursing education programmes, leading to registration on the nurses' part of the register, must be supported and assessed by mentors; and
- From September 2007 a 'sign-off mentor', who has met additional criteria, must make the final assessment of practice and confirm to the NMC that the required proficiencies for entry to the register have been achieved.

To develop this a little further, the NMC (2006b) identified outcomes for mentors, practice teachers and teachers so that there is clear accountability for making decisions that lead to entry to the register. There are eight domains in the framework, these being:

1. Establishing effective working relationships
2. Facilitation of learning
3. Assessment and accountability
4. Evaluation of learning
5. Creating an environment for learning
6. Context of practice
7. Evidence-based practice
8. Leadership.

Within this framework, mentors or practice teachers must demonstrate their knowledge, skills and competence on an ongoing basis, and 'placement providers' (NMC, 2006b, p. 8) must ensure that each mentor and practice teacher is reviewed every three years and that mentors who have the additional responsibility of 'signing-off' practice proficiency at the end of a programme are annotated on the local register.

A resource pack recently designed to support the educational and practice preparation for nursing students working with older people (RCN/ Age Concern, 2008) identifies the need for students to have more exposure to nursing older people in practice, supported by skilled mentors. Good mentorship should be provided by skilled, knowledgeable practitioners who are able to inform and support the development of practice learning. One example of this approach within dementia care nursing may be offered by Admiral Nursing. As mental health nurses specializing in the care of families affected by dementia (see box headed 'Role of the Admiral Nurse'), Admiral Nurses, as part of their role, provide educational and practice support to other health and social care professionals. As such they are in an ideal position to support practice learning for both pre-registration nursing students, Registered Nurses and other professionals interested in developing their skills further in working with people with dementia and their family carers (Thompson and Devenney, 2007).

In addition to mentorship the involvement of practice educators and/ or lecturer practitioners can provide an important link between education and practice settings. Joint clinical academic posts not only add to the clinical credibility of lecturers but also ensure that continuation of learning in practice is maintained (Owen et al., 2005). One such role is that of the Admiral Nurse Lecturer Practitioner whose core practice parameters are illustrated below:

- to provide teaching in care of people with dementia and their carers on pre- and post-registration courses;
- to take on a small caseload of carers of people with dementia and provide specialist care and support; and
- to act as a consultant/ mentor to other professionals and workers.

There are organizational and financial challenges to developing and maintaining such posts due to the difficulty in balancing requirements for contribution to research, teaching and clinical work. However, they provide an important developmental opportunity for the mental health nursing profession as a whole and demonstrate partnership working between NHS service providers and university/HEI settings.

The content and structure of the students' learning

The need for improved professional education for dementia care has been highlighted in the UK by a number of recent reports and policy statements (see, for example: NICE/SCIE, 2007; Alzheimer's Society, 2007; National Audit Office, 2007). Indeed, a key message within the service development guide, *Everybody's Business: Integrated mental health services for older adults* (DoH/CSIP, 2005), was that it was essential to develop a coherent and cohesive strategy for education and training for older adults' mental health services, including dementia care.

It has been demonstrated that education provision for dementia care as a whole is patchy, with many professionals, including CMHNs, having limited access to specialist knowledge to help them prepare for the role (Aveyard, 2001; Pulsford et al., 2007; Bryans et al., 2003; Manthorpe et al., 2003). Operating within the UK, the Higher Education for Dementia Network (HEDN) is responding to this identified professional imperative by developing a Curriculum for Dementia Education (CDE) to guide HEI providers in the key areas for inclusion in courses related to dementia care, at both pre-registration and post-qualifying levels, and to offer ideas for best practice in implementing the CDE.

The CDE represents a systematic attempt to set out the key knowledge, skills and attitudes that should be addressed in courses for health and social care professionals who work with people with dementia. It is offered as a guide to course developers as to what their courses should include – a 'checklist' for students of dementia care to help them identify their key learning needs, and a challenge to course providers to ensure that their provision is comprehensive and contemporary.

Methods

Within a mental health branch programme, students will be exposed to all four techniques of teaching and learning; namely experiential, written word, graphic and hardware. Whilst a balance of techniques are presented within the learning environment, Table 3.1 outlines that one of the key criteria to be able to practise as a nurse is to 'engage in, develop and disengage from therapeutic relationships through the use of appropriate communication and interpersonal skills'. For mental health nursing and for the care of people with dementia and their families in particular, educational value is placed on experiential and person-centred approaches. Role-playing situations and peer feedback of communication styles and approaches are essential in helping to equip mental health student nurses with a reflective and person-centred view of practice, and the world. In Derby Street this preparation is necessary if pre-registration mental health nurses are to approach the diversity, complexity and inter-dependency of the residents' lives in an informed and proficient manner, particularly if they then choose to specialize within CMHN work in dementia care. Reflexivity is a key part of mental health student learning and progress is demonstrated through a written portfolio that integrates both learning arrangements.

To return once again to the Bachelor of Nursing (Hons) Mental Health award offered by the School of Nursing, Midwifery and Social Work at one university for a practical illustration, in the undergraduate module 'Care of Older People with Mental Health Needs' (see Table 3.3, Year 3) the university-based learning is structured around a problem-based learning (PBL) approach. The unit uses a combination of classroom-based group work in facilitated PBL groups, supervised clinical practice and reflective practice, as well as more traditional lectures and seminars. Within the unit mental health nursing students are encouraged to identify their own learning needs following an analysis of PBL scenarios designed to stimulate thinking and learning about complex clinical and social situations. Moreover, within the practice environment, this learning process is also approached through role modelling and student reflection (Ferguson and Hope, 1999).

Table 3.4   NMC requirements for support and assessment

NMC requirements	Advice and guidance
Most assessment of competence should be undertaken through direct observation in practice.	Students must normally demonstrate competence in the practice setting. However, where experience is limited (for example, basic life support skills), simulations may be used. The majority of assessment should be through direct observation.
Mentors should be involved, wherever possible, when competence is assessed through simulation.	Summative assessment using simulation may occur where opportunities to demonstrate competence in practice are limited. Mentors should be involved in designing, using and evaluating such assessment strategies.
Mentors should consider how evidence from various sources might contribute to making a judgement on performance and competence.	The NMC recognizes that the total assessment strategy would include assessment through various means, such as direct care, simulation and other strategies.
Mentors should seek advice and guidance from a sign-off mentor or a practice teacher when dealing with failing students.	Inexperienced mentors may require support from a sign-off mentor or practice teacher when faced with a failing student to help them to communicate concerns, identify action and evaluate progress.

Assessment

The NMC (2006b) document, *Standards to Support Learning and Assessment in Practice: NMC standards for mentors, practice teachers and teachers*, acknowledges that nurses, midwives and specialist community public health nurses have different needs when applying the standards to support learning and assessment in practice. For example, for nursing education, mentors, practice teachers and teachers are required to provide the full range of support and assessment required to meet the needs of pre-registration, specialist practice and advanced nursing education (see Table 3.4). This is important as it allows mentors to assess learning in practice through a variety of approaches, as shown in Table 3.4 (NMC, 2006b, pp. 31–2).

Continuing professional development

Preceptorship provides structured support to newly qualified mental health nurses and facilitates their development during the first 12 months of their time in a new post. Preceptorship should be integrated with supervision, continuing professional development, and the NHS KSF (DoH, 2004b). If mental health nurses are to progress through a career pathway, as recommended in the NHS KSF (DoH, 2004b) and *Modernising Nursing Careers* (DoH, 2006g), then a clear educational development pathway needs to be made available for those nurses wishing to progress within dementia care. To this end, in the UK, there are a number of high-quality post-registration courses available within HEIs ranging from diploma level through to a master's level in dementia care. These courses can be accessed through attendance at a university (for example, http://www.manchester.ac.uk/postgraduate/taughtdegrees/courses/pgdiploma/course/?code=02142), or through distance learning (for example, http://www.bradford.ac.uk/university/ugpros/dementia-bsc.php). Naturally, these opportunities are open to nurses as well as other statutory or voluntary care providers in supporting their continuing professional development.

Current debates

It is now generally accepted that people who use health and social services and their carers should be involved in the planning, delivery and evaluation of those services, and in the education of professionals who will deliver their care (Callaghan et al., 2005; Lathlean et al., 2006). A growing literature has highlighted the extent that service users and carers have become involved in professional education, has offered principles for good practice in user and carer involvement, and has identified challenges to full involvement (Forrest et al., 2000; Repper and Breeze, 2004; Tew et al., 2004). There may, however, be particular issues with involving certain groups of service users and their carers in professional education, and one such group is people with dementia.

In supporting practice learning, service user and carer involvement may have a number of specific aims. A principal purpose is to assist students to empathize with the experience of the people for whom they are learning to care, by helping them gain a greater understanding of what it is like to have an illness or disability, or to care for a person with that condition. A related purpose may be for users and their carers to express their views to students as to their experience of care, and how professionals should work with the family group.

In most areas of health and social care practice and education, service users are more often involved than are carers (Repper and Breeze, 2004). In dementia care, by contrast, carers have traditionally held a more prominent position than people with dementia themselves, who have been largely excluded from active involvement in their own care (Cheston et al., 2000). It has been assumed in the past that people with dementia are unable to make personal contributions, due to the cognitive disabilities and the disabling effects of a progressive and enduring dementia. Also, it has been assumed that carers, with their intimate knowledge of those for whom they care, can act as spokespersons for the people with dementia. In recent years, however, both these assumptions have been challenged (Goldsmith, 1996; Aggarwal et al., 2003; Berenbaum, 2005) and it has become accepted that people with dementia are able to be involved in discussing their situation, which might inform practice. This includes facilitating ways of involving people with dementia in professional education and supporting learning in practice (Cheston et al., 2000; Cantley et al., 2005; Harris, 2007).

Some challenges remain in relation to ensuring that the experiences of those with severe dementia are integrated into practice learning. It is here that methods such as case study, role play, direct observation of body language, film, audio recording and life-story methods most need to be brought into play. There is also potential for mental health nursing students to draw on these methods as part of their learning, so that they are *'learning to ...'* rather than just *'learning about ...'* a particular approach or intervention. In this way practitioners will develop the skills of observation, reflection, interpretation and creativity that are so vital to working with all people who have dementia in a way that includes and values them (Thompson et al., 2007).

Future developments

Dementia care is a major public and social policy issue in the UK and, as such, is of significance to health care professionals charged with providing a response to identified need. Recent policy drives have reinforced the values, needs and supportive networks that people with dementia and their families require in order to live an active and fulfilling life (DoH/CSIP, 2005; DoH, 2005; National Audit Office, 2007), a dynamic that folds into the care professions (Brooker, 2006), including nursing (Adams, 2007). In 2009 this public commitment to people with dementia and their families was made manifest in the publication of a National Dementia Strategy for England (DoH, 2009).

Whilst the National Dementia Strategy will embrace training and education issues, it has, to date, identified three areas of particular importance, namely: (1) improving awareness; (2) early diagnosis and intervention; and (3) improving quality of care for dementia (Banerjee and Chan, 2008; DoH, 2009). Such initiatives are pressing, as the Alzheimer's Society has suggested that there are around 700,000 people with dementia living in the UK, representing one person in every 88 of the population, with the prevalence rising to 940,110 by 2021 and 1,735,087 by 2051, an increase of 38 per cent over the next 15 years and 154 per cent over the next 45 years (Alzheimer's Society, 2007). Advancing age is a notable risk factor for the acquisition of dementia, with one person in 1,000 aged 40–65 years; one person in 20 aged over 65 years; and one person in five over 80 years of age having dementia (Alzheimer's Society, 2007). Around two-thirds of people with dementia live in the community, with the remaining third in a care home environment; the annual economic cost of dementia to the UK is currently estimated at £17 billion (Alzheimer's Society, 2007).

The nurse education agenda and the student experience have been subjected to numerous changes and policy directions over recent years, some of which we have outlined in this chapter. Advances in all aspects of dementia care, along with the increasing numbers of people with dementia receiving both generic and specialized health and social care services, make it imperative that health and social care professionals receive education and training to equip them with the knowledge, skills and underpinning attitudes to care for people with dementia and their families. If nurses as key players in the delivery of dementia care are to be equipped adequately then it is essential that they are able to access educational courses in dementia at a variety of levels, wherever in the UK they are based.

Core text recommendations

Adams, T. (ed.) (2007), *Dementia Care Nursing: Promoting well-being in people with dementia and their families*, Basingstoke: Palgrave Macmillan.
Keady, J., Clarke, C.L., and Adams, T. (eds) (2003), *Community Mental Health Nursing and Dementia Care: Practice perspectives*, Maidenhead: Open University Press.
Keady, J., Clarke, C.L., and Page, S. (eds) (2007), *Partnerships in Community Mental Health Nursing and Dementia Care: Practice perspectives*, Maidenhead: Open University Press/McGraw-Hill.

Acknowledgements

Our thanks go to Dr Steven Pryjmachuk, Head of Division; Professor John Playle, Director of External Relations; and Helen Pusey, Lecturer in Nursing, all based at the School of Nursing, Midwifery and Social Work, the University of Manchester, for their invaluable advice and comments on earlier drafts of this chapter.

4   The doctor

Deborah G. Murdoch-Eaton and Trudie E. Roberts

Overview

Doctors on qualification are awarded an MBChB or MBBS (Bachelor of Medicine or Bachelor of Surgery). This is normally after a full-time training of a minimum of five years in a higher educational institution (HEI). A significant number of medical students will have extended their studies by one year to have additionally studied for a BSc. The medical degree is generic, aiming to produce a well-rounded doctor competent in core knowledge, skills and attitudes at a level appropriate to enter practice at Foundation Year on graduation. Newly qualified doctors then undertake a further two years of Foundation training, after which they are eligible for full registration with the General Medical Council (GMC), and able to commence clinical training in the specialty of their choosing.

The content and regulation of the undergraduate curriculum is under surveillance by the General Medical Council. Their publication *Tomorrow's Doctors* (*TD*) (GMC, 2003) outlines the content and method of delivery of undergraduate medical training within the UK. Medical schools are reviewed and evaluated by Quality and Assessment Board representatives of the GMC to ensure the adequacy of the undergraduate course and compliance with *TD* recommendations.

There has been a rapid expansion in medical school places over the last decade, in response to workforce pressures following both changing health care practice and a reduction in doctors' working hours to comply with the European Work Time Directive (EWTD). This has resulted in a number of new medical schools opening in the UK, bringing this to a current (2008) total of 27 medical schools, with an annual intake of around 6,400, and a total of 35,000 students in UK medical schools.

Current medical educational practice ensures early clinical contact from entry into medical school, increasing during the course such that by the final two years the majority of time is spent in clinical placements. Medical students' learning is supervised by a range of teachers coming from a number of academic and professional disciplines not only within medicine and the medical sciences. This reflects the multi-professional nature of health care delivery and involvement of patients as teachers. Formative and summative assessments of competence occur at frequent intervals during the undergraduate career. They encompass a variety of methodologies chosen to reflect the acquisition and range of knowledge, skills and attitudes required by graduation. There is no national qualifying examination in medicine (although this is under discussion), but standards and agreed competencies are laid down by the GMC, and external examiners ensure the comparability and adequacy of the degree awarded.

Recent developments

The publication in 1993 by the GMC of *Tomorrow's Doctors* (*TD*) changed the face of medical education. As a result of this publication, and its subsequent update in 2003, every medical school in the UK has changed the way in which it educates future medical practitioners. It not only impacted on what was taught but significantly contributed to the improvements in teaching and assessment methods utilized in undergraduate medical courses. The influence of *Tomorrow's Doctors* (GMC, 2003) has not only been on medicine within the UK, but it has also been the model for other health care educators to review their curricula both here and in Europe.

Historically, the medical curriculum had been divided into a two-year pre-clinical basic science course comprising mainly anatomy, physiology and biochemistry, followed by a three-year clinical course taking place principally in large teaching hospitals and taught predominantly by NHS doctors. The link between the two course elements was tenuous and not explicit. Each medical school taught its own curriculum which was not shared effectively with the NHS staff and was certainly not communicated explicitly to the students. Even within the preclinical academic disciplines, there was little or no communication and medical students were not infrequently taught the same course material as other science students with no acknowledgement of their subsequent different career. However, *TD* required each medical school to explicitly define the 'core' curriculum and the learning outcomes for that core. It also stated that students should be encouraged to go beyond the core by the provision of student-selected components (SSCs) which would allow them to pursue areas of interest to a deeper level, fostering the spirit of enquiry (Murdoch-Eaton et al., 2004). Recommendations on changes in course delivery were also included.

Consequently, the majority of medical courses in the UK are now integrated. The preclinical/clinical divide no longer exists and the scientific theory underpinning the practice of medicine is taught in context of the patient and their illness, or promotion of health. Most medical schools now have built-in early clinical exposure so that students meet and talk to patients and their carers in the first few weeks of their course. There are clear learning outcomes for each component of the course and assessments are blueprinted onto these learning outcomes in recognition of the 'assessment driving learning' doctrine. The overriding importance of the scientific basis of medicine, whilst still acknowledged, is tempered by re-introducing the 'art' of medicine. Curriculum time is being used to teach communication and teamwork skills, recognized as essential for medical practice in a new patient-led health service. There is now recognition of the continuing evolution of medical education as the pace of medical knowledge and societal demands continues to progress and, reflecting this, a new edition of *TD* is planned for 2008.

In the UK, students usually enter a five- or six-year programme directly from high school. In North America, following the Flexner report of 1910, graduates have been almost extensively admitted to four-year programmes. In Australia, an interesting mixture of graduate entry and traditional school-leaver entrants pertain. Although many medical schools in the UK have admitted a few graduates into their programmes, more recently some schools have set up graduate entry four-year programmes alongside and often integrating with their existing courses. Most commonly, these graduate entrants hold first degrees in either a relevant science or health-related area, although some (for example, St George's Medical School, London) consider applicants with a degree in any area. Delaying admission to medicine until after a first degree allows applicants to develop specific knowledge and generic academic skills. They will usually make a more mature and considered decision to study for a demanding career. Additionally, graduate entry programmes will offer the opportunity to enter medicine for those who develop a later interest in the subject, and the diversity of their previous experience contributes to the vibrancy of the medical school. However, these courses are intensive and demanding and, taking into account the cost of the first degree, they are not cheap; students may be deterred by the increasing amount of debt they will incur.

Models of teaching and learning

Different educational models in use range from problem-based learning (PBL) through to models of integrated or systems-based curricula. All encompass the principles of developing students as individuals, with elements of structured learning interspersed with apprenticeship and managerial models of learning. The principle of spiral learning is frequently used, with material being revisited at different stages of the students' learning. All models of teaching ensure focus around the patient and the clinical problem (Bruner, 1960; Harden, 1999; Harden and Stamper, 1999; Harden et al., 2000; O'Neill et al., 1999; O'Neill et al., 2002).

Interest in PBL has increased in the UK over the last decade (Finucane et al., 1998), with a number of medical schools (for example, Manchester and Glasgow) adopting this type of minimally guided instruction as their main method of teaching. The range of interpretation of implementation of PBL is large and practice often very different. Its proponents point to studies which show student enthusiasm for this mode of learning. However, despite many studies there is no unequivocal evidence to date that this method produces better teaching and learning outcomes (Colliver, 2000; Newman, 2003).

Personal development and reflective learning are key features of medical students' learning requiring them to integrate the knowledge, skills and attitudes with the development of the professional values and learning of the profession to which they aspire. Ethics and communication are key strands in any undergraduate curriculum (Kurtz et al., 2005; Mattick and Bligh, 2006). Discussion of interprofessionalism and experience of key issues for future professional practice (including confidentiality, self-awareness, self-evaluation and reflection for future development) are key strands introduced early into their undergraduate training and revisited in different clinical settings. This establishes the model for future lifelong learning and future appraisal.

Teachers of medical students come from across the full range of health care and community support providers. In the early years of the course particularly, their supervisors and mentors are likely to be from a wide range of health care professionals. Additionally there will be opportunities for interprofessional learning with students from other professions, usually in the format of small group work or joint clinical experiences; for example, visits into the community. Debriefing will then additionally include reflection on future professional working relationships, as well as the learning experience itself (Kember, 2001).

Illustrations of how this integrated model works in our medical school are shown below, demonstrating the interaction of students during their training with Derby Street residents in the Green Hill flats.

***

Avis Jenkins is an 84-year-old lady with deteriorating memory. She enjoys company and visitors. **Alison** is a first-year medical student and she and a nursing student have been for a pre-visit briefing with the practice nurse from Mrs Jenkins' primary care provider. Alison and the nursing student then went jointly to visit Mrs Jenkins at home to talk to her about not only her health care needs, but also the assistance and support she gets within the community to enable her to stay within her own home. Both students are required to write up a reflective account of their visit and what they have learnt about support for the elderly within the community. They will be required to make a presentation to their small group when they return to university.

Practice-based learning is woven in throughout the course to enable students to recognize the full range of health care requirements of populations and to consider health prevention and health promotion. Student-selected components (SSCs) provide individual opportunities for students to work alone or in small groups on areas that might not necessarily be included within the core curriculum, for example, on complementary health care provision. Such projects enable students to identify areas of particular interest and, through close personal supervision, to be able to investigate underpinning theory, evaluate the quality of the literature pertaining to the area of study and, having defined a clear question to investigate, write up an account based not only on a review of the literature but also on reflection about their own personal learning (Murdoch-Eaton et al., 2004).

Neal is a second-year medical student who is spending two weeks on a community-based SSC. His attachment takes him to a drop-in centre for homeless people. On his third day there, when he is assisting with lunchtimes, he meets **Jason Dean**, a volunteer who has recently completed a rehabilitation programme following drug addiction. Through Neal's contact with Jason, and the clients he meets at the drop-in centre, he becomes particularly interested in the effectiveness of drug rehabilitation programmes and decides this is the area he will concentrate on during his attachment and write up in depth for his SSC report.

Clinical skills and method are initially taught in clinical skills learning centres where students learn the skills of clinical examination in a safe environment on models and volunteers (Bradley and Postlethwaite, 2003). They are closely monitored and observed taking histories on selected patients by a range of health care professionals.

Ahmed is a third-year medical student who is on placement with a primary care practice for two days a week. **Zoë Benner** has brought her daughter **Kylie** in to talk to the practice nurse about her bed-wetting problems. Ahmed has been observing during the practice nurse's clinic, and participates in the training of Kylie and her mother in the use of an enuresis alarm. He is also interested in how the practice nurse agrees to contact the school to discuss Kylie's recent poor attendance and the factors that might have contributed to this. Ahmed has arranged to ensure that he is back with the practice nurse to review the progress in two weeks' time.

By the final two years of the medical course, students are virtually full-time in clinical placements, at this stage to gain exposure to a number of specialties, including paediatrics, obstetrics, gynaecology, ophthalmology, anaesthetics, and so on. In the final year, most medical students have a two-month period of study called the 'elective', which many students choose to spend abroad. A large number work in developing countries looking at health care delivery in resource-poor environments; some take the opportunity to pursue research; and some use this time for specialist clinical attachments, often in centres of international repute. After return to medical school for their final year, students are allocated in groups to senior clinical rotations in core medical and surgical areas before taking their final examinations. Prior to graduation students will usually undertake a period of shadowing the Foundation Year doctor they will be taking over from on graduation.

Sunita is a fourth-year medical student on paediatric attachment. She is on the ward when Zoë Benner brings in her 11-month-old baby daughter **Kara** with wheezing. Sunita takes the history from Zoë whilst the Senior House Officer is arranging an urgent nebulizer for Kara. Sunita also measures Kara's height and weight and plots them on the growth charts, which show that she is underweight for her height. The following day Sunita joins the dietician and Zoë to make a detailed evaluation of Kara's dietary intake. It is decided to keep Kara in for a number of days for observation, once she is over her asthma attack, to monitor her feeding.

Elaine is a final-year medical student. She is doing her final shadowing attachment and goes with the Orthopaedic SHO to the Accident and

Emergency department to see **Jim Rafferty** who has been brought in having fallen at home. He has a fractured neck of femur. Elaine helps the SHO prepare Jim for theatre by organizing the appropriate blood investigations and asking an anaesthetist to come and assess him prior to theatre. Elaine and the staff nurse jointly talk to Jim after the doctor has obtained consent for the operation to clarify some specific questions that he had thought about after signing the consent form. The issue of whether Jim has been able to read sufficient information on the consent form with his deteriorating sight is discussed. Elaine, on Jim's request, goes back to the SHO to ask that the operation be deferred until Jim's daughter has arrived and had an opportunity to read to him the consent form that he has signed.

Evidence-based practice and professionalism are key elements of being an effective health care practitioner and this is brought home to students throughout their course by increasing exposure to the principles. From early in their undergraduate careers, students will be required to search the literature to find answers to questions, initially using text books but, nearing graduation, using search engines to source the most up-to-date information including current published journals. By the final year, students will be expected to write to evaluate and critique management, referring to published guidelines and accepted practice recommendations from bodies such as the National Institute for Clinical Excellence (NICE) and be able to critique the management of patients they have seen (Sackett et al., 2002; NICE website). Medical students are thus encouraged to recognize the changing nature of evidence, and the importance of ensuring that practice is based on the best available evidence and adjusted on an individual problem-solving basis. Students are encouraged to critique management and to constantly evaluate and reflect on good practice.

The teacher in the practice setting

Funding for clinical placements comes from the Multi-Professional Education and Training levy (MPET), a funding stream from the Department of Health for the additional costs to the NHS of supporting the practice experience of medical and dental students. The Service Increment for Teaching (SIFT) component of MPET covers the costs to the NHS of supporting teaching of medical undergraduates (for example, reduced patient numbers in clinic as a consequence of the presence of students). Clinical placement contracts are drawn up annually between the university and the health care service provider stipulating agreements not only on access to staff and patients, but actual teaching and other requirements, including teaching space, IT equipment and overnight accommodation for students in residence.

Acknowledgement of the importance of learning in practice settings or 'on-the-job' learning has been at the heart of medical education since its inception and the apprenticeship model is often quoted: 'The student begins with the patient, continues with the patient, and ends his studies with the patient, using books and lectures as tools, as means to an end' (Osler, 1932).

Although the spirit of the apprentice is still present, it is now recognized that although medical students still need to learn from and with patients, patients are no longer in the environments they were even a decade ago. The majority of common illnesses are managed outside hospital inpatient beds through community and primary care practices and hospital outpatient appointments. Consequently if students were only exposed, say, to asthmatics who had to be hospitalized, they might regard it as a dreadful condition which interferes with the quality of people's lives in a major way, stopping them from working and leading to the ravages of medication side effects. However, in reality the vast majority of individuals with asthma live perfectly normal lives, mostly managing their condition themselves and occasionally requiring some extra help via the GP or practice nurse, but not necessitating either specialist hospital input or inpatient stay. This has meant that the term 'practice setting' now has a much wider connotation. It also means, therefore, that the term 'teacher', which even a decade ago in the context of medical students would have referred to other doctors, now needs to be interpreted in a completely different way. In today's medical education the term 'teacher' can refer to doctors, nurses, pharmacists; in fact almost any appropriate health care practitioner and now, increasingly, patients as well. These developments have done much to enrich the medical course but have posed challenges in terms of training educators from a wide variety of backgrounds. To illustrate this, three examples will be used covering doctor, nurse and patient educators.

The doctor as medical educator

It is enshrined within the Hippocratic Oath that doctors should 'gladly share such knowledge as is mine with those who are to follow'. With this expectation and the recognition that being able to teach requires training, *Tomorrow's Doctors* explicitly states that medical students should be taught how to teach within their undergraduate course.

Over 70 per cent of clinical teaching is undertaken by NHS doctors, both consultants and trainees. This is mostly in the form of 'bedside' teaching, although these days the 'bedside' is more likely to be replaced by the outpatient, GP's surgery or community setting, including sometimes the patient's own home. The training of NHS doctors to teach is provided by several bodies. Most immediately it is often provided by the medical education units (MEUs) which have been set up as repositories of expertise and training in many medical schools. One of the remits of such units is often to provide training for clinicians who teach or examine on their undergraduate courses and are not entitled to university teacher training. They often run a combination of generic and specialized training courses. For example, the University of Leeds runs courses on teaching in the ambulatory setting and examining in objective structured clinical examinations (OSCEs). Staff development units at universities provide generic teaching courses; however, these are usually only for substantive university employees and not available to NHS employees. Additionally, a number of institutions now run formally accredited postgraduate courses[1] in medical or clinical education, which are becoming increasingly popular with those involved in health care education. They combine the underpinning theory of teaching and learning with practical assignments involving their own teaching in their place of practice.

Nationally, specialist organizations such as the Higher Education Academy (HEA) Medicine, Dentistry and Veterinary Medicine Subject Centre (Medev) provide one-day specific training events for specialist medical educators. Other sources of training for those interested in increasing their teaching skills come from the local medical Deaneries, now within strategic health authorities (SHAs) and the Royal Colleges (for an example, see the RCP education website). Other organizations providing information specifically for those involved in medical education include the Association for the Study of Medical Education (ASME) and internationally the Association for Medical Education in Europe (AMEE). More recently ASME has linked with Harvard Medical School to put on a week-long leadership training programme for medical educators.

The nurse as medical educator

Increasingly, nurses are becoming more involved with undergraduate medical student training. In Leeds, for example, the clinical skills tutors are mainly from nursing backgrounds. In 1999, novel ward-based tutors were introduced in Leeds. These were nurses who helped medical students make the transition between learning in a classroom environment with manikins and interacting with real patients in the clinical environment.

---

[1] An example of the Leeds Master's in Clinical Education curriculum can be found at www.education.leeds.ac.uk/prospective/clinical_education/index.php.

Initially this only occurred in hospital but more latterly is also occurring in GP practices. The training for these nurses is usually initially provided by senior clinical medical academics but increasingly they too are entering the more formal courses provided by MEUs, universities and specialist associations (Kilminster et al., 2001). Readers will recall the key roles played in the learning of Ahmed as a third-year student on placement receiving supervision from the practice nurse. Alison's first-year presentation after her home visit to Avis is very likely to have been assessed by a number of health care professionals.

The patient as educator

In more recent years many medical schools have incorporated patients (and carers) as formal teachers, particularly in the area of communication skills. Often specialist academics with an interest in doctor–patient communication develop a group of patients who are trained to interact with students in a large variety of scenarios. This enables students to practise ways of communicating with different individuals in a wide variety of medical settings. These patients are trained initially by specialist academics but subsequently as they become experts themselves they are involved in training others. Networks of patient and carer teachers are currently being set up. In the future it is likely that patients will increasingly become involved in teaching medical students – even demonstrating how to undertake simple clinical skills like taking the pulse.

Ongoing support for all these groups of educators is provided mostly at the local level of the MEU, together with opportunities for wider training through the national and international groups as previously mentioned. Monitoring of the quality of the students' educational experience is triangulated from three sources: student questionnaires, peer observation of teaching and the results of student assessments. Increasingly the role of teaching is becoming more professionalized within medicine, particularly with the recognition that teaching is a skill which, like other skills, requires training and practice, and with the advent of medical education becoming a recognized speciality area to enter during postgraduate training. However, the standing of research in medical education is still a very long way from being equitable with research in other medical disciplines. There are good signs on the horizon and medical education as a discipline is, for the first time, to be returned in the 2008 research assessment exercise (RAE).

Financing of training for medical educators continues to be a cause for concern and will probably become increasingly so as training budgets, which currently reside with SHAs, cease to be ring-fenced and perhaps are raided to decrease overall budget deficits. Safeguarding the progress made in recent years in securing the future of teaching and learning is likely to be a story of constant battles. Despite this gloomy forecast, the desire to pass on knowledge, skills and professional attributes is well ingrained in doctors, being enshrined, as previously mentioned, in the Hippocratic Oath. The bringing-in of others to help educate medical students will help share the load of hard-pressed senior doctors who have increasing calls on their time – from government initiatives and targets plus an increasing managerial burden. However, the basic underlying pleasure of watching the blossoming of the next generation of doctors is a powerful and compelling one for most clinicians.

Content and structure of the students' learning

The main learning outcomes of the student's time in the clinical environment or practice settings naturally revolve around the core medical skills of diagnosis and treatment of patients with a wide range of conditions. This covers not only the usual clinical skills of history-taking, examination and ordering investigations but also the understanding of how the clinical team works with the patient to achieve the desired outcome.

Clearly defined educational themes run throughout the curriculum, incorporating areas such as communication skills, personal and professional development and ethics. All curricular models incorporate the principles of adult learning and interactivity, with students taking increasing responsibility for their own learning, evaluating their progress, and deriving their own goals through working in small groups or individually. Material is presented based around clinical material so as to increase face relevance. Large group teaching or lectures are still a feature to provide overview or structure to course elements; however, they are not the mainstay of teaching methods: for example, in the early years of the course there may be a total of four or five lectures per week, whereas in the later stages of the course there may only be one or two lectures at the beginning or end of the year.

The synthesis of information gleaned from taking a patient's history, their examination and the results of any investigations into a working hypothesis or diagnosis require complex higher-order skills which can only be learned by repeated exposure to common clinical conditions in a wide variety of individuals and settings. The capacity for a medical condition to surprise by its protean manifestations in different people is one of its great intellectual challenges. In the early parts of medical training students are taught specific individual skills, such as how to take a history of someone with chest pains, and the clinical environment allows students to practise this skill with a range of appropriate conditions. Initially the student uses a relatively rigid framework to do this, but as they become more familiar with the condition and its various manifestations they are encouraged to leave the inflexible structure behind and begin to develop information-gathering skills based on their own experience and the experience of watching others. Increasing expertise in clinical skills only comes from repeated and deliberate practice (Dreyfus and Dreyfus, 1986; Norman and Brooks, 1997; Schmidt et al., 1990; Eraut, 1994; Berliner, 2001).

To ensure these repeated practice opportunities are available, a large number of practice placements are required. Students are exposed to a large number of practice teachers to ensure that they get the maximum diversity of experience, which is essential. Consequently, in the initial parts of training, the activities that the student undertakes within the clinical placement are relatively prescribed with a number of 'hard' measurable outcomes. Look at the following learning outcomes taken from the University of Leeds medical course (other courses will have similar but not identical learning outcomes): '... at the end of this placement you will be expected to take a history of a patient presenting with chest pain and examine the cardiovascular system'. In contrast, later in the course, learning outcomes become directly related to the expected medical skills of a graduating doctor, for example: '... during this clinical placement you will be expected to finely hone your history and examination skills, demonstrate an understanding of the underlying scientific basis for common signs and symptoms and formulate and negotiate an investigation and treatment plan with the patients and their carers'. Clinical placements are therefore constructed to facilitate the achievement of these outcomes.

Methods

The methodologies used reflect the intended learning outcomes of the learning and teaching experiences, and have the overriding aims of ensuring both individual development of the student together with professional development reflecting future working practice. Recent texts from Newble and Cannon (2001) and Hays (2006) outline the current views on appropriate methodologies, many of which are additionally recommended by the GMC.

Experiential

A wide range of experiential learning experiences are used in the early years of the medical course. Role play or video clips are particularly used when developing communication skills, including a number of clinical skills, such as history-taking. Debates are a frequently used account within ethics components, together with group presentations. These are often followed by open simulation of practical situations posing real ethical dilemmas; for example, a research ethics committee or an ethical issue posed within the clinical environment. Small group sessions will frequently be broken down to include small exercises or activities promoting active learning using a variety of resources, including paper, video, clinical (simulated or real) or e-learning resources. In the later years of the programme, students will participate by observation and participation in a variety of clinical activities, ranging from ward rounds, outpatient sessions, acute and planned admissions, home and hospital visits, multi-professional team meetings, and planning investigative procedures, to name a few.

Clinical procedures

Development of clinical practical skills will initially be through use of models. This ranges from clinical examination, including learning surface anatomy, through to clinical diagnostic examination skills and a number of invasive and non-invasive procedures. On occasion, consenting peers may be used (either as self-study or in small groups). Simulated patients are used frequently, as are 'expert patients' who have been trained as trainers.

Lorretta and Luke Carter, from the Green Hill flats, have both undergone training as simulated patients, this being a potential source of additional income for them at flexible times to fit in with their other paid employment. They participate both in training of students, for example, in role play during communication skills training, and in objective structured clinical examinations (OSCEs) during the students' clinical assessments, again role-playing simulated clinical encounters which are observed and assessed by trained examiners.

Nearer graduation, real patients (with informed consent) are the main medium for learning (Maran and Glavin, 2003).

Graphic

A varied range of graphic materials are used, through the facilities provided within the university, NHS premises and dedicated clinical learning centres. In addition, students access facilities and resources through networked IT clusters or their own PCs. Small groups make frequent use of overheads, flipcharts and PowerPoint, rapidly becoming extremely skilled at presentations on material prepared before study sessions. Presentations are a frequent part of their learning and teaching with many actually being part of assessment (by both peers and teachers), recognizing the importance of this to future effective practice.

Hardware

A wide range of interactive material and e-learning resources are used, ranging from stand-alone websites to a number of rapidly evolving e-learning sites or resources devoted to providing reusable learning objects (RLOs) and virtual reality materials (Ruiz et al., 2006; Sandars, 2006). The clinical skills learning centres provide access to a wide range of interactive CD-ROM material specifically designed to provide material that may be difficult to access on the wards (for example, auscultation of heart murmurs or breath sounds). More recently, blogs and interactive websites have been an increasing site for managed learning environments. The use of technology-enhanced learning will begin to be used in the Assessment and Learning in Practice Settings (ALPS) programme undertaken by the Centre for Excellence in Teaching and Learning in West Yorkshire. RLOs are being developed which will be downloaded to enhance the learning by students in the workplace. For example, students in rheumatology clinics will be able to download video clips on how to examine joints on their smart phones whilst attending a rheumatology clinic. Students will be videoed undertaking assessments in the workplace using their mobile phones and this will then be uploaded to a tutor back at the university.

Written

Development of writing skills is a key part of undergraduate medical training, recognizing the importance of being able to document clearly and to communicate in a written format with a range of professionals and patients. Students are required to complete a number of reflective logs which may be in written paper format or be placed on an electronic portfolio. Items can be kept personal and private, or may in different situations be shared with peers and in some cases even be open to tutors for marking and commentary. Written work ranges from documentation of case histories, essays, short answers or reports to formal literature reviews, critical incidence analysis, preparation of patient information literature or drafting of letters (to professionals or patients, for example). A full range of paper-based and electronic resources are made available to students, who are required to access them for referencing of all written work. These range from books and articles through to peer-reviewed literature and journals, news items, journals, policy documents, guidelines and a number of websites that might include pertinent information; for example, patient information sites, Royal College websites or national statistics information bureaus.

Structural

Medical students need to be 'mobile' from the early years of the course, and be prepared to travel to learn! Whilst in the first few years in higher education, the majority of their teaching may occur on university premises, the nature of health professional teaching will involve them travelling to a variety of NHS and community premises as well as visiting patients and other professionals in their workplace and home environments. Students will work both individually and, particularly for safety when working in the community, may well be allocated in pairs. Increasingly, teaching sessions are backed up with access to information and resources held on medical school websites, which will link to national and international learning resources. Development of clinical skills will involve self-assessment in addition to peer, teacher and even patient observation and feedback.

Assessment

Miller's triangle model of assessment (1990) is used as the basis of assessment in most medical schools. In this model (see Figure 4.1), the base of the triangle is knowledge; then comes applying knowledge; demonstrating that knowledge can be applied to undertake clinical skills; and finally, at the top of the triangle, comes work-based or practice-based assessment.

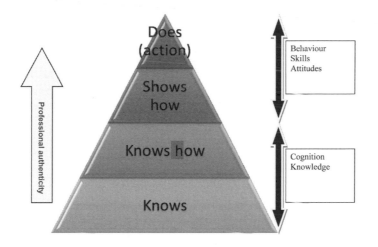

Figure 4.1   Framework for clinical assessment
Source: Miller, 1990.

Assessments, as 'biopsies' of a student's performance, need to be multiple and performed by several individuals for them to have a reasonable level of reliability. The range of assessment tools are chosen throughout the course mapping to the intended learning outcomes for that stage. Additionally, assessments need to reflect the type of practice setting in order for them to demonstrate face validity both to students and staff. Portfolios are recognized to be an important part of professional development, whilst the assessment of them remains challenging (Ben-David, 1999; Ben-David et al., 2006).

Consequently, medical students, during the large number of different practice placements throughout their undergraduate course, will often have several assessments during each placement. Practice assessments have recently become the focus for new developments in medical education, in both undergraduate courses and postgraduate training. The traditional previous solitary formal assessment of presentation of a case to the senior practice tutor is being replaced with several different tools measuring different aspects of education and training. Three such tools are now described to illustrate this.

Mini-CEX

The mini-CEX (mini-clinical evaluation encounter) was developed to assess the clinical skills that doctors most often use in real clinical encounters. It involves direct observation by the teacher of a student's performance in 'real' clinical encounters in the placement. It is designed to assess a variety of skills such as history-taking, clinical examination, communication, diagnosis and management of patients and their problems. In each placement a student is required to undertake a number of these encounters. Elaine, after her clerking of Jim Rafferty in Accident and Emergency, could well have asked the Orthopaedic SHO to have completed a mini-CEX on her observed performance for inclusion in her assessment portfolio.

Directly observed procedural skills (DOPS)

DOPS is a method of assessment developed by the Royal College of Physicians specifically for assessing practical skills. Although mainly used for postgraduates at present, many medical schools are planning to use it as part of their undergraduate assessments. It requires the placement educational supervisor to directly observe the student undertaking the procedure, make judgements about specific components of the procedure and grade the student's performance. As with the mini-CEX, the reliability of DOPS is increased by repeated assessments.

360-degree assessment

The 360-degree assessment is an objective systematic collection and feedback of performance data and is useful for assessing behaviours and attitudes such as communication, leadership, teamworking, punctuality and reliability. It asks people from all areas that the student has worked in to complete a structured questionnaire on the individual student's performance. This information is collated so that all the 'raters' remain anonymous and is then fed back to the student. All of the professionals and patients who had encounters with the medical students could have been asked to complete the questionnaire for that student in order to provide a wide range of feedback, thus going beyond the health care professionals.

For example, the ward nurse or dietician observing Sunita's performance on the paediatric ward could be asked to comment. The practice nurses or GPs involved with both Alison in Year 1 and Ahmed in Year 3 could certainly be included in the process, but also patients or their carers could be called upon (for example, Jason Dean could have been asked to comment on Neal's communication skills, or Zoë Benner on Sunita's developing paediatric skills when assessing her daughter Kara).

The student's placement assessment record is scrutinized by the medical schools examinations committee, and students with a pattern of persistent failures in any of the areas would be required to repeat and re-sit placements until satisfactory development is demonstrated. Normally the number of students showing a persistent failure pattern is very small (under 5 per cent).

Continuing professional development

There are currently major changes occurring in the postgraduate training of medical professionals. These changes are still in the process of implementation and are briefly outlined below (see also the PMETB and MMC websites).

Medical students graduate after four to six years in medical school with provisional registration granted by the GMC and apply through a national system for a place in a two-year Foundation Programme. Provided that they make satisfactory progress in the Foundation Programme, they are granted full registration at the end of Year 1. The first Foundation Year (F1) consists of four-month placements in medicine, surgery and another speciality. All F1 doctors have a named educational supervisor and during the F1 year undertake formal training based on a national curriculum for Foundation doctors. The doctors must maintain a national learning portfolio in order to progress and they undertake regular assessments of competence using the mini-CEX, DOPS and 360-degree tools described above. The F2 year again consists of three varied four-month placements and has a similar assessment structure. At the end of the Foundation Programme doctors can apply either for a place on a 'run through' speciality/primary care training programme or for a fixed-term specialist training programme. They are eventually awarded a Certificate of Completion of Training (CCT) and are then eligible to apply for a senior medical appointment such as a hospital consultant or GP.

Continuing professional development (CPD) is built into each stage of the training process and it is an ongoing expectation of all senior doctors (for example, currently 50 hours of CPD activity per year is required for physicians). At the present time, the method of revalidation for senior doctors is under debate but is likely to include evidence of ongoing professional development in their chosen specialty.

Current debates and future developments

Major impacts on the delivery of health care by the medical profession in the UK over the last decade have come from requirements to comply with the EWTD and, most recently, the implementation of the consultant contract. These have resulted in a limitation of the hours that medical professionals work at all grades, from consultants through to the most junior doctors. The consequent increase in shift working has impacted on delivery of teaching and training opportunities, both within the job environment and in designated protected time. Some of this has been very positive – a recognition of the need to ensure protected time for training, designed programmes with determined learning outcomes and an acknowledgement of the requirement for time to be dedicated to actual delivery of teaching.

However, a major knock-on effect from the significantly increased workload involved in more formal training of doctors in specialities after graduation (through the MMC agenda) has been on the training of medical students. In their restricted working time, qualified doctors have had increasing need to prioritize the pressures of clinical needs and managerial responsibilities with other pressures, including research and teaching. This has tended to result in an assumption by many doctors that teaching has come to be towards the bottom of their list of priorities, and particularly the teaching of undergraduate medical students. Whilst the SIFT contracts with NHS institutions stipulate the expectations of undergraduate teaching, the job plans of many doctors do not include identified sessions for undergraduate teaching, and many doctors now consider that the limited time they have outside their clinical role will be devoted to postgraduate teaching, or work for specialist colleges.

Another factor impacting on the training of undergraduate medical students includes the changing nature of health care delivery. Moves from centralized hospital-based services into health care management in the community has consequently resulted in a change in the ease of accessibility of patients, particularly for undergraduate students, who find that overcoming the resultant boundaries and organizational difficulties may be so inhibitory as to make it impossible for a meaningful learning experience to occur. This has resulted in an overall change in the volumes of clinical material that undergraduate students are likely to encounter and the need to develop other means of training, including use of e-learning resources, simulation and trained expert patient teachers.

Any programme is under constant review and pressure to incorporate an increasing quantity of information or skills, dependent not only on expansion in medical knowledge but also the requirements of a changing society. The move towards outcomes-driven curricula has led to considerable debate amongst the medical education community, with a shift towards a curricular reductionist policy, particularly in terms of the knowledge base of students, and an expansion in the development of skills. These are not only generic skills that may be pertinent towards lifelong learning, but also encompass skills that underpin the patient–health professional encounter, such as more effective communication skills. Current discussion amongst health care providers is questioning whether the 'new doctors' recently qualifying from medical schools, whilst being immensely skilled in areas like communication, are now deficient in knowledge, particularly of underpinning basic medical sciences. Concerns over the lack of the breadth of experience of these students indicate that this may have considerable implications for the speed at which they are able to progress through the training grades. Additionally, their preparedness for the variety of challenges that may occur in clinical practice, and their ability to judge the breadth of careers that are available within medicine (having had such a more restricted limited exposure in the undergraduate years), is considered by some to have significant longer-term implications for the medical workforce as a whole.

Currently, the regulation of undergraduate medical education comes under the control of the GMC which quality-assures the medical school courses through its Quality Assurance of Basic Medicine Education programme. Each medical school is visited a minimum of twice in ten years and the visits are conducted by groups comprising practising clinicians, medical educationalists and informed lay visitors. The inspections consist of extensive course documentary analysis and up to five days of visits to the school and its teaching sites to investigate course delivery and assessment. At present, each medical school runs its own graduatory examinations. However, concerns have been raised about the comparative standards at different medical schools (Boursicot et al., 2006). Consequently, the GMC has been consulting on the possibility of running a national exit assessment similar to the USA licensing examinations.

Until recently, efforts in the assessment of trainee doctors have been mainly focused on the areas of knowledge and skills. In *Tomorrow's Doctors*, for the first time it was made explicit that the assessment of professional attitudes and professionalism was expected. Until this time qualities such as integrity, honesty and altruism, although expected of doctors, were not explicitly identified in most courses. A major problem of teaching and assessing 'professionalism' is defining what is meant and encompassed by the term (Cruess et al., 2004). The Royal College of Physicians has recently published 'Doctors in Society: Medical professionalism in a changing world'. This is the final report of a working party which grappled with the idea, meaning and relevance of professionalism in the modern NHS and they provide a definition and a useful description (RCP, 2005). The literature on professionalism demonstrates that we cannot expect our students to merely osmose the ideas, beliefs and behaviours embodied by the term simply by being at medical school: the attitudes and behaviours required of a modern medical professional need to be explicitly taught and therefore also assessed (Cruess and Cruess, 2006). The assessment of attitudes is still an area 'under development' and currently the measurement of behaviour is more common (Epstein and Hundert, 2002; Stern, 2006). This area probably represents one of the current major foci for development in medical education. Many doctors have felt that the changing working practices in the NHS, the advent of the EWTD and the endless round of government initiatives and targets have eroded the fundamental nature of professionalism and demoted the doctor to the role of technician following pre-determined protocols or guidelines. Important initiatives like the RCP Working Group on professionalism seek to re-emphasize and reinstate the commitment of medicine and doctors to the central tenet of patient care. Devising evidence-based strategies to teach and assess the components which make up professionalism will be a major challenge in the next few years.

Core text recommendations

Dent, J.A., and Harden, R.M. (2001), *A Practical Guide for Medical Teachers*, Oxford: Churchill Livingstone.

Hays, R. (2006), *Teaching and Learning in Clinical Settings*, Oxford: Radcliffe Publishing.

Newble, D., and Cannon, R. (2001), *A Handbook for Medical Teachers* (4th edn), Lancaster: Kluwer Academic Publishers.

5   The health visitor

Fran Jones

Overview

Health visiting has a very long history, with roots in the nineteenth-century social and public health reforms that impacted positively on the mortality and morbidity of the population. Practitioners then worked to improve the living conditions and general health of communities, with a clear focus on hygiene, social policy and public health interventions.

By the mid-twentieth century a nursing qualification was the entry gate into the profession, delivered as part of higher education and regulated by the Council for Education and Training of Health Visitors (CETHV), a sister organization to the Council for Education and Training of Social Workers (CETSW). At that time health visiting was a community-based role, with health visitors employed by borough or county councils, working with the local Medical Office of Health, in the role of 'professional friend to families'. The work of the health visitor was based on community public health and health education.

Following the major reorganization of local authorities in 1974, health visitors were employed by the NHS. In addition, changes to regulation of the profession were made in 1978, when the profession was included in the regulatory structures governing the family of nursing disciplines by the UKCC (United Kingdom Central Council for Nursing, Midwifery and Health Visiting), later to be titled the NMC (Nursing and Midwifery Council). Some professionals *still* contend that for community and interprofessional working the service would be better managed away from the NHS, which, despite strong public health policy in the twenty-first century, still has a focus on treating existing disease in preference to targeting health improvement through prevention.

73

Since 2004, the NMC, in its capacity as a statutory regulatory body, has maintained three registers as part of its responsibilities to protect the public. These are:

Part 1: General Nursing, encompassing all branches of nursing
Part 2: Midwifery
Part 3: Specialist Community Public Health Nursing (SCPHN): this includes the following pathways: health visiting, school nursing, occupational health nursing and family health nursing.[1]

There are specific educational learning and standards for entry to these registers. Part 1 and Part 2 are attained by direct entry, with no previous professional qualifications required. Currently, to enter Part 3 of the register a practitioner must already be a registrant on Part 1 or Part 2.

Health visitors work across the age continuum (the 'cradle to the grave' or, more contentiously, 'the sperm to the worm') and within communities. Their clients can be individuals, families, groups or communities. It is this broad focus which adds to the complexity of their work and often generates a confusion and lack of understanding among the general public about the various roles a health visitor may adopt. Throughout the last two decades of the twentieth century, their work was very child-focused, in particular on the under-fives, although, even with this primary remit, health visitors addressed the whole family's health. Family and child health form the basis of an ongoing caseload, which addresses health promotion, health protection and health education. Health and well-being is the focus of the health visitor's work. However, the practitioner is very aware that to work successfully with individuals, families, clients and communities it is important to work with the wider determinants of health (Dahlgreen and Whitehead, 1991).

Health visitors are currently employed by PCTs (primary care trusts) (although practice-based commissioning will generate new opportunities), to offer a community- and family-centred public health service to the population. Many are attached to GP caseloads, whilst others have returned to the former geographical working pattern. Further, teamworking has been achieved with corporate caseloads that enable innovative working practices to meet health needs. Skill mix health visiting teams may consist of qualified health visitors, community staff nurses, nursery nurses and administrative assistants.

Currently, there are 43 qualification courses validated within the UK (2006); some 554 health visitors were trained in 2005–06. There are 24,965 practitioners (correct as of 2006) registered as health visitors. However,

---

[1]   This last pathway only applies in Scotland.

this does not represent the number of practitioners in the role within the workforce, as the health visitor can be seen as an escalator of transferable skills, taking these into areas of expertise such as consultancy, management and education. This workforce will be subject to the demographic changes related to the nursing community: for example, in 2004 one in six health visitors was over 55 years old.

Qualification courses are delivered over a 52-week period and can be taken on a full-time or part-time basis, during which time the student has supernumerary status. During the 52-week course students will complete to honours degree (Level HE6) or may take their studies to postgraduate level (Level HE7). There is a requirement for 50 per cent practice-based and 50 per cent university-based learning, followed by a minimum of ten weeks' consolidation of practice experience. Entry requirements include current active registration with the NMC on Part 1 or Part 2 of the professional register, at least one year of post-registration practice and evidence of study to diploma level (240 CATS to Level HE6), including recent study, and, as such, to have already completed a 'pre-registration' qualification. Many courses are currently sponsored through strategic health authority contracts, the Multi-Professional Education and Training (MPET) levy, in which case there is funding for the course and some 'backfill' monies for primary care trusts (PCTs). As 50 per cent of the learning is practice-based it is vital that a student is supported in that placement by their employer or sponsor. Close partnership working between the universities and the PCTs ensures quality audits of placements and excellent preparation of practice teachers to facilitate the delivery of the 50 per cent of learning in practice and assessment in practice.

The direction of the target-led NHS currently threatens the continuation of these courses. For example, in some areas of the country no health visitors were trained in 2006; further threats to courses exist now and in the future. It was estimated that in 2006–07 only 329 health visitors were in training. (Family and Parenting Institute, 2007). The professional body (CPHVA) and union (Unite) are lobbying for adequate numbers of practitioners to be trained (CPHVA, 2007).

Recent developments

Despite a very long history of health visiting, the title is now very much under threat. Currently, Part 3 of the register can be annotated in relation to the area of practice development within the course; that is, health visiting, school nursing, occupational health nursing or family health nursing (Scotland). One reprieve of the title occurred in October 2006, following a Prime Ministerial speech that highlighted the important role the health visitor has in relation to inequalities of health, working with identified vulnerable families. This was suggestive of a move back to the 'policing' debate of the early 1990s (Dingwall and Robinson, 1993).

The tensions around the role of the health visitor or the SCPHN are as strong as ever, with community public health and health improvement strategies pulling against a focus on child protection through targeted family health (complex, vulnerable, multi-problematical families) and safeguarding children. Health visiting has been viewed as a 'universal service' that works with the *well* population, as well as those with identified needs. The health visiting service is offered to all families and is therefore free of the 'stigma' associated with targeted intervention.

The *Principles of Health Visiting* were published in 1977 by the CETHV, and revisited in 1992 (Twinn and Cowley) and again in 2006 (Cowley and Frost). At each review core principles were reaffirmed which still continue to be the basis of the SCPHN work and are the domains within the *Standards of Proficiency for Specialist Community Public Health Nurses* (NMC, 2004d). Curriculum development and educational delivery reflect these principles and will feature further in this chapter. The principles of health visiting are:

1. The search for health needs
2. Stimulation of an awareness of health
3. Influencing policies that affect health
4. Facilitation of health-enhancing activities (CETHV, 1977).

As with other regulated professions the health visitor or SCPHN is a protected title, and the practitioner must complete and meet the proficiencies in order to register with the NMC. Courses are validated and accredited by both the university offering the course and the NMC. By September 2008, all courses must be revalidated to meet the *Standards of Proficiency for Specialist Community Public Health Nurses* (NMC, 2004d). The current specialist practitioner standards, first introduced in 1994, are being superseded – however, the shared learning with other community nurses (such as district nurses, general practice nurses and community children's nurses) will be retained to enhance interprofessional learning.

The latest review of health visiting, *Facing the Future* (DoH, 2007a), suggests that the core elements of health visiting continue the vital work to support families and children, by the promotion of health and the prevention of ill-health, safeguarding children and by early intervention and prevention. Working with parents and home visiting is pivotal to the work, as is 'progressive universalism'; in other words, a service that should be offered to all. However, high levels of need and complexity should be supported by intensive programmes of intervention. This review proposes that the primary function of the health visitor is to work with children and families, and to engage with wider public health programmes that target key public health priorities; in particular, obesity, smoking, alcohol, drugs and accident prevention.

Models of teaching and learning

The ideology of practice learning has long been used in the health and social care settings in the preparation of professionals. The days of an apprenticeship model in the nursing profession have long gone and health visiting education has been delivered in the higher education setting for almost 50 years. The pedagogical approach to learning in the practice setting has been related to developing practitioners who have capacity to practise safely in their chosen profession, having been assessed as competent in that area of practice. The practice placement has provided the student with the opportunity to apply their academic learning to practice and to develop skills and competencies, as stated in the latest *Standards* (NMC, 2004d).

Using a curriculum model to demonstrate pedagogical approaches

In an attempt to discuss pedagogical approaches, the model illustrated in Figure 5.1 highlights the factors that influence the work-based curriculum for the specialist community public health nurse and how these are supported by learning and teaching theory. Brennan and Little (1996), from whom the model is adapted, suggest that the requirement to meet students' learning needs is central to the work-based curriculum, with the needs of the HEI (higher education institution), the employer and possibly professional bodies influencing the learning requirements.

The adapted model presented clearly identifies these three main influences. The close partnership working and involvement between the commissioners, the employers and the HEI, both to develop and deliver the curriculum, is crucial to the student's learning. The influence of the professional regulatory body is considerable; for example, the NMC requires the curriculum to be validated against the professional standards. The *Standards of Proficiency for Specialist Community Public Health Nurses* (NMC, 2004d) outlines four guiding principles that should be reflected in all SCPHN programmes, which can be aligned to the main influences:

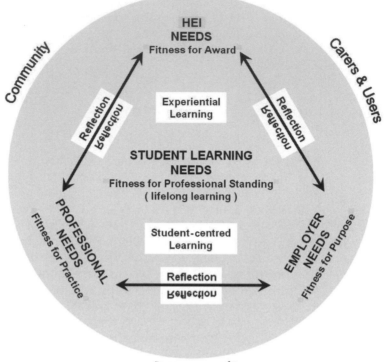

Figure 5.1   Pedagogical approaches to a work-based curriculum for the SCPHN

Source: Brennan and Little, 1996.

1. Fitness for practice: influenced by the professional regulatory body
   The professional regulatory body, the NMC, validates the courses to ensure that specified learning enables the student to meet the proficiencies to enter the practitioner onto the register. The NMC requires practitioners to be fit for practice, both at the point of registration and during the practitioner's working life, thus fulfilling their role of 'protecting the public'.
2. Fitness for purpose: influenced by the commissioners and employers
   Although a practitioner must meet certain proficiencies, the curriculum and students' learning must also meet the needs of the employer or commissioner to fulfil the role in the practice area. Student-led learning, in partnership with the practice teacher and manager, can facilitate structured learning. It is suggested that a work-based

learning curriculum is process-driven rather than solely a curriculum of content. Opportunities to continue self-directed learning and continuing professional development will enable the practitioner to remain 'fit for purpose'.

3. Fitness for award: influenced by the awarding HEI
   Each HEI will assure the quality of their academic awards to meet the QAA Benchmarks and academic standards. Learning, both in the university and in practice, must meet these standards.

4. Fitness for professional standing: influenced by the student/practitioner
   As a registered professional and lifelong learner it is recognized that there is a responsibility 'to provide competent, safe and effective care' and to maintain 'the highest standards of professional conduct and ethical practice'. The curriculum will prepare the student for this role and responsibility.

However, further influences can be added to this model; namely, the political agenda; the community; and the user and carer perspective.

The development of the curriculum must reflect current political policies. However, in a culture of constant change and development this requirement provides an ongoing challenge for the curriculum developers and the facilitators of learning. A plea for a period of stability in the NHS, to allow implementation and evaluation of policy and ways of working, is currently being heard. The ability to understand and respond to the political agenda is integral to the health visitor role and to fulfil the third of the main principles of health visiting, as included in the CETHV's 1977 list and termed 'Influencing policies that affect health'.

In the development of a curriculum model for SCPHN, particularly one which is work-based, it is vital to consider the community and clientele with whom the student/practitioner is working and learning. An understanding of and possession of skills required to 'search for health needs' of the wider community, groups, families and individuals is paramount to the development of the health visitor. Carer and user perspectives are now being highly valued within government policy. The NMC standards (2004d) require evidence of patient/clientele involvement in developing the curriculum, assessing practice and evaluating care given. The HEIs and PCTs are working both locally and strategically to ensure that user and carer perspectives are included at all levels of practice and education. Examples may include the following: feedback to practice teachers; client assessment in portfolios; attendance at course programme committees; or representation on curriculum development groups.

Returning to Figure 5.1, it can be seen that the pedagogical approaches highlighted in this model are student-centred learning, experiential learning and reflection. It is not by accident that the student learning needs are placed in the centre of this model. Student-centredness has been identified as one of the pedagogical approaches in work-based learning (Nixon et al., 2006), and builds upon the work of Rogers (1969). As a psychotherapist, Rogers applied his *client-centred* approach to the educational setting, leading to a *student-centred* approach. He contended that learning was enhanced when students could, firstly, recognize the relevance of the learning; secondly, participate and be involved in their learning; and, thirdly, self-evaluate in a non-threatening environment. The role of teacher is seen as a 'facilitator of learning'. These approaches to facilitating learning are demonstrated both in the university-based and practice-based learning through the roles of tutor and practice teacher. Student learning needs are supported by the curriculum design, with clear learning outcomes and 'proficiencies' identified. In the practice (work-based) setting, there is a tripartite approach (between the student, the practice teacher and the tutor) to identify and meet the student practitioner's learning needs. Learning opportunities are recognized and, through observation, discussion, action and reflection, the student's learning is facilitated through a process-driven curriculum rather than one based on content.

Several theories have been influential in the approach taken by the profession to learning. In particular, adult learning theories, or 'andragogy' (Knowles, 1990), support student-centred learning: these theories assert that adult learning should allow for self-directed and self-motivated approaches – approaches which are encouraged within work-based learning. In addition, Kolb (1984) presented a model of experiential learning which recognized the value of learning from 'doing'. This approach is based upon the notion of a student learning from a concrete experience. By cognitive recognition of the experience and reflection upon that experience, Kolb contends that the learner can form abstract concepts and generalizations – thus enabling the synthesis of new learning into new situations. Within the family of nursing, experiential learning theory has been well developed. Learning through experiences is raised to a higher level by reflecting and understanding the learning, which will enable the student not only to become proficient in that behaviour or skill, but also to be cognitively or affectively changed Schön, 1983; Gibbs, 1988; Johns, 1998). Both students and practice teachers are encouraged to maintain reflective diaries, which can be used during their learning sessions and can enhance the processes of debriefing a student and in-depth discussion of experiences.

The development of the curriculum is influenced by many factors which will impact upon students' learning needs. However, the approach to learning is shaped by the role and learning relationship that the student practitioner has with the facilitators of learning, both during the course and later as a 'lifelong learner': the learning styles aim to prepare the student for lifelong learning.

The teacher in the practice setting

The role of the 'teacher' in practice has always been a very important component of the health visitor course. Learning outcomes are met both in the university and in the practice setting. The role of the 'practice teacher' demands high standards of practice and of learning and teaching skills. The professional body (the NMC) has published standards for the 'fieldwork teacher' (applied from approximately 1960 onwards), 'community practice teacher' (applied from approximately 1980 onwards) and 'mentor' (applied from approximately 2000 onwards) and now has redefined this role as 'practice teacher', the standards for which must be met by September 2007 as specified in the publication, *Standards to Support Learning and Assessment in Practice* (NMC, 2006b). HEIs are working with their current mentors to enable them to demonstrate their skills as practice teachers, for example, by portfolio development, but those new to taking on this role will be required to complete the new courses, which will be at postgraduate Level HE7. The emphasis of the competencies relate to facilitating professional development of specialist practice students as well as working with pre-registration mentors and practitioners.

Partnership working and a close working relationship between the HEIs and practice teachers are paramount. Preparation days are held each year for practice teachers prior to the students starting their course, and ongoing updating meetings and evaluation are completed within the academic year. All nursing practitioners are required to maintain their professional portfolio and within this practice teachers demonstrate the quality of their continuing practice. Some universities have facilitated this development and have recognized the validated practice teachers' competence as *practice teachers* with letters or certificates. It is a professional requirement to maintain a live database of practice placements and practice teachers. The appraisal and maintenance of standards for such placements is now the responsibility of practice teachers, in partnership with the universities.

The motivation to fulfil the role of practice teacher is often founded on the desire to maintain high standards of practice and the enjoyment of facilitating learning in practice. Over the decades, financial recognition for this role has been patchy. However, it should be recognized in annual appraisal, and the pay-structuring *Agenda for Change* (DoH, 2001f) now recognizes the role.

Each student has a practice teacher based in a clinic or health centre. However, the teacher and student are not 'joined at the hip'; the practice teacher (in partnership with the student) has the responsibility for identifying learning opportunities with other professionals and in different areas. Learning outcomes are explicit in the course handbooks and assessment documents.

The *Standards of Proficiency for Specialist Community Public Health Nurses* (NMC, 2004d) now states that students must undertake at least half of their practice (6½ weeks of the 13 weeks) and 10 weeks' supervised practice directly related to health visiting. At least three weeks is set aside to gain experience in settings considered important but not central to the student's main area of responsibility. This allows greater opportunities to experience wider collaborative working; ideally that should include examples of innovative practice. Previously, courses would facilitate, if possible, one week of alternative practice, which was always evaluated by students very positively.

The relationship between the university lecturer and the practice teacher ensures currency of practice and innovative developments in the academic and clinical settings.

Content and structure of the students' learning

A common difficulty with health visiting education over the years has been the 'crowded curriculum'. Health visitor students will use their skills as graduate thinkers and lifelong learners to continue to develop throughout their professional career.

The process-driven curriculum requires the student to meet their learning outcomes both from the practice and university learning opportunities. The practice teacher and the tutor will facilitate this learning using reflection, experiential and student-centred learning. The NMC standards (2004d) must be met in the learning outcomes, and validated courses are explicit in these; however, they may be delivered and packaged differently. Although the curriculum is not prescribed, its essential content is set out in Table 5.1.

The relationship between the student and the practice teacher is one-to-one, and the student is placed within the practice setting of the practice teacher. As this is a new area of practice for the student at the outset, there is necessarily a continuum from observation to autonomy. Introduction to the physical location, community, services and individual clients provides an ongoing experience. As skills develop, so too will a small caseload, with which the student works.

Practice placement based around Green Hill/Derby Street: learning opportunities for the health visitor student

Jo has just moved into semester 2 of her SCPHN/Health Visitor course. She completed her Diploma in Nursing and registered as a nurse on

Table 5.1   The health visiting curriculum

Curriculum area	Curriculum content
Principles and Practice of Health Visiting	1. The principles of health visiting 2. Higher-level communication skills 3. Building therapeutic relationships, exploring advocacy, working with vulnerability 4. Working with families and children 5. Human development; physical, psychological and sociological 6. Nutrition, breastfeeding, weaning 7. Parenting 8. Behaviours 9. Working with communities 10. Safeguarding children 11. Domestic violence 12. Mental health issues, including post-natal depression 13. Special educational needs 14. Parenting 15. Identified health needs such as asthma, eczema, sleep disorders, behavioural problems 16. Working with teenagers – teenage pregnancy and motherhood 17. Working across the age span 18. Immunizations 19. Nurse prescribing
Evidence-Based Practice	1. Research and evidence based practice, including social policy 2. Using research to inform and develop practice 3. Sociological and psychological perspectives
Leading and Managing	1. Leading teams and managing change 2. Collaborative and partnership working 3. Developing health visiting practice 4. Group work and teaching and assessing skills
Health Promotion and Public Health	1. Assessing health needs – searching for health needs 2. Epidemiology and demography 3. Inequalities in health 4. Public health policy 5. Leading on health promotion 6. Planning health promotion strategies 7. Behaviour change 8. Health promotion, health protection and health education 9. Government targets on subjects such as coronary heart disease, obesity, sexual health, cancers, smoking 10. Community development

Part 1 of the register (NMC) three years ago. Jo entered nursing as a mature student, and has two children of her own, aged eight and ten.

Sue, her practice teacher, has worked with the Green Hill/Derby Street community for the last five years. She is based in the health centre which is a 30-minute walk from the flats – or two bus rides. The pharmacy is attached to the health centre, although they do offer a delivery service. Sue has an active caseload of 250 families who live on this estate and the neighbouring area which is a middle-class commuter area.

Since being placed in the health centre with Sue, Jo has been in practice two days a week, with two days in the university, and a study day for private study, problem-based learning, reading and assignments. Sometimes she finds it useful to swap her practice day, such as the day there was a case conference.

Her first few weeks were a whirl. She met so many people, including all of the health centre staff and other professionals with whom Sue worked. Jo had 'lost' her uniform and felt strange and vulnerable: did other people know she was a nurse? Apart from the community placement she had as a student nurse she has little experience out of the hospital setting and initially felt very out of place, even being unsure of whether to answer the phone! These feelings had been the subject of one of her earlier reflective sessions with Sue. This had helped her to recognize the many skills and life experiences that she was bringing to her developing role as a health visitor. Together, Jo and Sue had spent time considering her previous learning and identifying her initial learning needs.

Sue has a good understanding of the health needs of this area and has introduced Jo to many of her clients. Today they are reflecting on two aspects of Jo's learning, her work with the Benner family, Zoë and her children, and the wider community development work.

The Benner family

There is much for Jo to learn and many skills to develop in working with a family with such complex needs.

Health visitors are generally known for their work with young children and families. In the first instance Jo spent time with Sue, visiting families in their homes, observing the working relationships, working with families, observing infant clinics and child developmental sessions. She was observing how Sue worked with clients, how she confronted issues, and enabled clients to make their own decisions and promoted health.

Sue has known **Zoë Benner** since the birth of **Billy**, 3½ years ago at a 'primary visit'. This is the first visit undertaken by the health visitor following the birth of a baby – a service which each PCT has to statutorily provide. In partnership with Sue, Jo has worked with the family since coming out on placement.

Zoë has had a good relationship with Sue, the practice teacher, but Jo has built her own professional, non-judgemental, non-directive and therapeutic relationship. Jo has learnt that home visiting and working with clients is more than merely gaining access into the home. As she has developed her level of engagement, working in partnership and communication skills while working with Zoë, she has overcome some of her anxieties around making appointments and 'knocking on doors'. She is very aware that she is a 'guest' in her client's home. Zoë feels confident in working with Jo; she feels that the health visitor is interested in her and is letting her make her own decisions. Although her mother told her to beware of the health visitor – 'she can take your children away' – Zoë has found the service to be open and honest, straight-talking, and giving good advice. Zoë is finding life very difficult, yet she can talk openly to Jo about her worries, including her own health, relationship difficulties and dealing with other institutions, such as the police over **Jackson**, solicitors concerning **Kara** and social services with **Tilly**. In her practice placement Jo is relating her university learning and developing her communication skills as well as understanding advocacy and supporting vulnerable families.

Working with children and families, Jo will use her growing knowledge of child development to consider both Billy and Kara against expected milestones. In response to an identified need Billy is referred to the speech therapist for further assessment and intervention. She also makes a referral for auditory assessment (a hearing test). Although there is an emphasis on early physical and psychological development and parenting skills, Jo will consider human development across the life span. Jo has been working with Zoë concerning **Kylie's** bed-wetting and, in partnership with the school nurse and the school, is considering the wider psychosocial aspects of her behaviours. She is exploring the anti-bullying policies in school.

There are many health needs that can be identified, some of which Zoë would clearly identify herself and others which may become evident as Jo continues to work with the family. Jo recognized the health issues presented by Kara (asthma and allergies), and completes a literature search to ensure that her knowledge is current and that her practice is evidence-based. Sue and Jo discuss the problem and practical solutions, but also suggest Zoë and Kara visit the specialist asthma nurse at the surgery who liaises with the paediatrician.

Although Jo will not be able to prescribe any medication until she has successfully completed her course, her practice teacher, herself a nurse prescriber, will discuss prescribing situations, allowing Jo to reflect upon her developing prescribing skills. In the safety of a simulation, Jo will write practice prescriptions. She will also develop teamworking with pharmacists and GPs.

Jo has also been able to extend her learning around breastfeeding and weaning, and nutritional needs for the whole family.

It is important for Jo to help Zoë recognize her own health needs, enabling her to make her own decisions, increase her self-esteem and adopt healthy behaviours for herself and her family. These may include cessation of smoking, dietary changes, sexual health advice including contraceptive services and cytology, accessing benefits or even advice concerning educational or work opportunities.

The complexity of working with this family is supported by the interprofessional and collaborative working. These all offer excellent learning experiences for Jo, who has also used her skills of referral to other agencies. Jo has attended a case conference with Sue and has therefore experienced and learnt from the policies and procedures relating to safeguarding children. Although it was Sue who was required to write a court report concerning the custody of Kara, Jo shadowed her and later wrote a further report in a simulated exercise.

Jo will continue to work with this family in partnership with Sue. However, in her 10-week period of consolidation in the third semester, she will manage a reduced caseload of families in the area.

Jo also examines her learning with the wider community

In the university Jo had been introduced to the 'Principles of Health Visiting' which are also the domains that structured her practice assessment schedule relating to the standards of proficiency (NMC, 2004d).

In line with the first principle, 'Search for health needs', Jo began profiling the health needs of the community in which she was working. She collected various data from published documents such as the census and public health reports, as well as information about the area in which she was working. She had identified the health issues prevalent in the area, such as high levels of coronary heart disease and cancers, as well as asthma in children and obesity. Addictive behaviours, including smoking, and mental health were also identified. She could see that the local shop was boarded up, and talking to her clients it was clear that this caused some difficulty. A number of families and some of the older residents were very frustrated with the bus service that should have enabled them to get to the health centre and shops. One aspect that became very evident was that the collection of data included both the Green Hill flats area and the more affluent Paradise Gardens. This skewed the data and Sue highlighted the lack of services to Green Hill flats and the difficulties this presents for securing regeneration monies.

Jo, with Sue, is involved with the exciting community developments that are occurring in this area. The tenants' association has invited a number of professionals to join them and they are happy for Jo to join Sue in her work. This group has been successful in application to the local housing association, supported by the local council, to take over one of the flats as a community centre. Sue has been asked if she can arrange for the child development clinics to be held there. There is also a group of mothers with young children who would like to meet to support each other in parenting issues – they have asked for a 'weaning party'; Jo uses this opportunity to develop her group facilitation and teaching skills.

However, the use of this building is opening up so many possibilities, all made possible by the collaborative working of the people living in Green Hill flats and the coming together of the councillor, the police, the local headmaster, the vicar, a social worker, Citizens Advice Bureau and so on. Jo has first-hand experience of the benefit of collaborative working; she also experiences the conflicts and professional jealousies, but (using her higher levels of communication skills) does not get drawn into the conflict, rather considers ways to facilitate resolution.

One of Sue's colleagues has developed her skills around men's health and in particular smoking cessation. The landlord of the Green Hill Arms has spoken to her and is very concerned at the outcome of the introduction of anti-smoking legislation (July 2007). Jo is becoming involved in the planning of a 'lifestyle group'. There has been much interest from the regulars in the pub and the group is to meet in the events room. When Jo considers the principles of health visiting, she realizes this project relates to 'Facilitating health-enhancing behaviours and policies that influence health'. In the search for health needs it becomes apparent that smoking cessation is only one of the topics requested. The clientele, ladies as well, are also interested in diet, lifestyle and stress reduction. It is hoped that this similar group may develop in the community flat too. Jo is developing her health promotion skills – leading and planning strategies to improve the health of this community, in partnership with the community members.

Sue also identifies many other learning opportunities for Jo in the Green Hill community, such as working with cross-cultural issues, sexuality, mental health issues, chronic disease management, bereavement support and working across the age span.

Methods

The opportunities for learning in the community setting are many and it is the role of the practice teacher with the student to maximize these learning and teaching opportunities. Learning outcomes, assessment criteria and proficiencies are explicit in handbooks and portfolios of learning (including assessment schedules). Students will progress from working with their

Table 5.2   Methods used in practice teaching in health visiting

Methods
Role modelling
Reflection
Questioning
Discussion
Briefing and debriefing
Careful selection of small caseload – identified learning
Resources in the placement, such as books, policy documents, IT
Web-based learning – accessing information, Web CT, Blackboard
Practising and developing communication skills
Simulation – writing court reports and writing prescriptions
Workbooks on profiling – child development
Genograms and ecomaps
Teaching sessions – group work
Learning contracts
Attending meetings/case conferences
Portfolio development

practice teacher to autonomy of practice by the end of the course. Reflective diaries, discussion, briefing and debriefing are regularly used throughout the practice experience. An open and honest working relationship between the student and practice teacher is required. Most universities have well-developed assessment schedules to demonstrate the proficiency achievements which are used to identify the progress of the student. Learning contracts have also been regularly used to enable both the practice teacher and student to work together to identify learning needs and their attainment. Some of the most commonly used methods are given in Table 5.2.

Assessment

Integration between university- and practice-based learning leads to assignments that are practice-related, such as practice-based assessments, case studies, reflective analysis, project work and practice-based dissertations. However, the practice assessment of proficiencies is generally assessed by the practice teacher, who will also sign a final recommendation that the student is proficient for registration. Some courses have attempted to grade practice which has counted towards honours classification and sometimes practice teachers mark reflective assignments. Students' progression and competence are assessed in the portfolio of learning or practice assessment schedule by the practice teacher. All this calls into account inter-assessor reliability. Different approaches to address this issue have been adopted; these include moderation of portfolios by tutors and by other practice teachers. It is important that students, practice teachers, managers and the university have an explicit protocol for raising matters of concern, whether this is on account of a student's failure to progress, deficiencies in the learning opportunities or personal or professional issues. Issues of fairness and equity and learning experiences are also used to provide learning opportunities during the practice teacher study days that enhance and update practice.

In response to concerns about reliability of the standards attained by 'passing' pre-registration nursing students, there will now be mentors who are additionally qualified as 'sign-off mentors'. All practice teachers will be designated as 'sign-off mentors' (NMC, 2006b). In order for a student to complete the course successfully they must be deemed to be 'fit for practice' (that is, meeting the professional requirements of the NMC) and 'fit for award' (that is, meeting the requirements of the academic award). Working in partnership with the PCTs it is also important that students are 'fit for purpose'; in other words, meeting service requirements. Fitness for purpose can be enhanced with further continuing professional development (CPD).

In line with university regulations, students who are referred in assessed work have the opportunity to re-sit. Generally, the assessment schedules in practice are not only an assessment tool, but also used as a diagnostic tool throughout the course. Therefore, students should be aware of areas of weakness as they progress. Should a student require a longer period of practice to achieve their competencies, this is possible in agreement with their sponsoring placement. The NMC standards (2004d) do require a student to have completed their programme within 156 weeks full-time or 208 weeks part-time from commencement of their programme.

The attrition and failure rates on these courses are small, mainly due to the requirements of career progression, the sponsorship and competitive selection. The practice teacher role is supportive and developmental for the student. However, a small number of students do not meet the required standards and are 'failed', demonstrating that the universities and practice partners do take the role of 'protecting the public' and 'gatekeepers of the profession' seriously on behalf of the NMC.

Continuing training

On successful completion of the course, practitioners are awarded their academic and professional qualification. Notification is sent from the university along with a 'Declaration of Good Character and Good Health' to the NMC, who will, on receipt of payment from the practitioner, register their qualification on the third part of the register. It is then a requirement for that practitioner to maintain their registration through annual payments and triennial declarations that they have maintained their professional practice and met the updating requirements.

Preceptorship should be offered to any practitioner undertaking a new area of practice (NMC, 2006d) and as such the newly qualified health visitor should be suitably supported by their employer, who should also provide appraisal and supervision. Different models of supervision have been implemented and reflective sessions facilitate mutual support and learning. Issues of safeguarding children and working with vulnerable and complex health needs are challenging, and adequate support and supervision is needed.

The process-driven curriculum prepares the practitioner to practise as a specialist community public health nurse or health visitor. Lifelong adult learning will ensure that the practitioner continues to meet the health needs of communities and families and also provides the opportunity to continue to develop practice skills. Practitioners will access further identified learning, possibly at postgraduate level, within a CPD or professional qualifications framework, examples of which could include: advanced study in safeguarding children; parenting, leadership and management; further aspects of public health or community development. Alternatively, practitioners might access those aspects of professional practice that are related to their own practice, perhaps considering baby massage or alternative therapies.

Those practitioners wishing to teach SCPHN students are required to take the practice teacher course or may progress to tutor status (NMC, 2006b).

Current debates

Health visiting has once again come to a crossroads – and the direction it will take is uncertain. This impacts upon the development of the curriculum, the manner in which this is delivered and the roles of the teachers and facilitators of learning.

Facing the Future: A review of the role of health visitors (DoH, 2007a) clearly supports the role of the health visitor, which is focused very strongly on work with child health and with families – especially those identified as vulnerable. To successfully fulfil this role the review recognized the need for further emphasis on the essential learning about human psychological and physical development, relationships and parenting, both in the university and practice setting.

There are increasing tensions between the drive towards community-based working and the provision of family-centred working. Health visitor skills such as searching for health needs and facilitating health-enhancing behaviours are currently being focused on children and families, whilst the skills of collaborative working and community development are being sidelined. In the current climate within the NHS, it is unclear how services are to be developed, with an unfortunate effect that the numbers of training places for many nursing courses, including health visiting, are being severely affected. A major question to be asked is: 'what do PCTs want from their health visiting service?'.

Health visiting, now specialist community public health nursing, has its roots in public health practice. The 'new' curriculum to meet the 2004 NMC standards requires that students experience a wider breadth of practice learning in differing public health settings. The Royal Society of Public Health and Skills for Health are considering the wider public health workforce within the public health career framework (Skills for Health, 2007), yet it is uncertain how the specialist community public health nurse will relate to this framework and how the joined-up interprofessional working that is so pivotal to effective public health working will be implemented.

Future developments

The one certainty of the future is that there will be change. The tide of change appears to be moving at an ever-increasing rate, and academics are finding that a course which would normally be validated for at least five years is now being revised in shorter cycles, well within the five years, to meet the changing needs of service (PCTs), the contractors (SHAs) and also the professional regulatory body (the NMC).

These are also interesting times. It is very likely that within the next few years there will be no profession called health visiting – however, the specialist community public health nurse will undertake these roles, both with families and communities, working in different settings, such as the home, community centres, schools, places of work and leisure. However, the recent review of the role of health visitors (DoH, 2007a) suggests that the title may 'live another day'.

Across the country the recruitment to courses that prepare health visitors/specialist community public health nurses ranges from healthy to non-existent. The luxury of courses which are fully funded from the NHS education budget will probably be short-lived. The requirement for a specific 52-week course with supernumerary status will be contested – allowing practitioners to balance their university and work-based learning in more flexible ways.

However, my one prediction is that there will be 'direct entry' onto the third part of the register – that is, that someone wishing to work as a community public health nurse will start their training in that programme, and the practitioners that we are training today will, in fact, be our advanced practitioners in public health. Perhaps there will also be a clearer career pathway through the public health professions that is inclusive rather than exclusionary – all making for easier collaborative and partnership working and opening opportunities for greater career progression as a practitioner.

Core text recommendations

Canham, J., and Bennett, J. (2002), *Mentoring in Community Nursing: Challenges and opportunities*, Oxford: Blackwell Science.

DoH (2007a), *Facing the Future: A review of the role of health visitors*, London: DoH. Available at www.dh.gov.uk/cno.

NMC (2006b), *Standards to Support Learning and Assessment in Practice: NMC standards for mentors, practice teachers and teachers*, London: NMC.

6   The midwife

Val Collington

Overview

According to the Nursing and Midwifery Council, a midwife is:

> ... a person who, having been regularly admitted to a midwifery educational programme, duly recognised in the country in which it is located, has successfully completed the prescribed course of studies in midwifery and has acquired the requisite qualification to be registered and/or legally licensed to practise midwifery (NMC, 2004a).

Qualification is achieved through approved programmes that meet the standards of proficiency for pre-registration midwifery education (NMC, 2004a), as well as national and international standards (European Union (EU) Midwifery Directives 80/155/EEC, cited in NMC, 2004a; ICM, 1998; QAA, 2001a; RCM, 2003). At the point of registration, midwives must be able to supervise and provide care and advice to women during pregnancy, labour and the postpartum period, to conduct deliveries on their own responsibility and care for the newborn infant. In addition, the detection of abnormality in mother or child, execution of emergency procedures in the absence of medical help, the procurement of medical aid when necessary, parent education, family planning, and some areas of gynaecology are all within the scope of practice (NMC, 2004a).

The majority of midwives are employed in the National Health Service (NHS), practising in hospitals, community and health centres. Some work in the private sector whilst a small number of midwives have set up their own independent practices. Whatever the context, midwives are autonomous practitioners who are accountable for their own practice. They frequently work in collaboration with a range of health care practitioners including obstetricians, paediatricians, general practitioners, public health workers, and so on. Unique to the profession is the statutory requirement for supervision of midwives (NMC, 2006a). Each midwife must notify an intention to practise to the Local Supervising Authority Midwifery Officer in the area where they intend to practise (NMC, 2004b). Statistical analysis of the NMC Register showed that at March 2007 there were 35,177 midwives registered (35,038 female and 134 male). All of these submitted an Intention to Practise (NMC, 2007c) within the UK.

Historically, midwives have striven towards professional independence and autonomy. This desire to increase knowledge and self-determination has intensified over the years, leading to the integration of midwifery education into universities, as a professionalization strategy. The integration of midwifery education into higher education institutions (HEIs) was partly intended to confer greater academic credibility to the qualification. The outcome of a recent review of pre-registration midwifery proposed a move from the current Diploma of Higher Education to an all-graduate profession (NMC, 2008b). The review also changed the practice ratio to 'no less than 40 per cent theory', allowing more scope for focusing on practice education. All midwifery programmes are jointly validated by a higher education institution and the NMC, and are reviewed every five years. The length of the pre-registration programme is three years (156 full-time weeks), with 45 programme weeks per year. For registered nurses the minimum length of the programme is 78 weeks. Many universities offer a part-time mode of study for those students whose social circumstances require this option. Student midwives are supported in both the academic and practice setting by midwifery lecturers and clinical mentors who are prepared to meet the NMC standard for teachers of nursing and midwifery (NMC, 2006b). Although most of the curriculum content is delivered by midwife teachers, a range of multi-professional experts contribute to students' learning. In general, the pattern of delivery is blocks of study interspersed by varying lengths of time in clinical placements. In some instances, individual study days are also included to better integrate academic learning with practice experiences.

A variety of learning and teaching strategies are used to facilitate students' learning but in order to achieve the EU Midwifery Directives requirements for specific clinical experience (NMC, 2004a), direct contact with women and babies is required. When providing such care students should be supernumerary, under the direct or indirect supervision of a practising midwife (NMC, 2006b), and should be exposed to the full range of practice experiences needed to achieve the standards of proficiency.

For today's midwives, wanting to provide a woman-centred maternity service, the increase in technological interventions and the medicalization of childbirth remain challenging. It is expected that clinical experience should include varying models of midwifery care such as team midwifery, case holding, home births, midwifery-led care and birth centres, as well as care in the acute hospital setting. The focus of education is towards promoting normality in the childbearing continuum, whilst recognizing that the nature of the environment in which students learn clinical skills must also uphold a medical model of care. Assessment of students' learning will confirm depth and breadth of midwifery knowledge, practical skills and attitude. Development of professional attributes and the ability to work within the professional code of conduct is also assessed. (The recently revised NMC Code, subtitled 'Standards of conduct, performance and ethics for nurses and midwives', can be viewed on the NMC website, 2008a.) They are required to pass all theoretical and practice assessments to be eligible to register as a midwife.

There are over 49 HEIs offering midwifery programmes. They are commissioned by the local strategic health authority, based on workforce needs. Typically, the number of students commissioned to each HEI range from 15 to 70, the total figure for the 2007–08 academic year being 2,116 (Hansard, 2007).

Recent developments

The evolution of midwifery education has been influenced by legislation, with the first Midwives Act being passed in 1902. Also of influence is the development of a public health service, the setting up of the NHS in 1948, and reviews of the NHS over the years. Equally of relevance is the continued medicalization of childbirth that has led to active management, increased intervention and rising Caesarean section rates (Kitzinger, 2000). These issues impact on midwives' ability to work as autonomous practitioners within a medical (rather than social) model of maternity care (Symonds and Hunt, 1996). Even today the competing ideologies of women-centred versus a medical model of care are cited as a source of 'emotion work' in midwifery (Hunter, 2004). Midwives and students are encouraged to reflect on the impact of such practices on clinical decisions.

The 1902 Midwives Act was designed to secure the better training of midwives and to regulate their practice. At that time concern was not necessarily to do with professionalizing midwifery but with protecting mothers and babies. One hundred years later there is consistency in the key concerns about public protection and the connection between the quality of service, professional competence and outcomes of care (DoH, 2007b; Shribman, 2007).

It is a reasonable expectation that the quality of professional education reflects the quality of care provision (DoH, 2001a); hence the review and ongoing monitoring of professional education alongside modernization of the NHS and maternity services (DoH, 2007b; NMC, 2008a). The early profession's need for learning and developing technical skills has progressed to the current additional need for critical judgements, decision-making and critical analysis of practice required of midwifery practitioners.

Over two thirds of midwifery graduates have undertaken the direct entry three-year course at either diploma or degree level. The profile of students includes those with qualifications ranging from Access to higher education, the minimum qualification of five GCSEs (A to C grade, including mathematics and a science), A levels or previous DipHE or BA/BSc Hons degrees. Some mature entrants seeking a career change might hold master's degree qualifications. This variation necessitates particular consideration and flexibility in programme delivery and student support. The NMC figures show that 99.5 per cent of registered midwives are women (NMC, 2007c).

In the course of their practice, midwives have to make judgements in a variety of circumstances, using professional knowledge, skills and experience to inform decisions. These are key factors taken into account in the preparation of student midwives and the continuing professional development of current practitioners. Of importance is students' overall learning experience, the cultural context in which they learn and develop professional identity, their working relationships, and the level of supervision provided in practice.

There is some evidence to suggest that, on completion of their programme of study, some students are not equipped with the full range of clinical skills required for effective practice, such as lack of confidence in providing care when pregnancy is complicated (Kent et al., 1994; Maggs and Rapport, 1996; Fraser et al., 1997). It may be that some employers have unrealistic expectations of newly qualified midwives. Pre-registration education is just the beginning of their learning, providing them with the knowledge, skills and attitudes to perform competently. Key to their further development would be the support mechanisms in place for ongoing 'on-the-job' learning (Morgan, 2000) and the provision of continuous professional development programmes.

The *Standards of Proficiency* (NMC, 2004a) and the *Benchmark Statements* (QAA, 2001a) for midwifery provide a contemporary framework against which to map course outcomes. This provides national standards for the profession that might appear to be a 'national curriculum' for midwives' preparation. However, the reality is that it offers the basis from which curricula are developed to ensure that appropriate foundation for midwifery practice is achieved. At the same time there is scope for regional and local variation, different assessment schemes and contextual differences in care provision. Reviews of midwifery education have reinforced the need to strengthen the relationship between service providers and HEIs. Both are required to support learning and teaching in the context of practice (NMC, 2008b).

In order to ensure students acquire optimal practical skills much attention is given to practice learning support (Hall and Hart, 2004; Cook, 2006; Finnerty et al., 2006; Blaka, 2006; NMC, 2006b). Exposure to clinical practice should provide students with the opportunity to experience 24/7 care to develop understanding of the needs and experiences of women and babies (NMC, 2004a). In some institutions, conforming to a modular framework and semester pattern can adversely affect the structure and delivery of programmes and, in particular, the flow of students through practice areas. Despite these tensions, students' development of midwifery knowledge, competence and confidence in practice depends on the whole educational process.

Key issues for consideration are the process for commissioning midwifery education by the strategic health authorities, the focus on the practice learning environment and the possible impact of the changing student profile on resources to support their education in both the practice and academic contexts. Ongoing work by the NMC Midwifery Committee, the Royal College of Midwives and lead midwives working with the Department of Health all provide focus on the development of the profession, alongside improving the quality of maternity services (DoH, 2007b).

An essential part of the NMC decision-making process is the protection of the public through, for instance, focus on misconduct, lack of competence, physical and mental health, impaired fitness to practise and fraudulent entry to the register. In addition, the new standards for the preparation and practice of Supervisors of Midwives underpin the framework in place to support midwives in their day-to-day practice (NMC, 2006a), whilst enforcing the public protection strategy. Equally, the review of pre-registration midwifery considers the optimal education required to meet the needs of women and the maternity service. There are also new standards for those midwives trained outside the EU (NMC, 2008b) in respect of maintaining registration and fitness to practise, and return-to-practice programmes for those who have been out of practice for some time.

Models of teaching and learning

As with other professional education, there have been changes in the emphasis and style of learning in both the academic and practice settings. In pursuit of knowledge and understanding (of midwifery), both the learner and teacher have responsibility within the learning process. Midwifery education programmes, amongst others, have moved away from predominantly teacher-centred to student-centred education, with particular emphasis on the learner's active role in the process. The theoretical underpinnings of these processes are outlined here, with explanations of how student midwives, as adults, learn midwifery knowledge and skills, reflecting personal growth and development as practitioners.

The main theories of learning applied to professional education are behaviourist, cognitive, social and experiential. These explain in general terms how people learn, whilst principles of adult learning identify adults' unique and specific style of doing this. Practical application of the behaviourist approach is seen in education where the principles are applied in formal learning situations, incorporating the importance of feedback as reinforcement (Jarvis and Gibson, 1997). Module and course learning outcomes are often written in behavioural terms that can be measured. Recognizing that people's thought patterns continue to develop, developmental cognitive theorists such as Mezirow (1991) have focused on people's thinking, reflection and mental growth. Writing about adult development, for example, Mezirow explores the notion of the progressively enhanced capacity of an adult to validate prior learning through reflective discourse. His emphasis on meaning attached to experiences and how these are progressively transformed can be applied to the expectation of student midwives' development during their programme of study and, in particular, to their growth in understanding of practice experiences.

Social learning theory has its roots in social psychology and sociology and includes socialization, role and self-development (Hayes, 1994). The importance of role modelling was considered vital for achieving behavioural changes in attitudes, performance skills and adoption of the values and beliefs held. In addition, Lave and Wenger (1991) and Wenger (1998) identified learning and identity formation through participation in 'communities of practice'. Accepting that human learning takes place in social and cultural contexts, midwives, lecturers, other professionals and women/families influence students' learning, either consciously or unconsciously.

The concept of 'andragogy' (Knowles et al., 1998) incorporates core principles that could be applied to all adult learning situations, such as self-concept of the learner, readiness to learn, prior experience, motivation and orientation to learning. In the context of midwifery education programmes, application of this theory relates to the need to ensure that students are self-directing in their study, and their need to learn core midwifery knowledge and skills to achieve the desired learning outcomes for competent practice. Students' motivation to achieve these outcomes will influence their readiness and orientation to learning.

At the same time consideration is given to the role of the teacher as facilitator of learning (Knowles et al., 1998; Rogers, 1996; Cook, 2006). A variety of learning methods, including reflective journal writing (Moon,

2000; Collington and Hunt, 2006), allows independent inquiry to develop self-concept and enable students to take responsibility for their own decisions. Some degree of independence is noted in the completion of a portfolio recording their practice experiences, case studies of selected women for in-depth exploration and follow-up care. In these situations ongoing dialogue with midwives/mentors encourages students' learning in day-to-day practice, whilst integrating theory learnt.

Strategies employed in midwifery education programmes (such as reflective writing, critical incident analyses and student-led seminars) aim to empower learners to question established practices and to develop decision-making skills and confidence to act autonomously on qualification. Therefore, the nature of facilitation should be such that not only do students develop autonomy in their learning, but also in their professional actions. Clearly, the collaborative role of teacher and mentor in the practice setting is crucial in helping students to integrate theory and practice. Furthermore, having learnt reflective skills, it would be anticipated that, with support, application in practice would develop. These ideas relate to the fact that individuals need to understand the meaning of experiences.

Inevitably, students will use a range of these strategies to achieve learning outcomes in theory and practice. Methods used by teachers to promote learning recognize these differences, as well as the fact that individuals call upon the resources of existing knowledge and experience. With this in mind, reflective journal writing has been used in some midwifery education programmes to help students to focus on key issues in practice, to identify personal learning (Collington and Hunt, 2006) and development and to apply previously learnt knowledge to a given situation. Ghaye and Lillyman (1997), writing about the use of learning journals and critical incidents, affirmed this view and suggested that journal writing was a necessary skill for lifelong learning and also necessary for effective clinical learning.

Boud and Walker (1990) noted how learners constructed what they experience, and acknowledged the ways in which experience was interpreted within a cultural context. They recognized, however, that experience alone was not the key to learning but that certain measures needed to be in place to enable learners to gain maximum benefit from situations encountered. Schön (1987) argued that the skill of reflective practice should be started within the context of initial education. The main argument for teaching students in the professions to reflect is to develop their ability to be critical of their experiences in practice. During initial education, therefore, the problem could be that students do not yet have the body of knowledge and experience of day-to-day practice to benefit from the process. However, using a reflective cycle is useful in guiding students to draw on different types of knowledge/feelings to make sense of the experience as they progress through the programme of study.

Learning strategies such as reflection, critical incident analysis, problem-based and enquiry-based learning have been cited as useful tools to enable critical thinking, improve decision-making skills and increase confidence in practice (Jasper, 1996; Savin-Baden, 2000; Glen and Wilkie, 2000; Johns, 2000; Fisher and Moore, 2005). As a method of learning and teaching through critical analysis of experience, reflection helps students to develop knowledge, evaluate practice (Chambers, 1999) and question and challenge their established practices, convictions, basic beliefs and attitudes (Durgahee, 1996).

Many of these learning methods emphasize active learning and application of theories learnt to practice experiences. With reference to the Green Hill community, the following example demonstrates how students might develop understanding of the impact of social factors on health and well-being. Under the guidance and supervision of the midwife and other professionals working in that locality, awareness of the complex scenario of life at Number 1, Derby Street and Nicky's concerns regarding her social situation present a rich learning environment for a student midwife.

Nicky is the 17-year-old cousin of **Zoë Benner**. She is unsupported and living temporarily with Zoë in what is already cramped accommodation. She is 34 weeks pregnant and, after two bus rides, she arrives at the antenatal clinic where she meets **Andrea**, the midwife, and a second-year student midwife. Andrea notices that she looks pale and tired. When she enquires about this Nicky complains about the noise and poor living conditions where she is staying. She explains that having visited the housing department the previous day, she is distressed to learn that there is no guarantee that she will be housed before the birth of her baby. The midwife also learns that Nicky is still smoking and is not eating very well. The antenatal examination and further investigation reveals that the foetus is small for the gestational age.

In this situation the student midwife would participate in the consultation, and opportunity for dialogue with Nicky and the midwife would be afforded, especially for her to clarify issues raised. This scenario raises a range of psychosocial and physiological factors to enable the student to draw on theoretical concepts covered in class, particularly since promoting health and well-being is an important aspect of a midwife's role. For example, Nicky's age, social and financial status, limited social support, social and maternity benefits, access to health care in her locality and her housing problems are some areas of concern that could impact on her physical and mental health. There are a number of social, public and general health risk factors highlighted in the scenario that a student midwife should recognize, perhaps with the help of her mentor. She should reflect on the findings of the examination and medical/social history and begin to make connections between social issues, smoking and poor nutrition (for example) and pregnancy outcome. The scenario also presents exposure to interprofessional collaboration relating to child protection issues, for instance.

The teacher in the practice setting

Students need competent and confident teachers in the classroom and in the practice setting. Arguably, mentors have a key role in supporting students to develop knowledge and skills (Morton-Cooper and Palmer, 2000), and must, therefore, be adequately prepared to teach and assess students. In addition to obtaining approved qualifications and regular updating sessions, mentors/assessors need ongoing support in undertaking their role (Finnerty et al., 2006). Because of competing demands, many lecturers are unable to directly support practice learning (Gillmore, 1999; Cook, 2006), but can support mentors in this endeavour. Apart from their role in supervising students or contributing to assessment of practice, midwifery lecturers are encouraged to undertake some clinical practice experience for their own development. A small study by Cook (2006) highlighted lecturers' perception of the value of continuing midwifery involvement in practice, in terms of informing teaching activities and increasing confidence. The role of mentors and lecturers in supporting students was recently reviewed and the new standards highlight the need for collaboration and consistency in approach (NMC, 2006b).

With the increasing demand on practitioners to exercise personal and professional accountability, the importance of continuing professional development (CPD) cannot be underestimated. In order to mentor students, midwives must have at least one year's post-qualifying experience. Completion of an appropriate mentor preparation course, followed by annual updates, is also required (NMC, 2006b). The course provides an overview of learning/teaching/assessing principles, but guidance on midwifery programme-specific requirements is still required.

Midwives support 'on-the-job' learning for students to develop practical skills whilst helping them to relate what they learn in the classroom to the practice situation. Formally organized work-based learning is necessary for students to develop competence in clinical skills and in their role as midwives as a whole. To some extent the apprenticeship model still exists, with students learning on the job, working with mentors, learning by doing.

Audit of the practice learning environment and other quality monitoring activities allow consistency in approach to student support, and placement provision and the potential for learning is maximized. Begley (1999) recommends that those planning midwifery education programmes pay special attention to curriculum design and organization, student support and guidance in the clinical learning environment and the integration of theory and practice. In addition, Darra et al. (2003) devised a framework tool to help students combine theory and practice.

Content and structure of the students' learning

In general, midwifery programmes are modular in design. Although promoting a level of independent learning and development of key skills, the need to meet NMC requirements, QAA benchmarks and university regulations means there is little room for a liberal curriculum. However, in the practice context opportunity is provided to compare practices and different models of care. Typically, the curriculum contains relevant anatomy and physiology, with an emphasis on reproductive physiology, pathophysiology, applied sociology and psychology, social policy, midwifery studies (a major component), aspects of philosophy, law, ethics and research methods. Women's health, family planning and sexual health, and child health and development of key skills are also important components of the curriculum. Learning outcomes related to these can be achieved in either the academic or practice context. To enhance the curriculum service users are encouraged to contribute to its development and delivery. Generally the curriculum delivers an overview of the midwifery profession and its practice in Year 1, alongside physiological and psychosocial theories. More depth and a range of complicated childbearing issues are addressed in ensuing years. Students are required to keep a portfolio of evidence of achievement during the course, as well as recordings of practice experiences, demonstrating achievement of the EU Directives requirements; for example, 100 antenatal examinations, 40 normal births/personal deliveries. Proficiency in a variety of midwifery skills is also recorded.

Student progression is measured through achievement of the course/ practice learning outcomes that reflect the standards of proficiency (NMC, 2004a) required for registration with the NMC. An example of a student achieving a learning outcome relating to neonatal conditions in practice, supported by a mentor, is illustrated here. Evidence of a mentor's supportive role is demonstrated in this extract from a student's journal entry:

'It was my first visit to see this particular baby. The midwife had seen him on several occasions previously. The baby was very jaundiced and was sleeping. He was rousable, but maybe not quite as active as other babies of his age. The midwife questioned the mother as to whether the jaundice had worsened over the past couple of days. She thought it had in fact improved. The midwife then explained that she would like to take a blood test to ensure his level of bilirubin wasn't at a level where phototherapy treatment would be necessary. She also took the time to explain that the results would be ready that afternoon and if the level was elevated she would immediately contact the paediatrician who would arrange for the treatment to commence as soon as possible.' Student AEF (Collington, 2005).

'The blood sample was obtained and the mother advised about the care of her baby ... The test results returned and were 239 umols/litre, which is just below the rate at which most paediatricians would advise treatment.' Student AEF (Collington, 2005).

In this scenario, the midwife (as role model), by explaining the plan of care, was exposing her own reasoning and sharing experience and knowledge. This is a vital part of a mentor's role in helping a student develop reflective skills. Consequently, the student benefited through observing the communication exchange and later dialogue. The student's journal entry continues:

'Before I came across this baby, I had not realized fully the implications that jaundice can have, and when you should be concerned about it. I found the experience to be a positive one. The midwife gave all the information regarding the test, when the results would be available and how the mother would be notified. She later explained the wider implications of jaundice and the possible consequences if left untreated, therefore allowing the mother to realize how important it was to do the test and act upon the results as soon as possible. If the situation arose again, I would hope that I would recognize it for its potential hazards and, using my knowledge, act accordingly.' Student AEF (Collington, 2005).

In a situation such as this, a direct link with classroom learning would be enhanced if the student then considers the experience in light of further research/literature on the subject. This would allow deeper exploration of neonatal jaundice, using the experience and initial explanation as a trigger for learning. The concept of role modelling is adopted in the form of mentors and practice educators (Jarvis and Gibson, 1997; Morton-Cooper and Palmer, 2000). Mentoring relationships can be formal or informal, and in the context of the midwifery programme students may choose or be allocated experienced midwives who adopt a supervising, coaching, clinical teaching and assessing role in the practice learning environment.

Placing students' learning experience as the key purpose of the university's processes, Barnett (1997) focuses on systems and processes that create the framework for them to develop critical thought by making their own structured explorations and testing out ideas with teachers and each other. For optimal practice education, this is best achieved by academics working in collaboration with clinical practitioners. In this way, application of contextual knowledge is more likely to be meaningful to students. Bharj (2006) concurs with this view, stating that practice-based learning is central to the preparation of midwives for registration, but recognizes the problem of inadequate staff–student ratios in providing optimal support. To encourage development of critical abilities and incorporate its assessment in practice, three-way dialogue between midwife, student and lecturer is often used to increase reliability of the process. Also, to ensure 'fitness for practice', midwifery students' socialization into professional norms and values is given legitimacy by professional conduct statements and codes of conduct/ ethics produced by the professional body (see 'NMC Code', NMC, 2008a).

Methods

Preparation for practice placements, help with developing reflective skills, communication and professional conduct, for example, all tend to begin in the classroom followed by orientation in the practice setting. The range of learning methods used in midwifery education programmes to prepare learners for professional practice includes those that entail use of the written word, experiential methods and, more recently, the use of learning management systems to deliver e-learning materials. The concept of novice to expert (Benner, 2001) is still applied to curriculum delivery to enable practice elements to be achieved in a staged fashion, increasing in complexity as the course progresses. For example, the taxonomy of practice assessment criteria moves from having minimal knowledge, requiring full supervision, to needing minimal supervision, with the learner achieving independence on course completion.

Specific methods used include lectures, small group work, case studies, tutorials and discussion groups. Tutor-led reflective discussions and action learning sets are incorporated into some programmes. The opportunity for carrying a midwifery caseload is available to some students where this mirrors midwifery service provision. Depending on whether students are on community placements or within the maternity unit, they may be exposed to one-to-one supervision and individualized learning opportunities or involved in a team approach to planning learning activities. Allocation to various practice areas (for example, maternity wards, clinics, neonatal units, labour wards, gynaecology, paediatrics, community/primary care facilities) ensures sufficient exposure to enable achievement of programme learning outcomes and proficiency standards.

Apart from the didactic teaching used for some subject areas, midwifery students are exposed to a range of learning methods that help them to integrate theory and practice. Some authors have recommended the use of storytelling (Hunter and Hunter, 2006), using imagination to help students learn about disadvantaged clients (Hall and Hart, 2004) and using other forms of inquiry to help students construct knowledge (Brunt, 2003). The use of practice scenarios in this way is generally helpful in guiding students to consider alternative care management options and to facilitate in-depth thinking about care provision and appropriate decision-making. For example, storytelling as a creative teaching strategy was used in the context of limited exposure to practice. The benefits of experienced midwives telling students about their practice experiences included enhanced role transition, emotional clarification and increased cognitive learning.

In some instances opportunities to learn midwifery skills through simulation are provided in a skills laboratory prior to practising in real-life situations. Many institutions have developed a blended learning strategy, offering online learning in conjunction with face-to-face and other methods. Many of these methods require some degree of self-directedness, in line with the adult learning concept.

Assessment

Individual programmes have their own assessment strategies that adhere to university regulations whilst ensuring that the regulatory body requirements for registration and professional practice are met (NMC, 2004a). As might be expected, these change periodically; for example, recently the NMC has required that all practice assessments must be graded and introduced the notion of 'essential skills clusters'. In addition to the requirements set by the NMC, the Quality Assurance Agency qualification level descriptors are applied to each level of study (QAA, 2001b).

Continuous assessment of theory and practice is the norm for midwifery education programmes. In many institutions a tripartite process is in place where midwifery lecturers participate in the assessment of practice. Apart from theory and practice assessment results, the portfolio provides evidence to the assessment boards of students' achievement and progression towards demonstrating fitness for practice. Integral to the assessment process are professional conduct criteria that must also be met. On course completion, the NMC Lead Midwife for Education completes a 'Declaration of Good

Character and Good Health' (NMC, 2004a) for each student. Continuous assessment of conduct criteria is therefore helpful in making such decisions. It also supports the learner's personal and professional growth towards autonomous practice.

Assessment strategies/methods that draw on practice learning include examinations, coursework, case studies, extended essays, projects, viva voce and presentations. Objective structured clinical examination is increasingly being used to assess midwifery knowledge and attitudes. The documentation for continuous assessment of practice includes self-assessment at each stage to enable learners to reflect on their performance. In some instances practice learning contracts are drafted as an integral part of the process. Learners are normally given one reassessment opportunity in each practice assessment. If they are unsuccessful, discontinuation from the programme might result.

Despite differences in approaches to assessing learning in practice and readiness for professional practice, there is agreement about what constitutes fitness for practice. The benchmark is set within the proficiency standards for pre-registration programmes (NMC, 2004a). Fraser's (2000) study looking at effective assessment of practice schemes showed that whilst there was evidence that the majority of students are fit for midwifery practice by the end of the course, some assessment schemes were found to be unreliable. In particular, there was the potential for 'borderline' students to complete the programme if mentors were inadequately prepared for their responsibilities. Equally, if practice assessment documents were not 'user-friendly', evidence of competence was inadequately recorded. This and other evidence to date, plus quality monitoring procedures, have facilitated improvements in assessment processes.

Continuing professional development

The Post-Registration Education and Practice (PREP) standards set by the regulatory body (NMC, 2006c) provide the framework for practitioners to consider continuing professional development (CPD) and ways of developing their practice in order to maintain effective registration. Practitioners are required to maintain a personal professional profile identifying reflective accounts of actions taken to develop and meet the practice standards. They are responsible for addressing their CPD needs but generally there is employer support. In addition, the requirement for supervision of midwives (NMC, 2006a) provides a supportive developmental framework for them.

The drive for self- and organizational improvement requires adaptability and willingness to embrace new values, practices and concepts. Eraut (1994) concurs, stating that professionals continually learn on the job because their work entails engagement in a succession of cases, problems and projects. The view that CPD requires formally organized learning as well as work-based learning (Wallace, 1999) equally applies to midwives' clinical and mentoring role. For instance, formal preparation for mentoring students needs to include curriculum changes and developments within the profession. Therefore regular updating and ongoing reflection on practice is required.

In a later paper, Eraut (2000) explores the conceptual and methodological problems arising from several empirical investigations of professional education and learning in the workplace. His focus was on non-formal learning and tacit knowledge and the issue of whether tacit knowledge can be made explicit. In the context of midwifery education, for example, much learning takes place outside the formal context but contributes to achievement of learning outcomes and the award of a qualification. In addition, the in-service education of midwives and other professionals that contributes to practice learning tends to include elements of active learning from experience and sharing of expertise.

Research into professional development shows that the initial period, during which new professionals develop proficiency in their roles, continues long after initial qualification (Sookhoo and Biott, 2002). Eraut (1994) is critical of the way higher education institutions and professional organizations attempt to include all knowledge required for the profession, thus overcrowding the curricula. This approach demonstrates insufficient regard for lifelong learning. Hence, preceptorship and ongoing learning to meet workforce needs and changes in care provision are required of all practitioners.

Current debates

Changes in NHS provision overall and in the organization of maternity services and primary care services could impact on midwifery education in a number of ways. For instance, staff changes or shortages will result in inadequate numbers of mentors available to supervise students in practice. Also, service reconfiguration in some sectors has seen a reduction in the number of learning opportunities available. Such sometimes unpredictable issues require optimal partnership working between the HEIs and the SHA that commissions students. In general, flexibility in programme delivery and use of learning opportunities have aided management of practice education. Over recent years shortages in the midwifery workforce led to promotion of return-to-practice programmes, recruitment from abroad, and therefore the need for adaptation programmes for midwives from outside the EU. It is arguably important to consider such workforce changes alongside NHS changes and modernization, particularly to ensure that the workforce has the knowledge, skills and expertise to achieve NHS priorities. The above factors hold implications for the quality of care but also the quality of the practice learning environment (Buckley and Dunn, 2000; NMC, 2006a). In order to increase the range of learning opportunities some institutions have, for example, built in comparative care modules, enabling visits to other maternity services in the UK or abroad to consider different models of care.

A current concern surrounds the continued medicalization of childbirth and the increasing Caesarean section rate in the majority of maternity services. This does not uphold the view that pregnancy is a physiological state. The concerns drive voluntary groups and the midwifery professional organizations' promotion of normality. The focus on 'risk' partly explains the continued change in emphasis. Recent consultation on pre-registration midwifery and fitness for practice (NMC, 2006a) questioned the status quo and considered the possible impact on the education of future practitioners. Now, the definition of 'normal birth' is questioned, since the level of interventions in childbearing has increased. When completing their portfolio of practice experiences students might rightly ask, 'what counts as "normal"?'

Government health policy refers to the need for interprofessional collaboration in health and social care (DoH, 2000b) to benefit better patient/ client care. Professional education programmes, therefore, incorporate a range of interprofessional learning activities to initiate the process of interprofessional/interdisciplinary working (Furber et al., 2004). Specific learning outcomes of midwifery programmes include this element. For example, shared learning in subjects/modules such as physiology, communication and ethics is one way of bringing the professions together. In other institutions the curriculum allows continued themes to be studied together throughout the programmes. The *National Service Framework for Children, Young People and Maternity Services* (DoH, 2004a) also provides guidance for ways of working that requires consideration in the education of the future workforce.

Because of the changing student profile, including the number of mature women studying midwifery, a number of institutions offer part-time programmes to facilitate those needing flexibility. The rules regarding access to NHS bursaries have also helped to support learners with specific social/ family needs. The ability to step on and off a programme (for example, for maternity leave or special leave) has aided student progression rather than contributed to attrition. In order to meet government targets for widening participation in higher education, this degree of flexibility is also of benefit for those who require additional academic support.

Future developments

Political debates and changes relating to education and the NHS have a direct impact on the education of health professionals. For example, recent NHS workforce reviews have resulted in a reduction in the number of students commissioned for pre-registration programmes. Concerns about health care workforce issues are being raised via parliamentary lobbying, and so on, through the Council of Deans (CoD, 2006). The likely future of education and training is partly dependent on NHS priorities and it is difficult to predict the impact on practice education. In addition, there is still much uncertainty about the funding of health care education with the advent of standard national contracts and the benchmark pricing structure.

The need for midwives (a statutory requirement) and an appropriately qualified workforce to deliver optimal maternity services is unquestioned (DoH, 2000b; NMC, 2006a; RCM, 2008) but individual employers with minimal budgets are challenged by limited resources to meet needs. The development of 'assistant' grade practitioners in some service sectors has created some anxiety about future workforce patterns and, indeed, adequacy of supervision and role modelling for students.

It appears that HEIs will increase the focus on blended learning approaches, to include e-learning, a strategy that fits well with the flexibility required in professional programmes such as midwifery. However, the focus on face-to-face delivery and learning from experience will not diminish. Equally, the professions have much to offer HEIs with their new focus on work-based learning, since historically it has been central to professional learning. No doubt, the issue of evidence-based practice, a medical model of care, will continue to be a challenge to the desire for implementing a social model of midwifery care.

Consultation on the review of professional regulations (DoH, 2006d; DoH, 2006f) is yet to report formally following extensive consultation but the renewed focus on fitness for practice and public protection is warranted. Also, more consistency within the regulatory frameworks across the professions is anticipated. The NMC response reiterated the benefits of self-regulation, whilst maintaining public confidence in regulations that have a critical role in helping to deliver high-quality health care and patient safety. Finally, in addition to internal mechanisms for measuring quality, the range of quality assurance and monitoring frameworks for higher education (QAA, 2001b) and for the profession (NMC, 2006c) presents ongoing challenges for education providers (Watson et al., 2005), although such frameworks are necessary to ensure the maintenance of good standards.

Core text recommendations

Crosling, G., and Webb, G. (2002), *Supporting Student Learning: Case studies, experience and practice from higher education*, London: Kogan Page.

Meyler, E., and Trenoweth, S. (2007), *Succeeding in Nursing and Midwifery Education*, Chichester: John Wiley & Sons.

Moon, J. (2000), *A Handbook of Reflective and Experiential Learning: Theory and practice*, London: Routledge Falmer.

7 The nurse

Jenny Spouse

Overview

Nursing in the UK encompasses several disciplines – nursing adults, children, people with learning disability or people with mental health problems – and as it also relates to the international community of nursing practitioners across the world, finding a good definition that embraces all aspects of the profession is difficult. The most enduring definition has been agreed by the International Council of Nurses (n.d.):

> Nursing encompasses autonomous and collaborative care of individuals of all ages, families, groups and communities, sick or well and in all settings. Nursing includes the promotion of health, prevention of illness and the care of ill, disabled and dying people. Advocacy, promotion of a safe environment, research, participation in shaping health policy and in patient health care systems management, and education are also key nursing roles.

This definition specifies nursing as a collaborative activity with the patient (or client) and those closest to them and acknowledges that for many people complete recovery is not possible and even death will be the only outcome, but the nursing role throughout is significant to ease that person's life. Specific to the UK, the Royal College of Nursing (RCN) of the UK (2003) is more succinct:

> Nursing is the use of clinical judgement in the provision of care to enable people to improve, maintain, or recover health, to cope with health problems, and to achieve the best quality of life, whatever their disease or disability, until death (RCN, 2003).

The nature of nursing

The four branches of nursing can be further subdivided to provide nursing services to groups of people requiring specialist care in different settings. Nurses devote their time to supporting patients/clients and their families in a range of hospital and community settings. Popular media portrayals of nursing concentrate on the high drama of critical care departments in acute medical hospitals, omitting the more frequent experiences of the general population requiring the planned medical, surgical or mental health care that is provided by the majority of nurses in hospital wards, clinics and the community.

In March 2007 in the UK there were over 686,000 nurses and midwives (approximately 10 per cent male; 63 per cent over 40 years of age) registered with the UK's Nursing and Midwifery Council: of these, some 532,000 live in England. The vast majority of these registered practitioners hold the professional award of adult nurse. UK-trained nursing or midwifery students can apply for professional registration with the NMC only following successful completion of an approved academic course and if they can provide verified evidence of meeting various standards relating to competency, good health and character. Overseas recruitment activities, supported by the Department of Health, have been a strategy to increase the nursing and midwifery workforce during the past five years particularly, and attracted nearly 9,000 practitioners in the year ending March 2000. Most of these nurses have come from India and the Philippines. Unless the country of origin has a reciprocal agreement with the UK these practitioners are required to undergo a six-month probationary period and to take a programme of orientation with specific academic and professional outcomes to be achieved.

Nursing education in the UK

During the 2005–06 academic year there were approximately 73,000 students studying in England full time on either a diploma or degree course in pre-registration nursing (CoD, 2007). These students constitute a significant number of the total university students and are one of the few groups of students who receive their training free of top-up fees. Nursing education has changed considerably over the past century, moving from an ad hoc process provided by ward sisters committed to promoting learning, to a regulated and structured programme delivered by universities in collaboration with their health care partners and regulated by the professional statutory body (the NMC).

Nursing education in the UK has a long history, going back to before the time of Florence Nightingale. Nonetheless the UK was one of the last countries in the 'modern world' to establish professional registration of its nursing practitioners and to set standards for their training (Spouse, 1990; Maggs, 1981; Hector, 1973). Before the development of the National Health Service in 1948, many of the training hospitals were autonomous and were either small privately funded organizations with specialist areas of practice (such as fever hospitals) or district general hospitals, supported by public donation. Having a school of nursing was a means to recruit the workforce and this influenced the nature of training, the length of hours worked by the probationers and the quality of tuition provided. With the establishment of the GNC, standards of training gradually improved, but the quality of training and the high attrition rates was a long-standing concern, as reflected in numerous reports published by several bodies including *The Lancet* (the medical profession's journal) (Lancet Commission, 1932), the RCN (1964; 1971; 1984), the GNC (1969; 1974; 1983) and the government (DHSS, 1979; 1983). These reports focus on core issues, still prevalent, in England especially; in particular on the underfunding of nursing education and the use of nursing students to prop up an understaffed NHS.

Recent developments

Three reports published since 1971 have had the most significant influence on bringing nurse education into mainstream education: the Briggs Report (1972), the Commission on Nursing Education (1984) and Project 2000 (1986).

The Briggs Report

This report (DHSS, 1972) led to the establishment of the United Kingdom Central Council for Nursing, Midwifery and Health Visiting (UKCC) and four national boards for each of the countries of the UK (established in 1982, superseded by the NMC in 2002). It also argued that students preparing for different careers in health care should have a joint entry point to learn and work together for the duration of their programme until their chosen professional stepping-off point. This proposal has never been implemented largely because of the restrictions and entry requirements of the different professional groups.

The Commission on Nursing Education

The report (RCN, 1984) anticipated that nursing would decline as a career choice for school leavers due to increased prosperity and increased career opportunities for women (the traditional recruitment pool for nursing), leading to a huge shortfall in the numbers entering nursing. The report proposed that nursing should become an all-graduate profession on entry to the register, as a degree programme would be more attractive to young people and students would be supernumerary throughout the programme.

Project 2000

This more modest proposal (UKCC, 1986) was that nursing programmes should be approved by higher education but at the minimum level of a diploma in higher education rather than at degree level. It also proposed that students should spend only part of their programme in a supernumerary capacity. Scotland and Wales subsequently chose to prepare their nurses for entry to the professional register at degree level.

As anticipated, the government only reluctantly supported Project 2000 proposals and insisted that students should work as members of the workforce for 30 per cent of their programme. Schools of nursing in England have been affiliated to universities and pre-registration programmes now attract academic credits.

Application to a nursing or midwifery programme and entry requirements

Unlike the other countries of the UK where nursing students study for a nursing undergraduate degree, in England the majority of nurses study for a Diploma of Higher Education. Entry requirements to nursing programmes are defined by the NMC and include proficiency in the English language (spoken and written) and in numeracy skills. Applicants are encouraged to have some experience of working in the field of nursing they are choosing. As a condition to commencing the programme, all midwifery and nursing students have to be cleared by the Criminal Records Bureau, and meet the requirements of the terms of the Protection of Vulnerable Adults Act. If any student is likely to be working under supervision with children they must be cleared under the terms of the Protection of Children Act. All students are routinely screened for resistance to a range of infectious diseases such as tuberculosis, hepatitis and so on.

Models of teaching and learning

Throughout their programme students spend a relatively small proportion of time learning and practising in a skills laboratory. In this safe environment, students' learning is underpinned by classical behaviourist and cognitive constructivist theories. The latter series of theories proposes that humans relate to the world from within a framework of their own experiences, which provide insights and meaning to acts and events and an ability to utilize such knowledge in response to new experiences. Intention is important, and humans are seen to strive to make sense or impose order by establishing relationships or pattern closure, known as *Prägnantz*, hence the term 'gestalt'. Gestalt, or configuration, enables humans to understand the whole which is greater (more significant) than the parts. Thus, a professional skill is demonstrated, then it is deconstructed into its constituent parts and students given time to practise the parts before putting them together to perform the whole skill. Learners thus recognize the pattern of the skill and by reconstructing the skill achieve closure or gestalt. Learning is enhanced when the new skills are seen to have relevance to their practice experiences and links are made to existing knowledge and skills. Opportunities to engage in supervised and independent practice help students to consolidate their learning. Regular practice with reasonable breaks allows the skill to become integrated into their repertoire of knowledge (Borger and Seabourne, 1966). Many skills laboratories have video/DVD cameras, enabling students to observe their practice on a video link and thus recognize the areas that need further attention.

Transferring their skills to the real-life practice placement is often daunting and more complex, as there are additional layers of knowledge and expertise to add. Interpersonal skills support technical skill; professional knowledge is also vital to ensure the correct skill is practised at the right time on the correct patient. This is often compounded by fear, lack of confidence and the realization that a mistake could harm an already frail and vulnerable patient. This can be explained by Kurt Lewin's (1936) theory of topology. Challenges evoked by new experiences or the unexpected will create dissonance and can stimulate a search for solutions to the problem. Lewin argues this enables learning to take place and thus an increase in personal psychological life space or boundary of understanding (Lewin, 1936). As a result, new knowledge and understanding is acquired by using existing knowledge as a basis for further understanding.

Applying practice technical skills in real-life situations and often under pressure is complex and multi-faceted. Polanyi's work on tacit knowledge provides some useful insights (Polanyi and Prosch, 1973). For example, focal activities, such as giving an injection or undertaking an admission assessment, require considerable preparation in learning how to handle and use any associated equipment or how to develop a conversation with different types of patients in different circumstances. Once students have developed these kinds of subsidiary skills to a level that they no longer need to concentrate on them wholly, they are then able to develop the focal skill by combining all the different aspects of the nursing activity. A third stage would be to acquire the relevant craft knowledge. Having freed up their concentration from the focal task, students then have the psychological space to recognize the existence of questions waiting to be formulated, or they are able to make connections between what they were experiencing in their practice and what they had learned from their studies. As a result they are able to expand their zone of proximal development (Vygotsky, 1978).

Normative regulated action

Wertsch (1991) briefly discusses Habermas's (1984) concept of normative regulated action. As its title implies, individual action is influenced by situational norms, resulting in compliance and integration or rejection and consequent ostracism. The community, such as a placement setting and its staff, expects individuals to behave according to traditional norms, such as wearing a uniform, and to conform to informal codes of conduct, such as not fainting at the sight of blood. Failure to conform to these norms often results in students becoming ostracized or given a poor end-of-placement module (see Spouse, 2003). Adopting local customs enhances relationships (Schutz, 1970, pp. 92–5 and 298). Learning to identify these social norms can be a challenging experience for newcomers, as Melia described in her ethnographic study of pre-registration nursing students (Melia, 1984). Many of the processes newcomers engage in are to make sense of what is happening around them and attempt to recognize and understand acceptable (and desirable) behaviour. Such understandings are developed inductively through personal interpretation of the observed actions of others (Wertsch, 1991, p. 10). Habermas's (1984) theories of action-directed behaviour concern social interaction and provide a useful framework for viewing students' socialization experiences. Carr and Kemmis (1986) identify six essential features of critical social experience that lead to humans feeling oppressed but through which they can also find liberation. Four of these are concerned with the social experience; that is, concrete social experience, personification of participants, analysis of experience and contextual operating mechanisms (Carr and Kemmis, 1986, p. 139). So the importance of the mentor or sponsor to each placement setting is crucial in enabling students to adjust to their new environment and to learn the normative activities of that setting. Such activities, in addition to the everyday human interactions, include the specialist vocabulary, the jargon and abbreviations used as well as the techniques that are employed to nurse patients. Many students engage in impression management (Goffman, 1959; Spouse, 2003) whereby they construct a mode of behaviour that conforms to their beliefs of normative expectations so as to receive approval and thus a good end-of-placement report. Instrumental to students' progress is the ability to feel accepted by the community of practitioners in the placement setting and also their ability to function in the same manner as the other nurses of the placement by participating legitimately in the work of the community. Legitimized participation through partnership with an experienced practitioner bears a strong relationship to social learning experienced by humans from childhood. Socio-cultural theories of learning derived from Vygotsky's work (1978) help explain development of cognitive processes through social interaction and speech.

Integrating theory and practice

The integration of theory and practice is a challenge to students who have difficulty seeing the relevance of what they experience in practice and their reading or previous learning. Shulman's work with teachers suggests that learners need to reconceptualize their subject or theoretical knowledge in order to teach or use it in practice (Shulman, 1986). In a similar manner nursing students need to recognize the relevance of their professional knowledge to what they are encountering on a daily basis and vice versa. Normally this can only be achieved if students are supported by a knowledgeable companion (such as a mentor) who can help them make sense of practice.

Vygotsky (1978) came to develop a two-stage theory of development whereby a learner who was intellectually ready to move to the next stage but did not have the maturational ability, could be assisted to reach this potential through support and guidance of a more experienced other. This transition area he described as the zone of proximal development (ZPD). Intrapersonal speech in developmental activities, or alternatively in discussion with a more experienced person, provides necessary support to move through the level of maturation for which the novice is ready. However, this will only be achieved if such speech guides the individual to a level beyond that currently practised (the inner boundary of the ZPD) and providing the learner has already developed an understanding of the principles or has the theoretical knowledge – the outer boundaries of the ZPD (see Figure 7.1).

In the formal setting of the classroom, students are prepared for clinical placements with theoretical knowledge of (for example) nursing theory, psychology, pathology, and so on, but, not having seen actual examples, they need help to relate these forms of knowledge to their practice. Such knowledge constitutes the inner boundary of their ZPD and through mentorship they can extend their boundary towards the outer perimeter. By exposure to clinical practices alongside experienced practitioners students learn to relate their formal knowledge to informal situations. Ideally such learning is further stimulated by encountering unfamiliar situations that are viewed as problematic. This evolutionary process of assimilating new concepts to their practice and accommodating or shaping such knowledge relates to constructivist theories

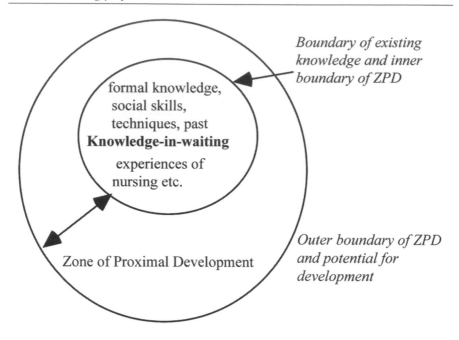

Figure 7.1   Boundaries of a zone of proximal development
Source: Spouse, 2003.

of learning (Von Glasersfeld, 1995). In coaching activities students can re-frame their theoretical knowledge within a clinical context.

'Scaffolding' – proleptic instruction

Wood et al. (1976, p. 90) coined the term 'scaffolding' to describe the process of providing experiences or challenges that move learners' 'knowledge-in-waiting' to 'knowledge-in-use' (from within the inner boundary to the outer boundary of their ZPD). The concept of scaffolding has since been developed in a number of ways but is particularly pertinent in nursing where students are given guidance by a coach who talks them through aspects of a procedure or concept where there is need for extra information to achieve understanding. The principle is similar but not the same as the coaching activities described by Schön (1987). In his examples, coaches take a lead in demonstrating and challenging the student which perhaps works well in the privacy of a design studio or rehearsal space but not in the public arena of clinical practice (Schön, 1987). The talk provided in scaffolded instruction has been termed 'proleptic instruction' (Wertsch and Stone, 1979).

Proleptic instruction or coaching assists students to use their theoretical or practical knowledge-in-waiting, so that it could be transformed into knowledge-in-use. Identifying and structuring a task which engages students actively helps them to apply knowledge within a social and professional context. It also enables achievement beyond current levels of practice to the level of potential at that moment in time; that is, through the existing ZPD. If the quality of supervision is appropriately supportive and challenging, students can acquire new knowledge which changes the boundaries of their own ZPD, leading to further development by stimulating them to ask questions or to read about their experiences. In contrast, should the mentor identify that the student is insufficiently prepared intellectually to make sense of instructions (that is, the level of development potential is less than anticipated), the scaffolding activity needs to be modified to accommodate the deficit. The importance of this process of novice (inexperienced in the area of practice) and mentor working together whilst giving care is vital. Students benefit from opportunities to undertake appropriate tasks beyond their perceived demonstrable level of skill but which are within range of what they have already learned in their studies or a previous placement (hence the importance of planning learning experiences). By guiding novices through such activities with coaching or proleptic instructions they become able to fulfil their potential. However, if the mentor is aware that a novice could not interpret these instructions correctly or fulfil implicit directions, then either the nature of verbal guidance (language used) or the task must be reviewed. For example, it may be that the mediating language used to describe the required activities is beyond the student's comprehension, so different (perhaps lay) terms need to be used. Alternatively, the task may be new and too complex and so a lesser legitimate, more peripheral activity could be offered. In both situations the expert must constantly assess the student's level of understanding or ability to learn and refine the nature of instruction offered. In assessing students' levels of knowledge and ability to put it into practice, the boundaries of their working knowledge and their developmental ability at that moment in time become apparent. Using Vygotsky's concept of development as a two-stage process and the ZPD as the difference between knowledge-in-use and potential knowledge-for-use (knowledge-in-waiting), a mentor can then use the concept of ZPD as a diagnostic or analytic tool (Spouse, 1998a).

Developing composite skills

Being able to witness the construction of practice through their mentor's activities of framing and re-framing patients' needs, added to the reformulation of their knowledge base, accordingly allows knowledge to become transformed into a vital and evolutionary reality. Students need to develop skilled performance in a range of psychomotor, interpersonal, therapeutic and management activities in preparation for every time they give care and this is best achieved when learning need is assessed and learning opportunities are planned, thus helping them to develop their technical and interpersonal skills until they are no longer conscious of using them or having to think about them, and can concentrate on the focal operation of assessing their patient's condition, of delivering the nursing care and their response to the care.

The teacher in the practice setting

Students are supported in placement settings by a range of teachers depending upon the funding arrangements of the local strategic health authority (SHA) and with the programme provider (the university). In clinical practice placements there is a mandatory requirement that students are supervised and mentored by a suitably qualified clinician, known as a *mentor*. Many strategic health authorities (SHAs) have funded additional posts to cover a more strategic educational role across placement areas used by pre-registration programme providers. Post-holders are variously known as *practice education facilitators* or *placement experience managers*. Other models of clinical educational support are also used by different educational partnerships such as the *link lecturer* role and the jointly appointed *lecturer practitioner*.

Practice teachers, mentors

During their practice placements students are required by the NMC to be supported for at least 40 per cent of their placement hours by a registered nurse with experience in the clinical discipline and who holds a qualification concerned with teaching and assessing in practice (mentorship). Mentors are members of the clinical nursing team. They receive no financial remuneration or work relief for this responsibility. The frequency and large numbers of students entails that most registered nurses become mentors who have a minimum of one year's post-registration experience in their clinical setting (for required standards, see NMC, 2006b). To support them to develop their mentoring skills they are required to take a recognized course of preparation with academic credit at diploma or degree level, normally assessed by a practical element and written assessment. Mentor preparation programmes are required to include: creating a learning environment, assessing learning need, developing a learning agenda, promoting learning in practice settings, assessing professional development, passing or failing a student, documenting progress, promoting equal opportunities, and supporting students with disabilities such as dyslexia. Mentors assess and certify a student's progress. Several research reports (Atkins and Williams,

1995; ENB, 1993a; ENB, 1993b; ENB, 1998; ENB, 2000) indicate that this is a difficult activity for mentors, especially when students are passing through their clinical setting for a placement of, say, 6–15 weeks. In 2006 the NMC introduced the requirement that experienced and specially prepared mentors, known as 'sign-off mentors', must take responsibility for certifying qualifying students as being fit for registration and that these mentors are given time (an hour a week) from their clinical workload to fulfil these responsibilities (NMC, 2006b).

With Project 2000, it was anticipated that the mentor support for students would improve. However, research by Wilson-Barnett et al. (1995) indicated that because of the low ratio of qualified nurses to unqualified staff and, as a result, to students, they rarely worked alongside their mentee and so students lacked the social and professional support that they needed. Other studies indicate that when students have opportunities to work alongside an experienced and knowledgeable practitioner their learning is exciting and profound (Spouse, 2003). Research undertaken for the National Board for Nursing, Midwifery and Health Visiting for Scotland found that the quality of mentorship was better amongst those nurses who had studied to degree level (Watson and Harris, 1999).

Effective mentorship requires a stable and effective skill mix of well-educated clinical staff, which, with demographic changes and the current crises in staffing the health care services, is almost impossible.

Practice education facilitators/placement experience managers

The development of this role by SHAs has transformed the partnership relationship between universities and placement providers, as the role holder is normally based in the clinical institution with responsibility to develop strong links with individual placement areas (wards, clinics, departments, community centres, care homes, GP practices, schools and so on) and with the university, particularly with the staff who are responsible for managing and allocating students to their practice placements. Hence, the practice education facilitator (PEF) has an intimate knowledge of the programme requirements as well as of the placement area. They take responsibility for ensuring there are sufficient placements for the anticipated number of students.

Lecturer practitioners

Creation of joint education and practice appointments and, in the 1990s, the lecturer practitioner role have also been used to resolve the issue of providing educational support to students in practice placements. Such joint appointments, where a clinician and an educationalist share a clinical role, have been praised by students and managers alike who saw improvements in nursing care as well as greater congruence between theory and practice (Ashworth and Castledine, 1980). Their particular merit was the appointment of well-educated and prepared practitioners into posts of authority (Lathlean, 1997). The aim of the appointments was to use practitioners with clinical credibility to teach in the practice setting and to support mentors, whilst also bringing the educational needs of students high on the clinical agenda. Inevitably clinical demands always took precedence over all others and resulted in many lecturer practitioners leaving the role within two or three years suffering from burn-out (Lathlean, 1997).

Link lecturers

Many nurse academics are linked with a clinical setting. Sometimes this involves undertaking patient care whilst working with a student or member of staff. Such clinical involvement raises questions about cost effectiveness and benefits. More frequently an academic will provide tutorial support to small groups of students on placement in a clinical area, or engage clinical staff in developing educational materials that are specific to the setting, such as welcome packs, workbooks and web-pages.

Content and structure of the students' learning

The programme

Preparation to become a registered nurse with the professional statutory organization (NMC) normally takes three years of full-time study or 4,600 hours and is 50 per cent theory and 50 per cent practice. Programmes are offered by over 50 universities in the UK, most of which require 'full-time' attendance. Students normally undertake their 50 per cent clinical practice experiences in local hospitals, clinics, voluntary and charitable sector institutions and in different sectors of the community (such as people's homes, clinics, day centres and so on). Successful registration requires students to have completed all academic and practice requirements of their programme as well as demonstrating proficiency in a range of professional attributes, including demonstration of competence, professional conduct and good health.

The pre-registration nursing programme is in two distinct parts: the Common Foundation Programme (CFP) and the Branch programme. Theory and practice experiences are equally provided throughout the programme. Those with evidence of relevant prior learning can take an accelerated programme. Most programmes are modular in nature with the practice element an integral part of a theory module or a stand-alone module that runs alongside the theory elements. Students work the same shifts as their placement supervisors including unsocial hours (weekends and night duty) so students experience care delivery over a 24-hour cycle. Learning with other health and social care professionals is a mandatory aspect of nursing programmes.

The Common Foundation Programme

The aim of the CFP is to promote good understanding between the different branches of nursing and midwifery, including the undertaking of 'taster opportunities' of each of the nursing branches. Students share academic sessions in all the core subject disciplines, such as biological sciences, psychology, communication skills, sociology, ethics and public health as they apply to nursing or midwifery. Students are also introduced to using information technology, study skills and research in nursing and midwifery practice. Many programmes now require students to have successfully completed the European Computer Driving Licence to develop skills in using electronic patient records.

During the CFP students are introduced to a range of essential caring technical skills, often to specific national standards. Before practice placements (normally ten weeks after commencing their programme) students must have attended and successfully completed a range of these mandatory training sessions (such as how to move patients safely, either with a mechanical aid or in collaboration with another person, from bed to chair or commode or from floor to chair). Sessions are normally provided in a skills laboratory (or practical room) where they are taught and learn under close supervision, often using simulations with manikin dolls or each other. Students also learn about the importance of infection control and safe hand cleansing as well as about the safe disposal of waste or dangerous materials.

The European Union Directives require adult nursing students to gain experience over the whole programme of caring for people with mental health or a learning disability, to gain understanding of: the needs of children and their families, of community care and of maternity care, care of older people, medical and surgical nursing.

Progression from the CFP to the Branch programme depends upon successful completion of the practice elements of the programme and achievement of specific outcomes. Assessment is of students' formal knowledge as well as their practical, professional performance. The latter requires a documented assessment of their placement performance and conduct from an experienced registered nurse who has supervised (mentored) them during the placement. To ensure students can conduct essential skills safely, they are often assessed in the skills laboratory at the end of the placement using objective structured clinical examinations (Nicol and Glen, 1999).

The Branch programme

This two-year (full-time) programme component is when students study in detail their chosen part of the nursing register. Students continue to have a combination of theory and practice, spending 50 per cent of their time in clinical placements and working the same shifts as their mentor. To meet professional and governmental requirements students studying for different parts of the nursing register have a wide range of placement experiences. All students spend their placements in different types of hospital and community settings for 10–15 weeks, learning to deliver care in increasingly complex settings and to take a more senior role of care management as well as care delivery.

Learning in and from practice experiences

Throughout their programme students are required to undertake specific placement experiences, and at different stages of their programme to demonstrate achievement of learning outcomes as applied to each clinical placement. These are clustered under the four domains identified by the Nursing and Midwifery Council:

- professional and ethical practice
- care delivery
- care management
- personal and professional development.

In other words, they are structured around the NMC Standards (NMC, n.d.) for progression from the CFP and successful completion of the Branch programme. The actual process and detail of each placement experience is negotiated between the mentor and student. The placement mentor typically welcomes a student with a list of learning opportunities that are available and the two agree a plan of action. Many placements offer workbooks for students to use to structure their learning and increasingly placements have intranet websites with relevant information and educational material for students to use. Often such educational material is developed as a collaborative activity between the link lecturer and the clinical staff. Students are also offered a range of hub and spoke experiences designed to provide an understanding of the patient experience of health care in that specific speciality. These experiences include visits with clinical specialists to patients' homes, attendance at specialist clinics, working with different health and social care practitioners such as physiotherapists, music therapists, teachers, and so on.

Throughout each placement students' progress is regularly assessed; this is documented on their placement report form or placement passport and an action plan is made to help them meet their learning needs. If students are making appropriate progress, they are encouraged to extend their clinical knowledge (both cognitive and practical) beyond the requirements of their learning outcomes, by undertaking increasingly sophisticated activities that contribute to the care of the patients and the workload of the clinical team (see Spouse, 1998a; Spouse, 1998b).

Methods

University- or campus-based teaching is concerned with introducing human sciences such as biology, genetics, pharmacology, sociology and psychology, applied sciences such as communication skills, nutrition, public health and epidemiology, as well as professional knowledge, including ethics, law, nursing theory and nursing practice.

An essential aspect of preparing students for practice placements is development of professional skills in the safe environment of a classroom or skills laboratory. Interpersonal skills training is an important aspect of the curriculum through the use of a range of experiential learning activities such as role play, simulation and games. Practical and technical skills are taught in laboratory situations using demonstrations, simulation models, and video recordings of students' practice followed by guided peer debriefing. Most sessions are taught by experienced practitioners, employed by a local care provider (such as an NHS trust) or by a link lecturer. Students are encouraged to visit the skills laboratories for practice sessions during their free time and are supported by a 'resident' skills trainer.

An essential aspect of skill development is competence in a range of technical skills, some of which students must have demonstrated to a required standard prior to entering their placements, for health and safety reasons. Such skills include moving and handling patients in a range of frequently encountered situations, resuscitation skills and prevention of and responding to accidents and fire. These mandatory sessions entail at least one updating activity each year of the student's programme.

The following case studies illustrate learning experiences that students are likely to encounter in nursing placement settings.

Case study 1 – Waheeda, a children's nursing student in a Common Foundation placement (first year)

Waheeda is 28 years old and a mother of two. She is in her first year and is on her community experience in Uppergreen School for three weeks. After an orientation to Uppergreen School and to the staff, Waheeda and her mentor spent some time discussing her learning needs and planning her placement experiences. She wanted to spend some time finding out about the Sure Start scheme and the work of the different staff members, getting to know the babies and their mothers when they brought their children in for the day, and learn how to make up formula feeds, as well as the importance of providing nutritious food and stimulation to their children.

Waheeda spent a day observing and participating in one of the daily clinics for expectant and new mothers. She saw the midwife conduct antenatal classes and give advice on how to manage some of the uncomfortable symptoms of pregnancy. She also observed the midwife undertake antenatal assessments and examinations. She went out for a day on a home visit with the midwife and again with the health visitor who conducts the post-natal care after the mother is discharged from the care of the midwife. Whilst Waheeda was observing in the antenatal clinic, one of the mothers came in with a black eye and some bruising. The midwife arranged for her to see a social care worker as she was concerned that the husband was mistreating her. Although Waheeda did not observe the interview, afterwards she was able to discuss with the social worker the principles of care that might be offered to a mother in an abusive relationship.

In her second week Waheeda helped in the Mini Tigers playgroup (part of the services offered by Tiny Tots) for three-year-olds and in the reception classes for children aged four to five years. Some of these children came to the school for a half or a whole day depending upon their parents' circumstances. Waheeda discovered that there was a range of resources available that might include wrap-around care for the whole day, starting with breakfast at 8 a.m. and planned activities, including tea, before the child went home around 6 p.m. She learned about the kind of activities designed to meet standards set by the Department of Education and Skills (2006) for children going to foundation or pre-school classes.

She also worked alongside the nursery nurse looking after children with learning disabilities for two days and learned about the kinds of resources available to them and the aims of the education they received. She attended the team case conference with the nursery nurse, social worker, child psychologist and speech and language therapist as well as the learning disabilities nurse with responsibility for the children and their families. This gave Waheeda insights into the complex range of resources available to such families and how these different professionals work together to provide seamless care.

Case study 2 – Josh, a third-year nursing student

Josh was on his final (15-week) placement at the rehabilitation unit attached to Eastern Hope Hospital for people with head injuries, to which he had requested to return. As with Waheeda he had a preliminary discussion with his key mentor to assess his learning needs and to develop an action plan for the first five weeks of his placement. As Josh was familiar with the organization of the unit and wanted to work as a qualified staff nurse on the unit when he finished his training he needed only an update on any changes to policies and procedures that might have occurred since his last allocation to the unit. Josh was looking forward to sharing a close working relationship with his allocated patients and the diverse health care team. As this was primarily a synoptic placement and Josh was wanting to further develop his organizational and management skills, it was agreed that he would take a full caseload of patients under the supervision of his mentor. He and his mentor would conduct a daily nursing round of patients at the beginning of the shift and assess the nursing needs of his patients. They would then discuss the prescribed nursing care and, in consultation with the patient, make any changes to the care plan. Josh would identify his priorities and make a plan of his actions for the shift. He had responsibility for implementing and evaluating these actions, with his mentor providing any guidance or support to ensure he was able to achieve the agreed goals. When his mentor was on a different shift Josh would work with another registered nurse and she would monitor his work. At the end of the shift Josh would write up his nursing notes and give a handover to the staff. He would also have a regular debriefing session with his mentor or his co-mentor so that he could discuss any issues relating to his management or his patients' condition. This enabled Josh to develop confidence in his management skills as well as increase his professional and craft knowledge.

An important activity that Josh enjoyed was participating in the weekly inter-disciplinary case conferences, where a patient's key nurse provided a synopsis of their progress. Often this synopsis was a joint presentation with the patient, who was normally fully involved in the discussion.

Initially, Josh had a small caseload of three patients. Two of his patients were wheelchair-mobile, whilst another was confined to bed and required full nursing care to prevent the common complications of bed rest. His workload included facilitating his patients to be self-caring as much as possible. This might involve standing by whilst a patient took over an hour to dress and get into a wheelchair, whilst all the time providing encouragement and support so they did not give up. During the day he might also be carrying out the rehabilitation activities designed by the physiotherapist (who visited daily for half an hour) or of the counsellor who also visited daily. Once up and in their wheelchairs the patients were able to go off the ward to a range of therapies designed to increase their physical and mental health. The patient who was bed-bound needed physical, social and emotional care and was coping with her feelings of bereavement at having both her legs amputated below the knee and her lower right arm as a result of a road traffic accident. She had also suffered some brain damage but was slowly recovering from this. Josh realized that the anger she was projecting stemmed from this loss and, whilst caring for her, worked with her to address this. One of his priorities in caring for her was to prevent her from developing any side effects of her immobility such as infection of her urine or chest, or pressure ulcers. Her appetite was very poor and although she had seen a dietician, it was Josh's responsibility to ensure that she ate and drank a suitable volume of food to promote her recovery. Caring for these patients enabled Josh to refine his care delivery and care management skills. Such care also provided opportunities to refine his communication skills and to explore the professional and ethical issues that arose. Case conferences inevitably raised a number of questions from different health and social care professionals that required Josh to develop an intimate understanding of his patients' personal and social needs. Caring for these patients inevitably meant that Josh was the key contact person for his patients' family and carers. This entailed learning how to provide them with support and encouragement even when their behaviour reflected projected anger and grief. To help him develop some of the necessary interpersonal skills, Josh spent some time sitting in with his mentor or another member of the nursing team when they were counselling or advising patients' carers. Similarly, if he encountered a new technical skill he would work alongside a registered practitioner to observe the technique and she would then supervise and coach him in using the skill until she was satisfied that he could practise it safely on his own.

At the midpoint of his placement Josh had an interim assessment of his progress which showed that he was ready to take on more responsibility and an increased caseload. He was also ready to practise managing the unit for a whole shift. This was documented in his action plan and Josh was encouraged to take on a similar workload as a junior staff nurse of the unit, always under the supervision of his mentor. With this increased responsibility Josh became more directly involved in planning rehabilitation activities for his patients, including short stays at home once he had arranged for the necessary adjustments to be made.

Another aspect of Josh's experience as a senior student was to learn how to manage the whole unit and deal with the unexpected, such as staff going off sick or patients having accidents. He also needed to learn how to prepare for the case conferences and be able to write reports on his patients' daily progress and to present these to the team.

Josh knew that he had to demonstrate that he had met the NMC proficiencies (see NMC website) for entry to the professional register as they related to this placement. His mentor had the enormous responsibility of verifying his competence in the proficiencies required for registration by signing him off. Because of the careful documentation of his progress and through consultation with her colleagues she was able to write a comprehensive summary of his progress during his 15-week placement. This report confirmed his readiness to be given a staff nurse job on the unit when he qualified. If Josh had not met his targets by the end of his placement he would not have been able to complete his programme or apply for registration as a nurse.

However, Josh was highly committed to being successful and often spent more hours than required for his placement. As a result his confidence grew and he felt able to deal with the everyday issues of the unit. His mentor and the rest of the team were impressed by his progress and looked forward to welcoming him back as a staff member.

Summary

The case studies of these two students at the beginning and end of their nursing programme illustrate how their learning needs were assessed against specific standards and then action plans were developed, implemented and evaluated at regular intervals throughout the placement. Students were supported by an experienced practitioner who had responsibility for monitoring and documenting their progress as well as making the final pass/fail decision. Whilst their mentor had the final responsibility, norm a decision is taken only after consultation with other staff members placement so that a fair assessment can be made.

Helping students to develop and extend their professional sk knowledge were opportunities to work and learn alongsi registered practitioners, to discuss their observations in debriefing sessions, to take responsibility for a caseload of patients that was within the boundaries of their capability, both actual and potential. Another important aspect of their learning was the opportunities to either document the care they delivered (along with the rationale for their actions) or to justify their actions, using evidence, with their mentor or in Josh's case with members of the multi-disciplinary team. Having the support and supervision of a critical friend or sponsor gave students the confidence to achieve their goals and to be successful. Other activities that broadened students' professional knowledge were opportunities to witness their patients'/clients' health care journey through the different elements of the service that they were using.

Assessment

Practice assessment is a core element of nursing students' programmes. The NMC requires evidence that the student is 'fit for practice' and 'fit for purpose' as criteria for registration: the university is bound to provide evidence that this is the case. Most pre-registration programmes now include academic credits for practice. Assessments tend to be in two parts – clinical and academic. Throughout their programme students are assessed against clearly defined clinical and theoretical criteria identified by the professional statutory organization (the NMC). These assessments require documentary evidence of the student's progress in demonstrating capability in specific clinical outcomes and proficiencies. These are defined in terms of the domains of professional and ethical development, care delivery, care management, and personal and professional development. Verification that a student meets these criteria is provided by their placement supervisor/mentor during each placement and by the end of their final 15-week placement by a senior practice placement mentor. Students have to demonstrate professional conduct and good health ~~that~~ ~~th~~ ey are fit to practise and fit for purpose. The
fitness for the academic award and draws
ent supervisor to support their application
, 2004f).
ns contain a number of attributes. Most
e placement modules to ensure students
ain as it applies to their stage in the
first year of their programme (the CFP)
tcomes for progression to the Branch
Branch programme, normally two years,
etency in each of the attributes of the
the responsibility for assessing whether

a student has met the required level of practice to have these signed off. In addition to evidence that the student can demonstrate these domains of practice the NMC also requires evidence of competence in several different essential skills clusters. These skills clusters include: administration of medications; provision of essential care such as hygiene, nutrition and hydration; prevention of infection; and health promotion. There is an assessment of competence in each skills cluster at different stages in the student's programme. Students are required to produce a practice passport that documents their progress from one placement to another and thus enables the mentor to monitor their student's progress.

Many programmes include objective structured clinical examinations (OSCE) of students' clinical skills which take place in the sheltered environment of a skills laboratory. An OSCE provides an additional means of monitoring progress and performance although they are not without their critics (ENB, 2000).

With continuous assessment of a student's performance whilst they are in practice the mentor is able to monitor their progress. Documentation is an essential aspect of this process and allows remedial action to be taken if the student is not making the appropriate progress or has specific difficulties.

The academic assessment of students' clinical performance is normally in the form of a portfolio where students are expected to write a reflective account of their learning related to specific clinical incidents and pre-defined criteria. By using this reflective and critical approach to their practice, students are able to further their understanding of their clinical experiences and recognize the relevance of formal knowledge to their practice and vice versa (Spouse, 2003). Assessing performance in the real world of clinical practice is fraught with challenges as each patient presents a different context for the assessment to take place. Inevitably the core features of professional conduct, courtesy, competence and patient safety are influential in decision-making.

Continuing professional development

On successful completion of their pre-registration programme and the academic programme students can apply for registration with the NMC. With registration they can then embark on their career. During the initial six-month post-qualification period their employer must provide preceptorship support. This is designed to help the newly qualified nurse to adjust to the role of being a staff nurse, to develop the necessary managerial skills and to consolidate their professional skills. Research by Eraut et al. (2000) illustrates what a challenging time this can be for nurses, describing it as working and learning in a pressure cooker environment owing to the constant pressures of rapid turnover of patients and high student throughput. Work by Cynthia Edmond demonstrated that some clinical teams are better at supporting newly qualified staff when they can describe their own work structures and processes and offer a structured induction programme in addition to preceptorship support (Edmond, 2001). Inevitably those students who spend the final 15 weeks of their programme working in the clinical setting and return as newly qualified staff nurses fare better than those who are unfamiliar with the setting.

All nursing staff are required to undertake mandatory training sessions each year. These are related to health and safety, such as moving and handling, fire management, accident prevention and infection control. Different branches of the Nursing Register require their staff to attend additional mandatory training sessions that are specific to their professional practice, such as child protection or aggression management.

Continuing education and professional development are also an essential aspect of the NHS education budget. Nurses working in specialist areas concerned with, for example, cancer care, renal dialysis, endocrine disorders and cardio-vascular disease all require further education and training. Most specialist areas such as care of the older person, intensive care, coronary care and accident and emergency will only accept new staff who already have at least six months' post-qualification experience. These staff will then undertake a six-month (or longer) course that provides an academic award as well as related competencies in the speciality. Many nurses use these courses as a stepping stone to top-up their Diploma in Nursing to an honours degree or, if they already hold a BSc, to study at master's level and beyond.

Current debates and future developments

The European Union (EU) has standard requirements for nursing education. In most European countries nurses are prepared as generalists with post-qualification specialist education. The UK is distinctive in having four branches of pre-registration preparation (mental health, child, learning disability nurses and midwives). As a result the EU decreed that all nursing students preparing for the adult branch should have a programme of 4,600 hours or three years' duration, which should include specific amounts of experience in nursing people in the four specialist areas in addition to care of older people, medical, surgical and community care. Many pre-Project 2000 programmes already provided students with experiences in these areas. The UKCC adapted this decree by requiring these nursing programmes to be 4,600 hours in three years, of which 50 per cent must be in practice, concurrently. As a result, the already heavily demanding nursing programme was telescoped into an extended academic year, which places huge stresses on students, clinical and academic staff alike (ENB, 1993a; ENB, 1993b).

Following implementation of Project 2000, the UKCC commissioned further research to evaluate its effectiveness. This was published as *Fitness for Practice*, otherwise known as the Peach Report (UKCC, 1999b) and many of its recommendations were implemented in curricula known as the Fitness for Practice curriculum. Significant amongst these changes were that students would be supernumerary throughout their programme, that their programme should be 50 per cent theory and 50 per cent practice, and that students should have their placements in what was described as a 'host' (NHS) trust.

Government policy, in particular the Department of Health papers (DoH, 1997; DoH, 1998a; DoH, 1998b; DoH, 1999; DoH, 2000a; DoH, 2000b; DoH, 2001e), has resulted in widened participation and access to pre-registration programmes for a wider, less cohesive group of men and women. The average age of nursing students is now closer to 30 than to 18, as reflected in the statistics for 2005–06 (NMC, 2006a). Attempts to broaden the curriculum to meet government agendas for provision of increased care in the community is hampered by the lack of registered nursing staff working in community settings and by the increased commissions of students to meet government targets.

Core text recommendations

Nursing and Midwifery Council (NMC) (2004f), *Standards of Proficiency for Pre-Registration Nursing Education*, on the NMC website: http://www. nmc-uk.org/aFrameDisplay.aspx?DocumentID=328.

Nursing and Midwifery Council (NMC) (2008b), *Standards to Support Learning and Assessment in Practice: NMC standards for mentors, practice teachers and teachers*, on the NMC website: http://www.nmc-uk.org/aFrameDisplay. aspx?DocumentID=1914.

Spouse, J. (2003), *Professional Learning in Nursing*, Oxford: Blackwell.

8 The occupational therapist

Sandra M. Rowan and Auldeen Alsop

Overview

Occupational therapy focuses on the nature, balance, pattern and context of occupations and activities in the lives of individuals, family groups and communities. It is concerned with the meaning and purpose that people place on occupations and activities and with the impact of illness, disability or social or economic deprivation on their ability to carry them out (Creek, 2003, p. 8). Occupational therapists work with a range of people including those who have physical, mental and/or social problems, either from birth or as the result of accident, illness or ageing, and are aware of the impact that change in circumstances can have on individuals' independence and confidence (see the website of the College of Occupational Therapists). Occupational therapists work with a person to design a management or treatment programme based on the individual's unique lifestyle and preferences, sometimes modifying the environment in which the person lives and/or works. Enhancing someone's ability to participate in everyday activities is central to occupational therapy.

Occupational therapists work in the public, voluntary and independent sectors. Employing organizations include hospitals, GP surgeries, social services and social work departments, charitable organizations, schools and colleges, equipment companies, wheelchair service providers, private rehabilitation companies and government agencies. Some occupational therapists are self-employed, working, for example, as independent trainers, consultants or in medico-legal work. Others work as advisors in large companies, supporting people in the work situation, especially those needing adjustments to their work environment following illness or injury.

Occupational therapy was introduced to the UK at the beginning of the twentieth century. The first recognized qualifications were at diploma level, latterly awarded by the College of Occupational Therapists (COT). Degree qualifications emerged in the late 1980s and by 1994 an all-graduate entry to the profession had been achieved (Alsop, 2006). The College of Occupational Therapists is the professional body that sets the professional standards and curricular expectations for those delivering education leading to the professional qualification. These reflect the standards established by the World Federation of Occupational Therapists (WFOT) (Hocking and Ness, 2002). The regulatory body for occupational therapists is the Health Professions Council (HPC) that sets both the Standards of Education and Standards of Proficiency for occupational therapists in the UK. Both the professional and regulatory bodies approve the education curriculum delivered by higher education institutions (HEIs) in the UK. Graduates emerging from approved courses are eligible to apply for registration with the HPC and thereafter to call themselves an 'occupational therapist', which is a title protected by law. Both the HPC and College of Occupational Therapists have now set the minimum qualification for occupational therapists at the level of a bachelor's degree with honours (Health Professions Council, 2004; COT, 2002). Some programmes, however, are delivered at a higher academic level.

Programme models

Two-year, three-year and four-year programmes are all well established in the UK. Two-year programmes, often referred to as accelerated programmes, are full-time programmes that lead to a bachelor's degree, postgraduate diploma or master's degree. It is usually a requirement that applicants already hold a suitable first degree so that they have well-developed study skills before entry to the course. These programmes are normally delivered over about 45 weeks in each of two years, slightly longer in the case of master's degrees.

Three-year full-time programmes (four-year full-time in Scotland) constitute the traditional and most common route to professional qualification. These programmes are populated by a mixture of school leavers, those with previous experience in health or social care environments and more mature entrants possibly seeking a change of career.

Four-year part-time programmes are those that allow students to complete studies leading to the professional qualification over a longer period of time. People with family commitments often choose to study on a part-time basis. Some part-time programmes are known as in-service programmes and are exclusively for those who are working in a health, social care or similar service and wish to work and study at the same time. They are seconded to education for the days required for study and practice learning; at other times they continue to fulfil the requirements of their role in employment. Attendance at the university is normally required on one or two days per week. Practice experience is often full time although this varies from course to course. Some part-time experiences are facilitated.

Occupational therapy education in England is commissioned by the Department of Health, currently via the strategic health authorities. Contracts are held with HEIs and the number of student places commissioned on each course is guided by contractual arrangements but determined annually by agreement. Contract reviews enable the commissioners to maintain an overview of issues affecting course delivery, particularly those that involve a relationship with NHS services. Wales, Scotland and Northern Ireland each have different arrangements for commissioning and funding occupational therapy education. The availability of practice learning opportunities is always of particular interest across the UK and interventions to secure practice opportunities are sometimes made by the commissioners. This may involve initiating investigations into the difficulties of obtaining sufficient practice learning opportunities or negotiating directly with health service managers.

Programme requirements

The WFOT sets the minimum length of a course leading to qualification as an occupational therapist at 90 weeks with 1,000 hours (approximately 30 weeks full time) being the minimum number of hours required in practice learning. These requirements still allow for enormous variation in the way in which an occupational therapy programme is structured. Each HEI, however, will use 90 weeks as the norm for planning the curriculum and 1,000 hours for practice learning, regardless of the qualifying award. Practice learning has to be integrated into the curriculum in each year of the course so that the learning that takes place in the practice environment informs academic work, and vice versa.

Students are required to gain practice experience in various organizations, with patients or clients of different ages and with different health problems or care needs. Although practice experiences will be structured differently depending on the curriculum developed at each HEI, students can normally expect to have three to five different experiences during their course. These will commonly be in blocks of between four and twelve weeks' duration, with longer periods of eight weeks or more scheduled towards the end of the course. It is a requirement that students be supervised and assessed in practice by an occupational therapist, but this stipulation still allows for a variety of supervisory models, as outlined later. Supervisors are expected to have a minimum of one year's experience in practice and to have completed the requirements of the College of Occupational Therapists' Accreditation of Practice Placement Educators (APPLE) scheme relating to student supervision before taking responsibility for assessing students. An overview of the APPLE scheme is provided later in the chapter. Occupational therapists may still contribute to student education prior to becoming accredited and are normally encouraged by their manager to gain related experience under the guidance of an accredited practice educator.

The profession's Code of Ethics and Professional Conduct (COT, 2005, p. 16) states that 'all occupational therapists have a professional responsibility to provide practice education opportunities for occupational therapy students'. Despite this statement, however, practice learning opportunities can be scarce and, once identified, often need ongoing support from tutors to maintain their availability and viability.

Terminology

Over time, practice learning, as it is now referred to by the occupational therapy profession, has been known as clinical practice and fieldwork. Changes have been determined by external factors. For example, clinical practice was rejected when, increasingly, occupational therapists accepted posts within the local authority and argued that their work was not at all 'clinical' in nature and that this term did not accurately reflect what they did. 'Fieldwork' offered a more universal term that was increasingly being used internationally. 'Practice education', 'practice learning' and 'practice experience' are terms more recently adopted in the UK to reinforce the educational nature of the experience and the expectation that students are in practice to learn and not just to observe or to perform in practice. Additionally, those who supervise have a responsibility to facilitate learning and create a broad range of learning opportunities and experiences for students that will complement their learning in the academic environment. Although the term 'placement' is still commonly used to denote practice learning, 'practice learning experience' or 'practice learning opportunity' are terms often adopted to denote a more flexible approach to learning rather than imply that a student is merely 'placed' at a practice site.

Recent developments

The last ten years have seen significant changes in professional education with new modes of learning and course delivery emerging for occupational therapy. The emphasis on widening access to education to students from all walks of life and to those with non-traditional educational backgrounds has resulted in a student group that is far from the traditional school leaver profile. The student population is diverse, with some of the adult learners already in possession of a first, and sometimes higher, degree as they embark on occupational therapy education. Some students are fresh from sixth-form college or school, some are already working as occupational therapy support workers and some have had previous careers, for example, in the forces, leisure industry, in teaching or banking. Some have been homemakers or full-time carers. All bring an array of life skills and experiences to their education. Programmes leading to qualification as an occupational therapist have been developed to meet the needs of this very diverse group and incorporate flexible learning and teaching methods into the curriculum.

The profession in the UK is aware of the move in North America and elsewhere towards the master's degree becoming the basic level of occupational therapy qualification (Allen et al., 2001) and of discussions around raising that in due course to doctoral level. The UK, however, currently maintains a variety of routes leading to various awards so that those with non-traditional qualifications and relevant experience also have the opportunity to gain entry to occupational therapy programmes and study for the professional qualification.

Between 2001 and 2005 the number of training places for occupational therapy students in the UK increased to meet the demand for appropriately qualified staff in health and social care, as specified in the NHS Plan (DoH, 2000a). New programmes were established; some were specifically commissioned to address local needs. For example, the first work-based programme in occupational therapy was approved to address the particular difficulty of recruiting occupational therapists in a very rural area (Alsop and Cooper, 2005). Efforts were made nationally to increase the number of therapists from minority ethnic groups and to encourage more men into the profession. Accurate figures are not known but representation in the profession of both these groups could be around 10 per cent.

The increased use of information technology (IT) over this period is also significant. Students are now expected to have basic IT skills as they enter a programme, or they are given support to develop relevant skills quickly so that they can make best use of the variety of web-based learning resources now available. Increasingly, aspects of the programme are being delivered online. The potential for delivery of occupational therapy pre-registration education through distance learning has also been the subject of some discussion.

Models of teaching and learning

Developments in learning and teaching methods over the last decade have led occupational therapy educators to focus far more on experiential and reflective learning than on didactic teaching. Problem-based, task-based and enquiry-based learning has gained strength as a mode of course delivery in both bachelor's and master's level education (Alsop, 2006) and there has been a major shift from formal unseen examinations to assessment via coursework. Each programme, however, will have an educational rationale for the chosen learning, teaching and assessment method. Practice education must fit with the overall educational philosophy of the programme.

While undertaking practice learning, students are expected to be active learners setting their own objectives, often using one of the established formalized learning outcome formats. For example, the student might set objectives relating to interview and report writing:

- engage with an identified client and undertake an initial interview
- accurately record information in an appropriate format
- from information gained, determine early needs and discuss future plans with supervisor.

Students must be able to make use of learning opportunities as they arise, reflect on those experiences and evaluate their own performance in practice. Practice educators expect students to be able to discuss their strengths, limitations and progress in this way.

The relationship between educator and student is one of partnership. It should be facilitatory, encouraging 'two-way enquiry and dialogue about practice' (Alsop and Ryan, 1996, p. 135) and avoiding the pitfalls of power in the relationship. The educator facilitates the student's learning and achievements using strategies that include informal and formal supervision, modelling, demonstration, observation, analysis of real case scenarios and problem-solving. The student takes the initiative to reflect on experiences and develop new insights into practice, which are shared with the practice educator in the supervisory process. Research has shown that much of occupational therapists' 'clinical reasoning' is tacit (Mattingly and Fleming, 1994) so students cannot readily observe the ways in which therapists make decisions. Therapists need to talk through the reasoning and decision-making process in order to help students appreciate not only the management strategies adopted for the client but also those that have been considered but rejected. Supervisory strategies and processes must engage students in experiences and interactions that enable the development of reasoning skills (Ryan, 1995).

Crucial to a successful learning experience is the availability of consenting clients. The student is required to work through real situations, devising assessment and treatment or care management strategies under the close supervision of the practice educator and in collaboration with the client and, in some cases, the client's carers. The student must develop good communication skills and demonstrate competence when communicating with both clients and colleagues. Students must have the opportunity to plan their time effectively and, in later practice opportunities, to manage a small caseload. In the early stages, planning is undertaken collaboratively with the practice educator during supervision. Later, students must demonstrate the ability to plan and organize work for themselves. Formal supervision takes place on a weekly basis for about an hour. Informal supervision is likely to take place more frequently according to student needs. Throughout the learning experience, students are enabled to identify their own learning needs, develop strategies for meeting those needs and are encouraged to evaluate their own performance in practice. There follows an example of how a student would learn in practice.

Milly is a first-year student who is spending her six-week placement with the community mental health team. She is working with her placement educator **Neil** who is an occupational therapist. She is also spending time with other members of the team. During her placement, Milly has been involved in the treatment programme for **Sam Weiner** who lives in Derby Street. Sam has had periods of severe depression and is long-term disabled. In spite of this, Sam has been an active member of the community and would like to find a way to get back to work. Neil and Milly are working with Sam towards this goal.

Early in the placement, Milly accompanied Neil on his visits to Sam and observed Neil and Sam work out a treatment plan. Neil then encouraged Milly to reflect on what she had observed and identify for herself the process Neil had undertaken. She spent some of her time researching the emerging role of the occupational therapist in the field of condition management and, in discussion with Neil, was able to identify this role and suggest how Sam could meet his goals. Later in the placement, Milly took a more active role in working with Sam. As her confidence grew, and with the support and supervision of Neil, she facilitated the sessions with Sam. At the end of each week, she reflected on her own progress against agreed objectives, and identified tasks and objectives for the coming week. Milly built a good understanding of how the team worked together by spending time with other team members when they were working with Sam. At team meetings, she had an opportunity to give feedback from an occupational therapy perspective on Sam's progress. In this way, Milly began to understand the dynamics of teamworking as well as the clinical intervention of an occupational therapist with a person who has a depressive illness. By working closely with Neil, Milly gained an overview of Sam's specific needs and treatment plan, whilst being involved with other people Neil was working with. Therefore Milly saw a wide scope of practice and identified how different models and approaches were practically applied. This is an important aspect of practice learning as it makes distinct links between the theory and the practice of occupational therapy.

The teacher in the practice setting

The preparation of practice educators

Practice educators are normally required to become accredited through the COT APPLE scheme prior to taking responsibility for supervising students. Accreditation can be gained in two ways, either via a basic course delivered by an HEI or by individuals providing evidence in a reflective profile of how they have met the learning outcomes of the scheme. The six learning outcomes, whether achieved through a course or personal experience, address the attributes of an effective practice educator, application of adult learning theory, the planning and facilitation of learning in the practice setting, the principles and process of assessing performance, evaluation of the learning experience and the process of reflection. Tutors within the HEIs are responsible for operating the scheme. The names of those who achieve accreditation are recorded on the COT database. Accreditation lasts for five years and those accredited are normally expected to supervise at least one student per year.

This national scheme is based on the Accreditation of Clinical Educators Scheme (ACE) of the Chartered Society of Physiotherapy (CSP) and operates under licence from the CSP.

Some HEIs offer a fully accredited module with CATS (Credit Accumulation Transfer Scheme) points. The core content, however, is fairly common across all programmes, including topics such as adult learning theories, developing an effective learning environment and coaching for improvement. In some institutions, occupational therapy practice educators learn alongside educators from other professions, sharing best practice and developing a greater insight into each other's roles. As with any continuing professional development (CPD) activity there are tensions for practitioners between the need to undertake the learning to support students and address the ongoing needs of service provision. Profile development and distance learning programmes may better suit the needs of educators.

These modules provide transferable knowledge and skills that can be used in staff supervision and management. No specific fee is payable for supervising students. Some therapists employed in health and social services have responsibilities for student supervision built into the expectations of their role and their salary reflects this duty. However, it is generally acknowledged that working with students offers therapists development opportunities for themselves. It is an expectation that therapists continue to develop professionally, not just as a professional responsibility but also to meet the requirements of the HPC in terms of demonstrating continuing competence to practise. Many therapists generally acknowledge that supervising students can be rewarding, helping them to develop their knowledge of practice and education.

Models of supervision

Professional standards require students normally to be supervised by an occupational therapist, although both close and 'long-arm' supervisory models are permissible. Some of the different models are described below.

One-to-one supervision by a designated practice educator

This continues to be the prevailing model used in practice education for approximately 95 per cent of students. The relationship between the student and the educator, who is an occupational therapist, is crucial to effective learning. A good working relationship needs to be established early in the learning experience. If the student and educator have different learning styles it can be challenging for both to have a successful experience (Alsop and Ryan, 1996). Practice learning experiences are not normally allocated on the basis of student/educator compatibility; rather they are allocated to meet student needs, ensuring that each student has a range of experiences across occupational therapy practice. Both student and educator need to have skills in communication and teamwork and must demonstrate a professional attitude in order to develop a working relationship that is conducive to learning.

Two students to one educator, or group supervision

Two or more students work with one educator who is an occupational therapist. This model provides the opportunity for peer support and learning to take place. It has been seen to reduce the pressure on the educator; however, it does require good preparation, planning and a robust caseload.

Two educators supervising one student

The student works with two educators who share responsibility for guiding the student. They may work in separate parts of the service, which can create enhanced learning opportunities for students. This model can successfully enable part-time workers to become practice educators. Occasionally, shared supervision may involve an occupational therapy educator and an educator from another profession. It is essential that learning outcomes or objectives for practice learning are agreed by all involved and that effective communication strategies are in place for both educators.

Supervision in role-emerging practice sites

Role-emerging practice experiences are those that occur 'in sites that have neither an occupational therapy service nor an established occupational therapy role. The student is assigned to an agency staff member supervisor as a contact person for agency issues and concerns and is supervised by an off-site occupational therapist' (Bossers et al., 1997, p. 71). These sites are often, but not exclusively, outside the NHS and local authority sectors and are more likely to be in the voluntary or private sectors. The on-site supervisor has to become acquainted with the learning objectives and needs of the student and be willing to facilitate learning experiences. At least once a week, the student will meet the visiting occupational therapist to review work undertaken, reflect on learning experiences and plan the week ahead. The student's abilities are assessed by the occupational therapist who would normally take account of perceptions of the on-site supervisor and relevant others, including service users. These learning opportunities take time to negotiate and establish as a quality experience for the student. However, they do allow the student an opportunity to develop personally and professionally by expecting him or her to draw more on personal resources for learning and to make decisions alone (Totten and Pratt, 2001).

Interprofessional practice opportunities

Some interprofessional practice learning opportunities already exist but with the Department of Health's increasing emphasis on interprofessional education, there is a growing intention to develop these further. Rosza and Lincoln (2005, p. 241) have observed that 'collaboration in workplaces is increasingly recognized as central to coordinated client care and some organizational structures have a focus on multi-disciplinary units or teams rather than professional departments'. Service delivery in the UK is increasingly based on multi-disciplinary or inter-agency teams. It is therefore vital that students have the opportunity to work within such teams if they are to be adequately prepared for the workplace. Learning opportunities could be developed in rehabilitation teams or services with a specific speciality such as orthopaedics or community mental health, where students from a variety of professions could work together and be supervised as a group. They would be assessed against specific criteria relating to practice competence by a member of their own profession but may be assessed by any educator against generic competence requirements such as report writing or teamwork skills. This model has been used in the context of a 'training ward' where all the care is delivered by students (see for example, Mackenzie et al., 2007). This model requires the educators to be excellent teamworkers who understand the skills and knowledge base of their colleagues and respect others' contributions to health and social care.

The content and structure of the students' learning

Practice education may either form part of a credit-rated module that is integral to the programme leading to the academic award or be totally separate from the academic structure of the award. There are wide variations across the UK and there have been controversies surrounding the choice of assessment for some time (Westcott and Rugg, 2001). If practice elements are outside of the honours degree classification structure, it can extend the course considerably as students must attain the necessary 360 credits from other academic modules and additionally complete their 1,000 practice learning hours. For practice learning to count towards an honours degree, it has to be given a percentage mark like other modules in order that the degree classification can be calculated. For this reason, most undergraduate programmes integrate practice learning into academic modules and establish a process for devising a mark for this element of the course. However, there is controversy about parity in the marking process, as for every student there will be a different educator and thus a different assessor. Moderation by tutors brings some parity to the marking process. For master's level awards, however, practice education is often outside the modular system as the profession requires that practice education be assessed at undergraduate level. The academic modules that constitute the award are all assessed at the higher master's level. In addition, no classification has to be calculated for a master's award, so there is less controversy about the marking procedure. Recording either a pass or a fail for the practice element is generally acceptable to all.

There will be a curriculum for students to address whilst undertaking practice learning. For example, students may have to explore the evidence base that underpins practice, gain a working knowledge of the theoretical models used in the practice area or explore contemporary issues affecting the profession at that time. Through the different blocks of practice education, students will be expected to take on increasing levels of responsibility. At the beginning of each practice learning opportunity, the student and educator will define and agree learning needs and goals. Weekly objectives will be set and reviewed at the next supervision session. Some universities expect students to use a learning contract as a guiding tool.

It is important for both the student and educator to be aware of the assessment process and criteria against which the student's professional knowledge, performance and behaviour will be judged. The criteria will reflect the learning outcomes that are expected by the HEI based on national and international standards. As students have practice learning opportunities in each year of their course they can demonstrate a growing understanding of the application of theory and practice. They can also practise skills of communication, negotiation and professionalism. Overall, the process ensures that, by the end of their studies, students will be recognized by all parties as being competent to practise.

Methods

The following example follows **Steve**, a third-year student who is undertaking his final 12-week practice experience in the local authority office located near Green Hill flats. He has been working with **Jim Rafferty** who is having problems coping since he started losing his sight. Jim has also lost confidence in going outside because of his poor sight and this has worsened since he was widowed three years ago. The referral came into the office shortly after Steve started his practice experience. His practice educator, **Claire**, decided that Jim would be a good person for Steve to work with as Steve would practise a range of occupational therapy skills and would build on previous placement experiences in rehabilitation and care of older people.

Steve has already established his practice learning needs with Claire and together they have looked at how Steve will fulfil these needs. Steve has brought some good practice knowledge from his previous experiences but has never worked in a local authority office before, or worked with clients in their own homes. He needs to build his confidence in using community services and applying the occupational therapy process in the community.

Before they visit Jim, Claire and Steve agree on how Steve will work with Jim. They practise some of the questions Steve wants to ask and Claire ensures that Steve understands the pathology of Jim's sight loss. Following this first joint visit Steve and Claire reflect on the outcomes and the plan Steve agreed with Jim. Steve now continues to meet with Jim and implements the agreed plan without Claire. At each week's supervision,

Claire checks on progress and offers suggestions and feedback to Steve. Before the end of the practice experience, Claire will visit Jim with Steve and observe how they are progressing. She may also speak to other members of the team who have been involved with Jim. In addition to working with Jim, Steve will also have responsibility for a small caseload of perhaps six clients. He will continue to have supervision throughout his practice experience and will work towards achieving his objectives. He may also work with Claire undertaking aspects of occupational therapy intervention with clients who have very complex needs. In this way he can gain additional skills and learning without carrying the full responsibility of a complex case. For his own small caseload Steve will be responsible for liaising with other members of the team, negotiating a treatment plan with individuals and sometimes their advocates, completing records accurately and in a timely fashion, and acting professionally and ethically. For all these activities he gathers evidence and uses this evidence to complete his objectives and learning outcomes. In supervision Claire will expect Steve to talk knowledgeably about models and approaches and she will expect this knowledge to become increasingly apparent in his practice as a therapist.

Naturally, the experience for each student in practice will vary depending on the nature of the practice setting, any previous experience and the student's personal motivation and interests. All students will experience a different range of practice settings in different organizations (prison, hospital, community) with people with different needs (physical, mental health, learning disabilities) and from across the age range. Some of these settings will be more prescriptive in nature than others. This usually depends on the needs of the client group and the need to ensure the safety of both client and student. For example, in a forensic psychiatry setting the student may have less opportunity for autonomous practice than in a day hospital for older people. Each experience will be different but collectively these experiences will provide the necessary opportunities for the student to fulfil the requirements of the course.

Assessment

Assessment of practice education may either be graded to conform to the educational requirements of a modular system that requires a mark to reflect the level of achievement, or be recorded as a pass or fail. Sometimes a mark is awarded for written work associated with the practice experience and the experience itself is recorded as a pass or fail. As already stated, this will depend on the structure and approved procedures of the individual course. Students must have accumulated 1,000 hours from the experiences where they have been awarded a pass mark (as opposed to a fail) in order to qualify as an occupational therapist.

Assessment processes for practice education will include ongoing formative assessment and feedback and a final summative assessment. Each HEI sets the criteria for the final summative assessment as either learning outcomes or performance criteria in a number of key areas. These areas include verbal and written communication skills, teamworking skills, practice skills, application of theory to practice, skills of organization and planning, and affective skills such as professionalism, ethics and values.

Students are encouraged to self-assess and provide evidence of their achievements throughout the learning experience, particularly in the opportunities afforded for formative assessment. This evidence is usually recorded in the learning contract. Some students may also collate a professional portfolio of evidence. Evidence may take the following forms:

- observed practice: for example, the educator sees the student undertaking a successful treatment session
- product: for example, a written report
- testimony of others: for example, a verbal report from team members, a client or a carer regarding the student's ability or approach to practice
- simulation: for example, a fire drill or trial activity with the educator.

The practice educator normally takes responsibility for the final assessment of the student's performance and achievement. This final assessment is made in a written report, which is sent back to the HEI. The practice educator will confer with other members of the team involved with the student and add their observations to his or her own judgement of the student's performance. If two practice educators have worked with a student, one of them will normally take a lead in undertaking the assessment.

Practice educators should always use the learning outcomes or assessment criteria set by the HEI when assessing the student. A student who struggles to meet learning outcomes should be coached for improvement. Clear, unambiguous feedback should be given. Feedback and reflection will enable the student to identify areas of strength as well as areas of weakness. A written plan should be agreed that builds on strengths and addresses the weaknesses. This written plan can then be reviewed and modified as necessary. It is good practice to keep a written record of the expectations of the student, should performance continue to be an issue. Practice educators can call in help from tutors when dealing with poor performance. The role of the university tutor in this instance is to support both the educator and the student through what can be a very difficult situation, particularly where poor performance is related to professionalism and personal values. A third party can often bring a new construct to resolve issues and identify a way forward.

If the student does not meet the learning outcomes and fails a practice learning experience, the final report should state specifically where the deficits are and suggest future learning objectives. These can guide the retrieval of the practice learning experience where the regulations allow. Students in occupational therapy may normally only retake a practice learning opportunity once. Subsequent failure will normally result in termination of studies. The reasons for failure are various and can include:

- lack of knowledge of occupational therapy theory
- failure to apply theory to practice
- unsafe practice
- unprofessional behaviour such as lack of respect for others, poor timekeeping
- inability to communicate effectively with the team or clients or keep relevant people informed of events or progress in the care management process.

Continuing professional development

Once students gain their degree in occupational therapy they are eligible to apply to the HPC, the UK regulatory body, for registration. Registration is mandatory for those employed anywhere in the UK as occupational therapists including in higher education if engaged in the teaching of occupational therapy students. Registration is dependent not only on the professional qualification but also on the applicant having no convictions or cautions that might affect their suitability for registration, or health issues that are deemed by the regulatory body to constitute lack of fitness to practise. Applicants must declare their health and criminal status and the HPC will determine whether they are fit to be registered as a measure of public protection.

Once registered, individuals may apply for any relevant position of employment of their choice. The occupational therapy qualification is generic, allowing qualified individuals to work in any field of practice. Opportunities for new graduates are developing all the time in new and emerging areas. Sometimes graduates who have gained experience at role-emerging sites return to work at the site, so developing occupational therapy practice beyond the public sector.

There is no probationary period for new graduates. Graduates entering the public sector often try to secure a rotation post that will allow them to consolidate their learning and gain further experience by working in three or four different areas of practice over about a two-year period. Later, occupational therapists may choose to specialize in a designated area of practice. Some organizations have in-service programmes for newly qualified staff that provide support for graduates and enable them to continue their professional development in a structured way. In the NHS, however, preceptorship programmes are now gaining momentum with the aim of assisting new graduates to manage the transition into practice (Morley, 2007). These programmes are linked to pay progression and integrated with the *Knowledge and Skills Framework* (DoH, 2004b). They address standards of practice and professional behaviour, working practices, reflective practice and involve a supervisory relationship with a senior occupational therapist. Graduates' responsibility for recording their CPD is a key feature of the programme. A portfolio with evidence of CPD in relevant areas can assist a practitioner to gain employment in a different area of practice or to achieve promotion.

The onus on all occupational therapists, as detailed in the profession's Code of Ethics and Professional Conduct (COT, 2005) is to remain competent to practise. The HPC has now finalized arrangements for registrants to demonstrate ongoing competence to practise in the chosen context of employment and provide evidence of continuing professional development. A sample of registrants each year will be required to produce a personal profile indicating how they have maintained their competence in practice and more specifically in the specialist area of practice. This will apply to all registrants wherever they work, whether they are employed in the public, voluntary or independent sector, in health and social care or in education, or whether they are self-employed as consultants, advisors, or in medico-legal work. The College of Occupational Therapists has put some structures in place, available through the members' website, that enable occupational therapists to identify potential development needs and possible resources and courses that might assist them to meet those needs.

Current debates

The availability of appropriate learning experiences will continue to challenge the HEIs despite the efforts of education commissioners and the College of Occupational Therapists in supporting the HEIs and occupational therapy managers to identify student learning opportunities (see, for example, Wilby, n.d.). HEIs are becoming quite creative in their attempts to widen the scope of learning experiences. Whilst service restructuring and pressures on practitioners working in the more traditional areas of practice have combined to reduce opportunities for students, the profession is actively promoting new areas, such as vocational rehabilitation and condition management, as offering relevant experiences.

The increasing emphasis on interprofessional education can open up practice learning opportunities but these are not without their difficulties. Only a limited number of students may be allowed at one place. Opportunities may be limited by physical space or by the demands of a number of students at any one time on the available resources or by the impact of too many students at a time on client care. There also has to be some reasonable way of relating interprofessional practice to the profession of occupational therapy so that students can meet their learning outcomes.

The move to community and primary care has already had a major impact on the practice situation with the loss of supported learning environments in large institutions. The norm now is for lone practitioners, working single-handed across a large geographical area, to provide a very different model of occupational therapy. Inadequate, temporary or otherwise cramped accommodation offers a much more restrictive environment for student education, and practitioners often feel unable to offer an adequate, let alone an ideal, learning situation. However, many would argue that it is just the scenario that students need to experience in order to prepare them appropriately for work as a new graduate. Some community environments can also be challenging and raise issues of student safety. Risks must be assessed and reasonable precautions taken during the practice experience.

An increasing number of occupational therapists are moving into private practice. Whilst they have the same professional obligations and expertise to teach and assess students, they sometimes consider students to be a drain on their resources and to adversely affect their income. There is no financial remuneration for supervising students to compensate for work-time lost. This drift to independent practice thus reflects a loss of expertise available to provide practice-learning opportunities.

The issue of shortages of suitable learning opportunities also challenges the quality of practice education. Many experiences offered to students are of very high quality with extremely committed practice educators taking the lead. However, a shortage of learning opportunities can force university tutors to place students in environments offering lower-quality experiences in order to meet demand. There are tensions between waiting for and working towards gaining high-quality experiences for students and delaying their practice education, which could upset their total programme of learning. Students naturally become distressed when they find that they have not been allocated a practice learning opportunity, or that a previously allocated opportunity has been cancelled at short notice. These are common occurrences despite the fact that university tutors have worked closely with practitioners to secure suitable and timely learning experiences for students.

A significant number of students on a course may also wish to study close to home because they have dependants and family commitments. They make demands on university tutors for locally based practice experiences, which may not always be available. Even if they are available, they may only provide the student with a restricted view of occupational therapy practice. Whilst tutors may be sympathetic and offer experiences close to home, this may be to the detriment of other students who must travel further. The financial costs of these experiences thus fall on those without family commitments but who otherwise may have part-time jobs in order to meet their needs. The situation is fragile as university tutors try to manage the various expectations of students, which is not always possible. The ultimate response of the student whose needs are not met is to leave the course, which impacts on attrition rates and results in a loss to the profession.

Widening participation initiatives and recent legislation have resulted in an increasing number of students with special needs that must be met. Whilst systems are in place in the university for assisting students with, for example, dyslexia or with mobility or sensory problems, these issues also have to be addressed to enable them to undertake practice education. Students have learning contracts that can extend into practice learning but the practice learning site is only a temporary feature that does not demand full-scale accommodation by the employer. Negotiations must take place so that reasonable adjustments are made in the practice environment and assessment processes allow students to demonstrate competence in non-traditional ways. The judgements about competence can be extremely difficult to make in a fair and objective way.

In assessments, students have also become more astute and prepared to challenge the practice educator on the final grade awarded for their practice experience. A low grade could seriously affect their final degree classification if practice education is embedded within a credit-rated module. For this reason, many programmes are now reverting to a pass or fail for the assessment of practice rather than bands and marks denoting different levels of attainment. Practice experience is a professional rather than academic requirement and so, as previously discussed, can be structured to occur and be assessed outside of the modular system.

Given the greater use of IT support for learning, students now have high expectations that they will have access to IT systems in practice in order to be able to continue to access university learning resources and library material to support their practice education and to keep in touch with issues related to their course. This is not always possible or realistic given the changing nature of practice experiences. A good deal of work has to take place with students in university prior to practice learning in order to ensure that students' expectations are not unreasonable. It is also up to the HEI to ensure that no assessed work from practice learning depends on access to university resources.

Future developments

Entry routes to occupational therapy education

Increasingly, students entering occupational therapy education have a variety of educational backgrounds. Whilst the norm might be Advanced or Higher level education awards obtained at school, those mature applicants wishing to enter into a new career may take a relevant Access course. This helps them to develop a knowledge base and study skills as preparation for higher education. Even so, many mature students tend to underestimate the demands of an occupational therapy course, the challenges of being a student and the impact on family life (Ryan, 2001).

In order to attract young people to occupational therapy there is more work to be done promoting occupational therapy as a career amongst younger schoolchildren and establishing Foundation degrees for those unsure of their academic potential or career aspirations. Generic Foundation degrees are intended to alert prospective candidates to the attributes of a range of careers, for example, within the NHS, and to prepare students for ongoing education in a chosen field or career. Occupational therapy cadet schemes have also been discussed as potentially helping to prepare students for a professional career, although none are currently known to exist for occupational therapy.

Work-based learning

The ability to integrate practice and academic learning is illustrated in the work-based learning programmes now being delivered in selected areas of the country (Alsop and Cooper, 2005; Alsop, 2006). Programmes can either be university-based or community-based and can be delivered at either undergraduate or postgraduate level. Students have several extended work-based learning opportunities, normally for three days per week for about three months at a time during their course, undertaking academic studies at the same time. Students are expected to draw primarily on their ongoing learning experiences to help them to develop knowledge and understanding of practice and to locate relevant material to underpin their assessments. Those supervising students in these learning experiences must be prepared not only to deal with the normal practical arrangements and the supervision and assessment of students in practice; they must also gain an appreciation of the ethos of the course and their wider remit in terms of facilitating learning. It is crucial that the learning environment and student experience be developed to allow a broader range of learning experiences in order to enable students to fulfil their learning needs. In parallel, students are supported by tutors and mentors who ensure that curricular requirements as well as personal and professional needs are addressed.

Service learning

> Service learning is a strategy through which students engage with a community so they learn and develop together through organised service that meets mutually identified needs. Service learning helps foster civic responsibility through coordinated activity with a higher education institution and a community (Lorenzo et al., 2006, p. 276).

Service learning has been adopted by a number of occupational therapy programmes within HEIs in South Africa as a means of introducing students to a different range of learning experiences to reflect the communities with which they may find themselves working when qualified. Occupational therapists in the UK are increasingly likely to find themselves working with communities such as refugees, asylum seekers, travellers and homeless people. Each community will have its unique characteristics but each might benefit from engaging collaboratively with occupational therapists on projects of an occupational nature that promote health and well-being and that eventually become self-sustaining within the community. There are benefits for HEIs, students and the participating community in implementing service learning as a collaborative educational process (Alsop, 2007).

International developments: Tuning across the EU

Occupational therapy has been one of the first health professions to be involved in the Tuning programme. Tuning is the practical application of the Bologna Process. It is concerned with developing reference points at subject level and harmonizing the outcomes of learning across Europe. One of the key results of Tuning will be the increased mobility of the workforce throughout Europe. Subject reference points are expressed as competencies. These competencies represent 'a dynamic combination of cognitive and metacognitive skills, knowledge and understanding, interpersonal, intellectual and practical skills, and ethical values' (Gonzalez and Wagenaar, 2006, p.1).

For occupational therapy this process has brought together academics from the European Network of Occupational Therapists in Europe

(ENOTHE) and practitioners from the Council of Occupational Therapists in European Countries (COTEC) into a Tuning Project Group. They have developed a set of competencies, which should be used across Europe to underpin curricula and to establish baseline competencies for the new graduate. This development has undergone a series of rigorous consultations with all stakeholders and both the process and the competencies have been validated by professional bodies, non-governmental organizations, service user groups and regulators.

The agreed competencies have been built around existing frameworks, such as QAA benchmark statements and HPC standards of proficiency. This should ensure their compatibility within the UK context to existing curricula learning outcomes. For the first time Europe has a measure of the competence of new practitioners in occupational therapy.

Other international learning opportunities

Occupational therapy students are increasingly seeking opportunities for learning in international settings in order to gain relevant experiences beyond those available in the UK; for example, experience of working within different cultures. Some may take time out of their course to pursue projects of personal interest; others may use an 'Independent Studies' feature of a course to draw up a learning contract and negotiate access to resources to attain their goals. Individual students may make personal arrangements to have a practice learning experience abroad; other students may take advantage of exchange schemes made possible by an HEI in the UK having developed a partnership with an HEI in another country. Care has to be taken to ensure that students can fulfil the learning outcomes for the relevant aspect of their course whilst abroad and that suitable insurance, supervisory and assessment arrangements are in place.

Further developments in practice education are being called for to promote knowledge and awareness of political, social and economic factors and lack of education and health services in impoverished areas of the world (Pollard and Sakellariou, 2007). These authors acknowledge that a reconceptualization of occupational therapy has commenced (Pollard et al., 2005), recognizing the existence of occupational injustices and occupational deprivation, but they advocate that more needs to be done to develop a critical mass of occupational therapists who are well versed in the issues and can contribute globally to initiatives that address these problems. Curricular developments need to take place to promote awareness amongst students of these issues to help them develop the skills that the profession needs to counteract restricted access to occupation for disadvantaged people. Opportunities for practice learning in services devoted to community-based rehabilitation might assist. These would need to be supported by a guiding framework for the experience, possibly developed by the WFOT with input from professional and regulatory bodies. Pollard and Sakellariou (2007) see the growth of 'global citizenship' to be a professional objective.

It can be concluded that practice learning for occupational therapists has evolved over time to reflect the changing nature of practice. One thousand hours of practice experience remains, however, the international benchmark for qualification. Practice education is nevertheless shifting to embrace not only preparation of students for work in traditional health and social care services but also preparation for emerging roles in support of national and international imperatives.

Core text recommendations

Alsop, A., and Ryan, S. (1996), *Making the Most of Fieldwork Education: A practical approach*, Cheltenham: Stanley Thornes.

Rosza, M., and Lincoln, M. (2005), 'Collaboration in Clinical Education', in M. Rose and D. Best (eds), *Transforming Practice through Clinical Education, Professional Supervision and Mentoring*, London: Elsevier Churchill Livingstone.

Tuning Occupational Therapy Project Group (2008), *Reference Points for the Design and Delivery of Degree Programmes in Occupational Therapy*, Bilbao and Groningen: University of Deusto and University of Groningen.

9   The physiotherapist

Barbara Richardson and Beryl Gillespie

Overview

Physiotherapy is one of the oldest of the allied health professions, having its origins in 1884 with a group of nurses interested in massage and physical healing. It is now a profession of more than 41,000 members (2006) in the UK (that is, England, Scotland, Wales and Northern Ireland) who have clinical autonomy to assess, diagnose and treat patients. Physiotherapists work to restore or improve movement disorders and dysfunction, as a result of injury, disease or following surgery, with a wide range of patient groups and ages, encompassing broad variations in health status over the lifespan. Using physical and interpersonal approaches physiotherapists aim to maximize potential through promotion, maintenance and restoration of each individual's physical, psychological and social well-being. According to the Chartered Society of Physiotherapy,

> The profession is science-based, committed to extending, applying, evaluating and reviewing evidence that underpins and informs its practice and delivery, and has the exercise of clinical judgement and informed interpretation at its core (CSP, 2002).[1]

Since 1992, three-year full-time physiotherapy programmes have led to a BSc (Hons) qualification (four years in Scotland) and since 2001 a number of two-year full-time MSc Physiotherapy accelerated programmes have been introduced for those who have already gained a BSc in a relevant subject.

---

[1]   The Chartered Society of Physiotherapy is the national professional body for physiotherapists.

Academic award is followed by mandatory registration as a physiotherapist with the regulatory body, the Health Professions Council (HPC)[2] and optional registration as a chartered physiotherapist with the professional body, the Chartered Society of Physiotherapy (CSP). In total there are 36 higher education institutes (HEIs) offering physiotherapy programmes nationally; 14 of these now offer an MSc qualification (for further details, see CSP, 2006b).

Physiotherapists work closely with other members of the multi-disciplinary team (MDT) in a variety of health care settings. The majority of physiotherapists are employed by NHS trusts, to work in hospitals or in the wider community as part of the primary care team. This may be in residential care homes, outpatient departments, day-care services or within schools. Others work in the independent sector hospitals, in private clinics and the sport and leisure industry. Practice-based learning opportunities are intended to reflect this mix of working environments that students will encounter on qualification.

The traditional pattern of practice education in the UK set by the Chartered Society of Physiotherapy, the professional body, and now approved by the HPC, requires students to complete 1,000 hours of practice in health care settings. This is equivalent to one year of a three-year full-time course. Practice must be supervised by an experienced HPC registered physiotherapist. Practitioners who take the role of teachers in practice settings are called placement educators (PEs) and will normally have a minimum of two years' experience with evidence of regular updating of skills and knowledge, and a positive commitment to conform with Standards of Physiotherapy Practice (CSP, 2000; CSP, 2003). Placements should take place within a variety of settings that reflect the breadth of experience expected on qualification. Most practice education is delivered in the form of placement blocks spread throughout the three years. Established programmes in the UK have provided leadership and models of education emulated internationally in English-speaking countries such as Canada and Australia. Countries in the EU and Scandinavia have developed from technical-based programmes which are beginning to move into higher education (for example, Germany) and those which have developed alongside and been strongly influenced by medical education in universities over many years (for example, Norway and Sweden). For practitioners moving to the UK, licence to practice is controlled by the HPC who can require a requisite period of supervised practice before registration.

In a period of major modernization of the NHS, policy and funding are affecting the delivery of physiotherapy programmes. Department of Health

---

[2]   The Health Professions Council is the national regulatory body for 14 allied health professions.

policies to re-structure health professionals' pay and working conditions within the NHS (DoH, 2004b), alongside organizational restructuring (DoH, 2004f) of health service delivery, have led to significant changes to the traditional role of physiotherapists and their deployment within health care. Despite some uncertainty about the organization of future work in health care and possible reduced employment opportunities for physiotherapy graduates in the NHS, these programmes remain very popular and many schools of physiotherapy, as our own, may process three times the number of applicants for the places available.

Recent developments

A broadening access to higher education programmes in the UK to reflect the demographics of the general population has led to mixed-ability classes of students with a wide age range from both traditional and non-traditional routes of entry (Morris, 2002). Changes in health and social care provision have led to caseloads with an increasing social and cultural diversity, and ethnic mix. Current global and national health policy promotes client-focused care and lifelong management of independence and mobility for individuals (DoH, 2006b; World Health Organization, 2001) in the context of the changing demography of an ageing population. There is a continuing transition from acute sector work to practice within primary care settings and a move to health promotion and prevention to maintain peoples' independence in their own homes. Increasingly students are placed with educators working in admission avoidance, falls prevention schemes and rapid response/discharge and community-based multi-disciplinary teams. An apprenticeship model of practice learning (Wenger, 1998), mainly concerned with development of psychomotor skills in an acute care setting, is being replaced by a model of self-directed career-long learning (CSP, 2002) in which students see themselves as lifelong learners who are critical in evaluating practice and flexible to respond effectively to change as autonomous practitioners (NAO, 2001; CSP, 2002) in the uncertain world of health (Eraut, 1994).

The continuing professional development (CPD) of each UK practitioner is seen as a systematic and planned process (CSP, 2005) that moves practice away from a behavioural model of competence towards a holistic model of competence (Thomas et al., 2003) fitting of autonomous professional work. It is considered that students' continuing professional development starts at the point of commencing education. A culture of workplace learning promoted within physiotherapy departments (CSP, 2005) that supports a shared responsibility for mentoring and educating the next generation is strongly promoted in the role of all physiotherapists and physiotherapy assistants (CSP, 2003). These are core competences required of all health professionals (DoH, 2004b).[3] Management of physiotherapy placement education thus places an emphasis on structured information for both placement educators and students to ensure a common understanding of placement expectations and a quality of practice experience.

Models of teaching and learning

Learning outcomes drive physiotherapy education nationally, being the standard of quality assessment for both the HPC and the Quality Assurance Agency (QAA).[4] This can create a tension for many programmes where the learning process is considered equally important to students as adult learners (Knowles, 1990) who will be lifelong learners. As Eraut comments, 'the deliberative processes of planning, problem-solving, analysing, evaluation and decision-making lie at the heart of professional work' (Eraut, 1994, pp. 112–13).

Equally, experiential knowledge gained in placement education is seen as key for students to integrate propositional and procedural knowledge (Richardson, 1999). An overarching premise of teaching and learning strategies is increasingly based on a constructivist perspective of knowledge which is the product of a 'dynamic and indeed difficult process of knowing or striving to understand' (Higgs and Jones, 1995, p. 130), with increasing recognition of the value of articulating physiotherapy practice epistemology (Richardson et al., 2004).

Conceptual models of problem-solving, clinical reasoning and evidence-based practice are central learning processes that drive physiotherapy assessment procedures to evaluate the physical, cognitive, mental and emotional needs of patients within their social and domestic circumstances. It is argued that clinical reasoning (Stephenson, 1998) integrates subjective symptoms and objective clinical signs in a process of framing physiotherapy problems. It is expected that solutions to address physiotherapy problems

---

    [3]   *The NHS Knowledge and Skills Framework (NHS KSF) and the Development Review Process*. This was the statement of the Department of Health's policy intended to identify the knowledge and skills NHS staff need to apply in their post, help develop individuals, and provide a fair and objective framework on which to base review and development of staff.

    [4]   The Quality Assurance Agency (QAA) was established in 1997 and is an independent body promoting continuous improvement in the quality of higher education (www.qaa.ac.uk). Its mission is to 'safeguard the public interest in sound standards of education', through regular inspection reviews of HEIs in the UK.

are informed by reference to relevant, high-quality clinical research (Herbert et al., 2005). As in many health professions, there is debate on the use of problem-based learning (PBL) (see, for example, Wood, 2003), in which students work in team groups to identify a solution intervention appropriate to the needs of an individual patient in the context of a health care service provision. The lack of evidence of success of PBL and the high resource burden has led to preference for a problem-led model of learning in which additional structured teaching material is provided for the student in the form of lectures, or practical demonstrations to support a problem-based scenario. This allows faculty to guide students to relevant information, from a potentially vast expanse of data.

Purposeful socialization in practice education, as in other areas of the syllabus, is based on educational principles that facilitate growth from concrete to abstract thinking with increasing ability for integration and synthesis of ideas which embrace professional attitudes and values (Bloom, 1954; Bloom, 1956). A process model of teaching supports a central aim of physiotherapy education to assist students to learn how to learn. From the beginning of the study programme, student-centred learning is encouraged through reflective practice. Students are guided to Kolb's learning cycle (1984) as a means of recognizing the 'messy swamps of practice' highlighted by Schön in his seminal work on how professionals think (Schön, 1983; Schön, 1987), and to other models of reflection which utilize pre- and post-activity reflection (see, for example, Boud et al., 1993) to assist in the deconstruction of complex processes of decision-making in physiotherapy (Sim and Richardson, 2004).

Learning outcomes for early placements are normally comprehensive and explicit whilst in the later placements they become increasingly complex to demand a demonstration of analysis and evaluation. Reflection-on-action (that is, the self-assessment and critical review of personal practice) is considered essential to enable the implicit theories used by practitioners to be brought to the surface (Donaghy and Morss, 2000) and encouraged through keeping a personal portfolio. Personal learning outcomes formulated with reference to the portfolio are agreed with each placement educator via a student learning contract. This model of student-directed learning is contingent on support of appropriate information. Placements are negotiated to purposefully include an induction to personnel and hospital policies. Annual student handbooks detail course units, learning outcomes, assessment procedures, allocation of credit rating in relation to development as an autonomous practitioner and also reiterate their rights and procedures for grievances.

We now look at another case study from the Green Hill flats community.

David, as a third-year student physiotherapist, worked with **Avis Jenkins** after a fall in her home which left her bruised and shaken and following a GP referral to a physiotherapy service in a 'rapid response'[1] or community care team. As part of his caseload of eight or nine patients, he would visit Avis with his placement educator, **Claire**, a Band 6[2] senior physiotherapist with four years of post-qualifying experience. David would contact Avis directly by phone or letter to arrange the visit or indirectly through another health professional such as a district nurse. During the rituals of introducing himself as a student and establishing how Avis liked to be addressed, he would observe the general living conditions, noting any physical obstacles of risk to mobility such as doorsteps, loose rugs, lack of solid furniture for support, poor footwear. Aware of gender issues in working with an older lady he ensured a respectful and supportive approach and, with her agreement, remained physically close to her for her safety. Keeping a central focus on the client he would briefly test Avis's mental state and cognition and listen to what she considers to be her main problem, before asking her to carry out a number of daily activities, such as transferring in and out of bed, walking around the house, negotiating stairs and personal care. In this process of collecting baseline data he would continually develop working hypotheses that would guide him to select a sequence of tests, carried out in sitting and lying positions that Avis could adopt, to ascertain her range of movement and muscle strength, proprioception and innervation coordination and balance. Results will be accurately recorded in a conventional style in a patient record. He would note her ability to understand, to follow and remember simple instructions. Following this assessment he would, in collaboration with Avis, create a problem list which identified and prioritized her problems in maintaining mobility and independence. In the process of evaluating the assessment data in relation to the context of this patient, he would draw on his knowledge of recent relevant research to plan an evidence-based intervention and would then explain to Avis alternative approaches to her physiotherapy. He would negotiate a final programme of intervention with her, including an agreed long-term goal of maintaining independence in the home, and identify short-term goals to address each of the problems.

[1]   Rapid response teams in community trusts are intended to provide a first contact service for recent injury within a stated number of hours.

[2]   *Agenda for Change* banding extends from Band 2 to Band 9. A newly qualified physiotherapist would start work in Band 5.

The teacher in the practice setting

The placement educator (PE) has a number of supervision roles. Initial administrative duties include ensuring orientation to the hospital bleep system, relevant telephone numbers, departmental policies and procedures for accident, health and safety, manual handling policies and complaints procedures. PEs facilitate student experience to meet placement learning outcomes and give regular feedback on performance through meetings negotiated by the student. The PE monitors the quality of care to the patients and liaises between patient and student as necessary. As counsellors, PEs monitor students' emotional well-being, help to reflect on difficult or distressing incidents, and encourage the development of a holistic and empathetic approach to care. Although one allocated PE takes responsibility for collating and judging the final grade for the placement, students may work with many 'supervisors' of their own profession and have periods of joint supervision with other members of the multi-disciplinary team (MDT).

The quality of practice education is monitored by placement providers via a system of formal and informal placement audit, student and educator feedback, and visits to placement sites. Most HEIs work to establish and maintain the quality of practice-based learning by offering regular training for both new and experienced educators through a variety of workshops; attendance at training can be used as evidence of personal CPD. Workshops encourage small group work to examine topics such as: preparing to take new students; models of student supervision and learning; students with special needs; supporting students' performance; and assessment and grading guidance. In addition there is orientation to documentation and policies relating to practice supervision, and opportunities for networking with others and to share a common approach to practice education. The lead PE is responsible for practice education assessment (in consultation with relevant others). Members of faculty, as visiting tutors, liaise with both the student and the PE half-way through the placement. This formative assessment is documented using standardized assessment forms that give each student structured personal feedback on aspects of their safety and professionalism, clinical reasoning, information processing, interpersonal skills, and client management. The visiting tutor can offer practical help and advice to either party and can be used as an advocate or arbitrator if difficulties arise. In the case of a failing student it may be necessary for the tutor to make a return visit to assist with the final assessment and grading. Although it is rare for students to fail placements, it can be a stressful situation for both the student and the educator and at that time good communication between the PE, the university and the student is vital. Ideal procedures for supporting a failing student are outlined in the educator handbook and will include discussions with the visiting tutor and university placement team. In exceptional cases where a student is deemed to be unsafe (for example, in handling a patient or using electrotherapy equipment) the student may be withdrawn from placement and, having failed, would be required to re-take the placement at another time. Students are normally allowed one opportunity to re-take, after which they will be withdrawn from the course.

Following his assessment of Avis, David would discuss his plans of intervention with Claire who would highlight any strengths or weaknesses in his approach; for example, his appropriate level of communication and pacing of treatment for an elderly person might be commended. Claire would explore his clinical reasoning and countersign David's patient record which forms part of the multi-disciplinary team notes maintained in each patient's home. As a third-year student David would interact with his supervisor as a 'consultant' or advisor, using informal supervision according to his perceived need. A formal supervision session would take place at least once a week for one hour. In this 'protected time' David and Claire would discuss any issues relating to his learning, such as professional behaviour, rationale for treatment interventions, agreeing plans for future practice experience, and feedback on performance and assessment grading.

The content and structure of the students' learning

Practice education is designed to build in complexity at each year of study and to develop transferable skills fundamental to professional practice such as assessment, critical appraisal and evaluation, clinical reasoning and problem-solving, self- and caseload management, communication and teamwork (CSP, 2002). Fostering a growing independence throughout the placements is aimed to promote a strong professional identity (Lindquist et al., 2006), enabling students to take responsibility for their own learning and to be critical of individual and social factors in concepts of health. It is expected that the process of placement education complies with placement guidelines of the professional body (CSP, 2003) whilst the quality of placement experience is monitored by the university (HPC, 2006).

The content of the students' learning to Level 3 is similar in both the BSc (Hons) and MSc pre-registration programmes in the UK. Both are likely to be modularized. Difficulties in placement recruitment can lead to a varied pattern of placement. Some HEIs are beginning to pool their placement resources to facilitate this. The sequencing of theoretical and practice modules is considered important to student learning in many HEIs and some still seek to retain the ideal of placements practice structured around university-bases study of related anatomical and physiological systems.

The University of East Anglia provides an exemplar of the structure of student learning in the UK (School of Allied Health Professions, 2006/07). Placement experience is demonstrated in the following examples.

Level 1 learning

Level 1 learning in the first, or Foundation, year familiarizes students with work in multi-disciplinary teams as part of the health and social care system in the UK. A general mix of settings can provide learning opportunities for competence to practise a range of specific psychomotor clinical skills and early development of transferable client-based skills. They are closely supervised as they start to bring their theoretical knowledge into the workplace. Demonstration of safe practice, professional behaviour and a reflective approach to work is fundamental to Level 1 learning. Assessment is through a combination of placement report (from the PE) and a linked problem-solving essay generated and assessed in the university. A pass must be obtained to progress to the second and third years for the BSc (Hons) award.

> **Tracey**, a first-year BSc student in a community placement (such as Derby Street and Green Hill flats), would observe her PE carrying out a patient assessment, and note her interactions and the varying professional roles within the MDT working together in the care of **Frank and Edith Sunderland**. She would become aware of professional, communication and client-centred skills such as confidentiality, note-keeping and history-taking. She would be supervised in giving simple treatment and patient-handling.

Level 2 learning

At Level 2 learning, students are expected to take more responsibility for planning and managing their caseload, demonstrating increasing skill and care in their work, and demonstrating links between academic theory and practice. It is expected that they are placed in settings which reflect the profession-specific studies of the taught syllabus. Assessment includes placement reports from the PE and a substantial written assignment set by the university which calls for clinical reasoning and reflection on practice to integrate diverse factors of patient details, stage of condition, environment and social circumstances, along with awareness of health provision and resource allocation.

Karim, a second-year BSc student in a musculoskeletal placement, would manage a full caseload of patients which could include acute care of the sports injuries of **Lorretta and Luke Carter** or care of the chronic back pain of **Jim Rafferty** from an old industrial injury, as well as long-term management of the exercise in respiratory care of **Kara Benner**'s asthma. He would have regular discussion with his PE regarding assessment, evaluation and plans to progress treatment. He could see patients in an outpatient clinic at the local GP surgery or in domiciliary (home) visits. His assignment would require him to select and anonymize a case study in which he can show a holistic perspective of a client within their environment, drawing on knowledge from a range of identified sources. In the case of Jim this might include interactions with health personnel such as his GP and practice nurse, his relatives (if accessible), and his neighbours, the Carters and the Kiyanis. It would also include comment on potential for independent mobility relating to transport access and the presence of social amenities for older people in his local social environment of Derby Street.

Level 3 learning

Level 3 learning is aimed to further develop autonomy of practice with decreasing reliance on direct supervision in preparation for working independently. Students have the opportunity to demonstrate increasing skills of management in organizing and prioritizing a patient caseload. Within curriculum options, a choice of placement can reinforce recognition of student self-directed learning. Assessment is through placement reports and a further written assignment selected to link with work as a newly qualified physiotherapist.

David may have chosen this placement to further a personal interest in community-based rehabilitation or to augment a perceived lack of skills in working with older people. He would consult with his PE only if necessary and take full responsibility for assessment, treatment and evaluation of his caseload of patients. In addition he could be asked to manage referrals from a selected geographical area, such as Derby Street, or a particular patient group, such as an elderly ward in the local district or community hospital. He would be expected to show complex clinical reasoning and reflective skills to explain the role of the physiotherapist to the multi-disciplinary team, to colleagues, patients and carers. An assignment of an evidence-based journal article gives him the opportunity to engage further with a selected practice problem and to synthesize research and practice evidence to raise debate through the conventions of professional discourse.

Methods

Whilst teaching methods may vary between schools in the UK, they will commonly focus on interactive dialogue with teachers as facilitators of student-led group seminars. A range of methods can be used to support the integration of propositional and procedural knowledge with personal practice experience to maximize student development. School-based teaching methods include lectures, case-based tutorials, seminars, presentations which utilize anatomical models, video and Internet material, and guided practical sessions to develop clinical reasoning or summaries of critical appraisal of literature. Together these provide a strong base to underpin the confident debate and critical thinking of an autonomous practitioner. Placement educators will purposefully facilitate other learning activities such as shadowing expert physiotherapists and other health professionals in activities with specific patients. Placement negotiation ensures student involvement in in-service education, regular individual and group supervision sessions, ward rounds, staff meetings, and attending clinics/theatre as appropriate. A university-generated learning framework of reflective diaries, learning contracts and significant learning events provides a structure for discussion and negotiating placement experience that relates to the later management of personal CPD in appraisals as a qualified practitioner. Students use portfolio-based evidence to generate personal learning contracts that raise awareness of their specific learning needs in each placement. Peer review of practice through case presentation forms an important preparation for participating in team discussions of the effectiveness and efficiency of therapy interventions and processes and of the monitoring of quality of care expected of the qualified therapist. Access to library, study areas, reference literature, computer/Internet is essential to structured and unplanned, incidental learning (CSP, 2005).

In a Level 3 placement, towards the end of his education programme, David would be conscious of the need to articulate his knowledge and understanding of his role as Avis's physiotherapist within the wider MDT. He could suggest a range of activities to facilitate this, such as spending time with the local Falls Coordinator or attending a local falls prevention exercise group. He would want to access any relevant documentation, such as the *National Service Framework for Older People* (DoH, 2001d) that suggests standards of care following falls. His learning contract would include some of these goals. On later reflection on his practice performance he may add further goals such as improving time management in making patient assessments, ability to write notes succinctly, and so on. A case study presentation to the physiotherapy department would integrate his client management information with evidence or experience recorded in his professional development portfolio.

Assessment

Assessment of students is a collaborative process between the university and the placement educator to ensure that physiotherapy students develop the skills and competences to qualify as competent and safe physiotherapy practitioners. Both academic and practice modules must be passed to evidence students' effectiveness as practitioners. Formative and summative assessment of the student's performance is documented and, although minor differences may exist between universities, will include a record of the process, criteria for grading and assessment of performance at the half-way and final stages of placement experience (CSP, 2003). It is expected that students will be given regular feedback about their performance through the process of supervision. The university provides educators with guidance (placement standards) and offers training in applying the academic grading process to practice situations to ensure equity through the annual workshops. Currently, grading descriptors are given for traditional first to fail grades, although there is a move towards pass/fail grades within some HEIs to address issues of students being 'grade obsessed' rather than valuing learning on placement, and of difficulties of gaining parity of experience and grading consistency across a number of placements. A main concern of a pass/fail system is the withdrawal of the motivating factor in grading for degree classification. The academic aspect of practice can also be reflected in a portfolio of placement experience verified by the PE and assessed by the HEI. Completed assessment forms are returned to the HEI for checking and any anomalies in the grading system, such as comments that may be at odds with the mark awarded, brought to the attention of the placement educator. Internal audit of the placement quality will begin with collation of data from evaluation forms from student, educator and visiting tutor. Any issues of concern from any party would be dealt with by the placement coordinator who has the responsibility for collating and tracking the quality of physiotherapy placements for the HEI, and maintaining placement profiles identifying the individual student's experiences, related evaluation and assessment documentation. S/he would contact a student's university personal advisor and/or the visiting tutor in the first instance. An audit trail of documentation would then be maintained at each stage of discussion until the problem was resolved. Any mitigating circumstances surrounding placement grading would be brought to the attention of the examination board by the student for their consideration. These standards of quality ensure students have parity and equity of experience as far as is possible given the wide variety of placement locations available. They are in line with QAA standards.

David would use the assessment proforma to self-assess his performance in relation to grading descriptors before both mid-way and formal final assessment meetings, when he would discuss these with the placement educator. As an example with regard to a dimension of client management that 'demonstrates a systematic approach to assessment', guided by the university descriptors David might feel he is working at the level of a student who is taking responsibility for his own assessments, has good communication skills, is timely in executing the assessment, and confident in his approach and choice of diagnostic tests. He could be pleased to hear that, based on his assessment of Avis, and several other patients she has observed, Claire feels that he is consistently showing a level of high professional work beyond that expected of a student at this stage. Similar discussion would take place around each area of physiotherapy practice: interpersonal skills, clinical reasoning, information management, safety and professionalism. Typically David might judge himself quite harshly in some areas, and might show less insight into his performance or behaviour than in others. Constructive feedback from his PE (and others in the MDT) that commends good practice, and identifies how to improve his skills where necessary, would assist him to shape his behaviour and attitude to practice. He would be reassured that a process of external scrutiny of HEI courses includes the examination of placement assessment documentation and processes of assessment by a team of external examiners who, along with the HEI exam board, ratify placement grades.

Continuing professional development

A concept of work-based learning in a range of workplaces (CSP, 2005) commonly embraces the continuing learning of qualified professionals. Staff development is central to the NHS Improvement Plan (DoH, 2004f) and *Agenda for Change* (DoH, 2004d), with annual appraisals of each practitioner that examine evidence of development within a current salary band and achievements for appointments to a higher band. At the point of commencing work in an NHS trust, the current policy of continuing quality improvement of services and the explicit career pathways in the *Knowledge And Skills Framework* clearly indicate milestones of continuing development for a junior physiotherapist. These are not related to any specific 'postgraduate training programme' but must be individually negotiated with the manager in the workplace with regard to the needs of the organization and the CPD of the individual. PEs have the opportunity to attend a number of meetings/conferences held by the local HEI and join the national HEI Placement Coordinators group hosted by the professional body which can be used to provide evidence of individual CPD. Although not mandatory, some PEs will have completed additional study to achieve an 'Accredited Clinical Educator' status (CSP, 2006a). A series of reflective pieces of academic work, with a portfolio of supporting evidence, assessed and graded by the HEI, gives eligibility to be registered with the CSP for five years, after which evidence of maintaining expertise in practice education must be given to remain on the register.

Current debates

Placement recruitment is crucial to sustaining the quality of practice education. Concerns with redressing the substantial financial deficit in most health care trusts have currently upset the established routines of obtaining placements. This, along with the changing panorama of health care and views of health, has led to the increasing use of non-traditional placements as well as the traditional placements in acute care hospitals. There is continuing discussion nationally of the numbers of practice hours and the length of placement in any one area of practice. A move to a single year-long placement model within a 'host trust' in the second year of some MSc programmes allows the placement provider to utilize student skills within the real-world practice concerns of allocation of staff in response to illness absence or contract demands. It also supports the government policy of a flexible workforce to underpin the continuing planned change from secondary-based care into the community and the contracted NHS tariff system (DoH, 2004e) which will mean very rapid discharge management by therapists. There is beginning to be a related debate of other models of practice education in which the substantial number of requisite hours could move into a first probationary year of employment preceptorship.

A split between skills learning in HEI and health settings is another focus of debate since the *Agenda for Change* and *Knowledge and Skills Framework (KSF)* expectations of important skills learning in a specific workplace may not match the national professional agenda or individual aspirations. The NHS and wider health care sector competences-based agenda is drawn from national workforce competencies: in *Assuring and Enhancing the Quality of Healthcare Education* (Skills for Health, 2006), competence emerges as a sum of separate units of competence. This has highlighted the tension of a holistic professional view of competence, based on professional artistry, and a behaviourist, technical rational model of competence (Thomas et al., 2003) which, in the short term at least, can be more easily audited. Demand for risk management in clinical governance of health services and explicit accountability of the quality and effectiveness of practice (Healthcare Commission, 2006; NICE, 2006) has fuelled debate on the skills and knowledge required for competence to practise in all professional groups.

Many programmes are engaging service users and carers in sessions within the taught syllabus to enable students to experience real-world practice needs early in their education and to help inform curricular development. Service users also may be recruited to course or course development group management committees (DoH, 2004h) and examination boards. In addition, in many schools they form part of the interview team for recruitment onto courses.

Future developments

The current trend to MSc physiotherapy programmes which yield small numbers of highly educated physiotherapists, alongside a broadening syllabus for larger student cohorts in BSc programmes and assistant practitioner training programmes (14 MSc programmes with cohorts of 20 compared with 36 BSc (Hons) programmes with student cohorts of 50 to 80), points to a move towards health care provision underpinned by a large generic workforce capable of carrying out the day-to-day care of a large proportion of the population, leaving the more advanced practitioners to manage care and undertake the specialized care of complex conditions or individual clients. A strategy of genericism with increasing use of non-professional health care assistants as a short-term solution to long-term problems of health management may have implications for the further development of professional expertise and suggests an increasing importance of the development of professional identity.

If managers, who are currently cautious in recruitment or in creating jobs, see the potential of the single-spine salary scale and the *Knowledge and Skills Framework* of *Agenda for Change* for rapid advancement and reward of expertise and ability, the labour market will become more relevant to the local needs. This will have implications for graduating students who will need to be prepared to negotiate job changes in order to gain experience as juniors rather than expect the rotational posts which have traditionally offered short spells of work in a number of areas. In the context of expanding practice into primary care there is now a drive to deliver services, such as stroke rehabilitation, traditionally provided in secondary care settings, within the community or primary care environment. It will be important to ensure that practice education management remains flexible to closely follow these changes and to avoid constraints on placement quality and numbers. Further use of non-traditional placements in the public and private sector should help to prepare and even give precedent for a changing pattern of health services.

A growing understanding of the principles and practice of adult learning and lifelong learning can lead to an increase in use of a 2:1 model of practice supervision which encourages student peer support alongside supervision from a PE. This could be enhanced with improved use of IT support for virtual classrooms and distance learning if difficulties with opening access to the intranet systems of HEIs and the NHS are addressed to overcome current security and confidentiality policies in which users of intranet systems in education and health services cannot 'talk' to each other effectively in order to share information.

Consumers of health are becoming better informed and have easier access to information for maintaining healthy lifestyles. There is improved choice for patients through 'choose and book' (DoH, 2004h), development of seven-day-week services, electronic appointment and text-reminder systems to reduce non-attendance, along with a flexible health workforce who will be responsive to change and who can utilize IT and new ways of working together with clients over their lifespan. These developments point to a challenging future for physiotherapists but one in which they look forward to playing a major role in lifestyle management to maximize individual potential and one in which practice education of students will continue to play a central role.

Core text recommendations

Herbert, R., Jamtvedt, G., Mead, J., and Birger Hagen, K. (2005), *Practical Evidence-Based Physiotherapy*, Oxford: Elsevier.

Higgs, J., and Jones, M. (eds) (2005), *Clinical Reasoning in the Health Professions* (2nd edn), Oxford: Butterworth Heinemann (1st edn 1995).

Hong, C.S., and Harrison, D. (eds) (2004), *Tools for Continuing Professional Development*, Salisbury (Wiltshire): Quay Books.

Acknowledgements

Our thanks go to Jane Cross, Director of Teaching and Learning, and Catherine Wells and the placement educator team at the School of Allied Health Professions, Faculty of Health, University of East Anglia.

10 The social worker

Joyce Lishman

Overview

In this chapter we will consider professional education from the point of view of the social worker and with a context of Scottish professional education.

There are some limitations to note in this chapter. It will be based upon social work professional education in Scotland. Since devolution each of the four countries of the UK has developed rather different, although aligned, social work degrees under different regulatory bodies.

When a Welsh colleague mentioned a 'daffodil curtain' going up in Wales I was anxious that a 'thistle curtain' might be going up in Scotland. Let us hope this is not so and that each of the four countries can learn from each other, but we do have to acknowledge differences in legislation, policy and organization of social work and social services which influence practice learning and education. For example, in Scotland, criminal justice remains part of social work and children's and adults' services have not been split as completely as appears to have happened in England. Furthermore, I draw on my direct experience of developments in practice learning and education in the North East of Scotland; while this is not geographically mainstream we may perhaps offer some useful examples of innovative practice for colleagues in the rest of the UK. Whatever the specific differences, practice learning in the four countries derives from a common history and shared principles.

Between 2003 and 2005, the Scottish Institute for Excellence in Social Work Education (SIESWE) commissioned three Scottish universities in partnership with other Scottish universities to undertake a study of 'learning for effective and ethical practice'. This chapter will draw on the findings (SIESWE, 2005), which concentrated on three main themes:

- the integration of university- and agency-based learning
- interprofessional learning opportunities
- agency-based learning.

Social work has been and is notoriously difficult to define: this is both a weakness and a strength. It is a weakness because it can be seen as amorphous, with no clear boundaries and no clear discipline knowledge base. It is a strength because it addresses individuals and their problems in the context of the societal and structural worlds they live in. At its General Meeting in Montreal, Canada, the International Federation of Social Workers (IFSW) defined social work as follows:

> The social work profession promotes social change, problem-solving in human relationships and the empowerment and liberation of people to enhance wellbeing. Utilising theories of human behaviour and social systems, social work intervenes at points where people interact with their environments. Principles of human rights and social justice are fundamental to social work (IFSW, 2000).

Elsewhere, I have similarly outlined these fundamental aspects of social work:

- a concern about individual people and the enhancement of their lives and relationships
- a commitment to social justice and the eradication of poverty and discrimination
- a commitment to social work as a moral and ethical activity
- a holistic approach to practice, where relationships and processes as well as outcomes are addressed
- a commitment to partnership and involvement with users in developing services to meet their needs
- a commitment to evaluating practice as a means of developing it
- a recognition that the worker's use of self is integral to social work activity (Lishman, 2002, pp. 95 and 96).

The practice of professional social work also involves up-to-date knowledge of and application of the law and of social policy initiatives, attention to the views and requirements of carers and service users and a much greater emphasis on research-based knowledge, evidence-based practice and evaluation of outcomes.

This examination of the complex nature of social work is the context of social work education and practice learning. It is practised in local authorities, health services, health and social care partnerships, children's services, voluntary sector services and independent sector services. We also need to consider how we prepare students to embrace and manage change, led by service user or carer requirements, policy, legal or organizational change and by a developing evidence base.

Social work education is now delivered in the UK by an honours degree (four years in Scotland) and also in Scotland by a postgraduate diploma in social work. In Scotland, the honours and postgraduate degrees are required to meet the Standards in Social Work Education (SiSWE) which combine the requirements of the QAA Benchmark Statement for social work degrees in the UK and assessment of transferable skills and National Occupational Standards. The Scottish Social Services Council (SSSC) is the approving body. The honours and postgraduate SIESWE degrees replace the previous two-year DipSW (CCETSW) award introduced in 1990 and which was entirely competence-led, rather than knowledge- and research-led. The new degrees are better aligned to the Scottish Qualifications and Credit Framework, at honours or postgraduate levels, than to the Diploma of Higher Education (as the Diploma in Social Work was) and reflect the complex requirements of knowledge, ethics, skills, reflection and evidence of the new award. The new degrees are provided in full-time, part-time, distance-learning and employment-based modes.

Students applying for entry to social work professional degrees approved by the SSSC must:

- meet the universities' requirements for entry;
- be registered as a student by the SSSC and thereby undertake a police check/Disclosure Scotland check. The registration as a student on the SSSC register and the other countries' registering bodies is currently unique in the health and medical professions;
- have relevant language, literacy, numeracy and IT skills. Students throughout their course and subsequent practice are required to meet the SSSC Codes Of Practice (SSSC, 2003);
- in terms of the Standards in Social Work Education, meet the prescribed overarching standards for entry.

For qualification students must meet the following requirements:

- prepare for, and work with, individuals, families, carers, groups and communities to assess their needs and circumstances
- plan, carry out, review and evaluate social work practice with individuals, families, carers, groups, communities and other professionals

- assess and manage risk to individuals, families, carers, groups, communities, self and colleagues
- demonstrate professional competence in social work practice
- manage and be accountable, with supervision and support, for their own social work practice within their organization
- support individuals, to represent and manage their needs, views and circumstances.

Each of these standards and their accompanying knowledge and transferable skills translates into detailed outcome requirements of competence for the honours or postgraduate degree which need to be achieved, not only in a university setting but also in practice. A major aim of the new degrees is to integrate knowledge, theory and practice across university and agency settings.

Practice learning is a major component and requirement for qualification. Providers are required to:

> ... make sure that all social work students spend *at least* 200 days in practice learning of which *at least* 160 must be spent in supervised direct practice in direct delivery settings. This practice learning must be assessed. Up to 60 days of the supervised direct practice element can be subject to credit from prior experiential learning (Scottish Executive, 2003, p. 15).

This allows for employment-based students who study by distance learning to have work experience credited as RPL (recognition of prior learning, previous prior experiential learning) (Scottish Executive, 2003, p. 18) and therefore 'fast-track' to an honours degree. It also means that for full-time students 40 of the practice learning days may be spent undertaking skills and/or practice learning in the university setting. This option is not available to students in England and Wales.

Assessed practice learning is required to provide contrasting experiences in terms of service delivery settings and user groups: students are required to undertake statutory social work tasks.

These are the SIESWE requirements. The *Framework for Social Work Education* clearly states:

> Practice is seen as an essential element of the new qualification. Development of the students' skills and abilities in practice is based on the fact that practice is *a setting* for learning, a way of learning and an *essential part* of the learning students must complete (Scottish Executive, 2003, p. 19).

Recent developments

Since the SIESWE requirements were introduced two new relevant developments have occurred; the first, a major review of social work in Scotland, *Changing Lives*, and the second, the introduction of 'Key Capabilities in Child Care' as mandatory in the social work degrees.

Commissioned by the Scottish Executive, *Changing Lives* (Scottish Executive, 2006a) is a policy context for social work education in Scotland. It was a fundamental review of social work in Scotland following two major tragedies: the first was the Borders case (Scottish Executive, 2004) where long-standing abuse of people with learning disabilities had been ignored over a number of years by a local authority and where lessons about performance management and corporate responsibility emerged; the second was the Caleb Ness case (O'Brien, 2003) where a child died in Edinburgh. Lessons here were about criminal justice workers failing to see a child protection responsibility, but also about wider interdisciplinary communication and responsibility, in particular health and social work including criminal justice.

The implications of *Changing Lives* (Scottish Executive, 2006a) keep changing and with a change of government in Scotland in 2007 remind us of the high profile social work has in a volatile political climate. Key themes relevant to social work education include the need for autonomous and accountable social work professionals, performance management, leadership, governance and reconfiguration of services.

Key Capabilities in Child Care and Protection (SSSC, 2006) provided another challenge to social work education in the middle of implementing new degrees; again, it arose out of the political implications of the Caleb Ness case of 2002 (O'Brien, 2003). Essentially, *Key Capabilities* requires all social workers in training to undertake detailed assessment, observation and intervention with a child in order to ensure that all trained social workers do not become defined by their role (for example, criminal justice workers) in working with adults, but also have a 'third ear' (Lishman, 1994) for implications for vulnerable children. Social workers who predominantly work with children also need this 'third ear' for adults in vulnerable situations (Trevithick, 2005).

Models of teaching and learning

In the Scottish Audit of practice learning (Loxton et al., 2004) almost all respondents used reflective practice and evidence-based practice (both discussed later in this chapter and in Lishman, 2007b). A majority (but much smaller number) used adult learning. Adult learning was a central component of the two-year CCETSW competence-based model of training (the former DipSW) but the population of social work students has changed, with an increasing number of young school leavers entering the profession.

Observation, modelling and role play in the audit were highly valued as enhancing skills development in social work education. Didactic or direct teaching was seen as a less useful model, but should not be discarded, for example, in considering the inhabitants of Derby Street where didactic teaching in relation to the impact of inequality and relative poverty (Hills, 2004) would be critical. A student might be asked to consider the following: What is the employment status of each of the inhabitants of Derby Street and what impact does this have on their social situations and their respective power? How might government employment and pension policies (in London and Edinburgh) affect each of the inhabitants of Derby Street?

It can be argued that inequality and relative poverty derive from geographical, social class, gender and ethnic inequalities in income and education achievements. Age and disability also contribute to inequality and relative poverty. Poverty has an impact on health and social exclusion and so has an impact on the effectiveness of the work of all the professions represented in this book. The social worker might be the person most closely in touch with this association.

The two main Models of teaching and learning that emerged from the audit were reflective practice and evidence-based practice. These will be explored further.

It is probable that theories of adult learning have become subsumed into reflective learning where we ask both 'how did I reflect on action?' and 'how do I reflect in action?' (Schön, 1987). Both of these questions draw on our previous experience to help us understand how we are now interacting professionally.

Schön's reflections *on* action include:

- how did I engage?
- what previous experiences influenced me?
- what did I do and why?
- how might I have responded differently?

Reflection *in* action can be reframed:

- what do I feel now?
- how do I present?
- should I change how I am presenting?

Reflection *on* action in relation to Derby Street could ask the student social worker to reflect on their own previous experiences (for example, in terms of their class, gender, age and ethnicity) and how these contribute to their perceptions and consequent interventions with the different individuals and families living in that community. Reflection *in* action involves us in being aware of how our own knowledge, values and experiences influence us in current professional interactions with service users, carers or interprofessional colleagues.

Models of adult learning encourage and are re-enforced by reflective practice; questions about learning and teaching in social work in both university and practice settings include:

- how do we learn or not learn from our previous educational experiences?
- how do we best learn from different teaching models; do we learn (as individual learners) from didactic or written material (books or the web) or enquiry and action-based learning? Do we learn best from doing in practice and then applying knowledge and theory?
- how do we learn best for a particular focus using the spectrum of models? For example, we probably learn most about the law by didactic teaching and strict multiple choice assessment; skills are best learned by practice, initially by video in universities followed by direct practice in agencies and assessed by video, observation and the judgement of a practice teacher.

Evidence-based learning and practice is now a major requirement of social work education, but what does this involve? Evidence-based practice in medicine was defined as 'the conscientious, explicit and judicious use of current best evidence in making decisions about the care of individual patients, based upon skills which allow the doctor to evaluate both personal experience and external evidence in a systematic and objective manner' (Sackett et al., 1997, p. 71). MacDonald and Sheldon (1998) apply the principles of this definition to social work and social care: 'Evidence-based social care is the conscientious, explicit and judicious use of current best evidence in making decisions regarding individuals.' I have recently argued (Lishman, 2007a, p. 384) that:

> It is impossible to argue with this definition. As professionals in social work and social care we have a duty to make sure we are using the best possible knowledge and evidence on which to base our assessment and intervention. We should do this with the intention of minimizing adverse consequences to users of services.

A current debate concerns what should be considered as a valid evidence base. Research and evaluation findings and service users' and carers views' are clearly central to evidence-based practice but so are theories of understanding and meaning of individual experiences, ethics and professional judgement. What is *not* evidence-based practice includes the use of outdated knowledge and over-reliance on practice wisdom where what appeared to have a successful outcome may not be generalizable. The critical basis of social work education encourages students to reflect on the different power bases of the various perspectives that might, or might not, have a place at the table of evidence-based practice.

What are the implications for practice learning in social work? Practice teachers need current knowledge, both of available outcome research and of the views of service users and carers, and they need to be clear about their ethical base and the way in which they exercise professional judgement and act as reflective practitioners.

Social work students could find themselves working with any of the residents of Derby Street and, in all cases, they will be learning how to exercise professional judgement, for example, in relation to **Avis Jenkins**, as part of a risk assessment of her ability to look after herself and what areas she will need help with. Service users' views in relation to depression and mental health are important in working with **Sam** (Beresford and Croft, 2001). In relation to **Zoë**'s child and parenting issues the student can be asked to draw on evidence from attachment theory (Aldgate, 2007) and assessment and children (Daniel, 2007).

The teacher in the practice setting

A new practice learning qualification has been introduced in Scotland. This is at SCQF (Scottish Credit and Qualification Framework) level 10 (honours degree), and modules include teaching and learning styles, methods and models, assessment, interdisciplinary learning, evaluating the effectiveness of learning environments for the learners, reflective practice and evidence-based practice. Practice teachers and link workers are also invited to relevant training sessions, for example on Key Capabilities and working with students with disabilities. Practice teachers and link workers are also supported in these meetings by colleagues from agencies and the university: individual practice teachers and link workers are supported by individual personal tutors from the University. A model piloted in the LEEP (Learning for Ethical and Effective Practice) project involved a university tutor co-facilitating student placement groups with practitioners and engaging in continuing professional development activities, including changes in the law and social policy and changes in practice and service delivery identified from evidence-based practice (SIESWE, 2005; Clapton and Daly, 2007). This model was perceived as extremely effective in integrating theory and practice, and in breaking down divides between universities and agencies. However, it required considerable resources in terms of university time allocated to practice learning and a more diluted model has been adopted, with university tutors providing relevant continuing professional development for agency colleagues. The 'trade' (Doel, 2006, p. 32) is two-way, with practice teachers involved in assessing preparation for practice, class teaching, course management and the practice assessment panel.

The practice assessment panel is not formally required by *The Framework for Social Work Education in Scotland*, though it had been a requirement in the DipSW by CCETSW. In general, it has been retained as a way of maintaining an overview of practice learning experiences and their quality and of providing feedback to all practice teachers about general issues and specific feedback to individual practice teachers where improvements appear to be required, either in the student learning experience or in the assessment.

The LEEP practice audit and literature review (SIESWE, 2005) identified a number of key themes about good practice in practice learning in terms of enhancing both the quantity and quality of practice learning experience (see also the SSSC/SIESWE publication, *Confidence in Practice Learning*, 2004). These included:

- the need for new approaches to ensure an adequate supply of practice learning experience
- the need for the involvement of senior and operational managers in ensuring practice learning opportunities are available and valued by the agency for the student's contribution both to service delivery and team learning
- the need to share responsibility across a team or teams for the teaching, learning and assessment of social work students.

These recommendations do reflect how practice learning and teaching in Scotland *had* tended to become somewhat marginalized (as the business of training teams) from the main operational service delivery of local authorities in Scotland. Voluntary organizations were more likely to see students as enhancing service delivery and as part of general staff learning and development.

Tania and **Jack** are students on their first placement in a service user-led community project working in the Green Hill community. Their placement has a project element, namely working with service users in the project to make a video which will show the work of the user-led group. It is also intended that the video will be used to promote the community group as a good setting for social work student placements, so it will be played to Year 1 students to encourage further involvement with the community group.

One concern for Tania and Jack was how this experience was 'social work' and, whilst they valued the experience of the service users, whether they could expect the service users to be able to help them to make links between their work with the project and the theory and practice of professional social work. However, they have weekly contact with an 'off-site' practice teacher with whom they can discuss their experiences and who is able to help them understand 'the social work'. The off-site practice teacher keeps in regular contact with two of the service users, who are designated as work-based supervisors for the students, and these work-based supervisors have also undertaken a two-day introductory course in practice learning to help them understand their role with social work students.

As well as the community video, Tania and Jack are also involved in the tenants' association and each of them has a link with one of the social workers who works in the Green Hill area. Their situation is indicative of the way in which social work practice learning is moving away from closed, one-to-one supervision with 'my' student to a broader team which might well include users of the service. What is particularly important is that this experience is properly coordinated.

Practice teaching and student supervision has traditionally played a major part in promotion prospects in local authorities and was also seen as a normal part of professional development; however, an increasingly managerial approach to service delivery and organization has not been kind to practice learning and teaching. More generally, barriers to professional development and learning in social work include:

- a tension between a local authority's requirement for a technically competent worker and a professional requirement for critical, reflective practice, which may include criticism of agency practice
- a lack of agency recognition in terms of pay and status for the achievement of professional development, the practice teaching award being one example

- a lack of time allowed for professional development (Lishman, 2002).

So why become a practice teacher or link worker? The new requirements for registration with the Scottish Social Services Council (SSSC) do recognize practice teaching as a way of meeting registered social workers' continuing professional development (CPD) requirements, which are 15 days over three years. Agencies have begun to recognize that taking students may help their problems in recruitment as students with good practice learning experiences are likely to seek a job in the agency which had provided these good experiences (Parker et al., 2006). Practice teaching has therefore become more valued for its indirect contribution to service provision. *Confidence in Practice Learning* (SSSC/SIESWE, 2004) argued that it is *everyone's* job to ensure the learning and development of students and new entrants into the profession and the SSSC's Codes of Practice reinforce this.

Following the publication of *Confidence in Practice Learning* in 2004, the Scottish Executive allocated funding to universities to pay for practice learning via a daily rate to the agency providing the practice learning. While this has not, in Scotland, been universally successful in providing the required quantity and quality of practice learning, in the North of Scotland it has. The reasons for this success include:

- considerable university and agency investment in developing specific service level agreements specifying numbers and kinds of practice learning opportunities to be provided by agencies
- creative use of practice learning money to fund full-time practice teaching posts in the voluntary sector and local authorities
- a commitment from local authorities and the voluntary sector to fund practice learning as part of recruitment and professional development strategies
- partnership working between the university and agencies for joint funding of posts.

A further major contributor has been the development from the LEEP project (SIESWE, 2005) of a different model of practice learning and practice teaching. Singleton practice teachers (social workers who supervise one student at a time in addition to their regular work as practitioners) remain an important and valued part of practice learning. However, another model involves using full-time practice teachers funded by the daily rate supervising and taking overall responsibility for the assessment of the student and taking six to eight students twice a year. They share the teaching and learning in the practice curriculum with team colleagues, managers and link workers who also contribute to assessment, as indicated in the example of Tania and Jack (above). Further teaching and learning sessions are contributed by university staff, and agency colleagues can use these as part of their continuing professional development.

The content and structure of the students' learning

The students' learning in practice is prescribed by the requirement to meet the Standards in Social Work Education (SiSWE) which include six key roles underpinned by more detailed learning foci and practice requirements. The key roles are:

- prepare for, and work with, individuals, families, carers, groups and communities to assess their needs and circumstances
- plan, carry out, review and evaluate social work practice with individuals, families, carers, groups, communities and other professionals
- assess and manage risk to individuals, families, carers, groups, communities, self and colleagues
- demonstrate professional competence in social work practice
- manage and be accountable, with supervision and support, for their own social work practice within their organization
- support individuals to represent and manage their needs, views and circumstances.

Students also have to demonstrate that they meet key capabilities in child care. There are two requirements in practice:

- A requirement of the key capabilities is that whatever practice learning opportunity a student is engaged in, they must be able to evidence their knowledge and application of child care and protection as it is relevant to their setting. The intention here is to help students avoid the effect of working in a child or adult setting without thinking more broadly of child protection in working with adults and vulnerable adults in working with children (see the Caleb Ness case, O'Brien 2003).
- A further requirement is that, during one of the assessed practice learning opportunities, students should undertake an assessment of a child or of parenting capacity.

Clearly, students over two or three practice learning experiences have to address these requirements and therefore for each placement a learning agreement is drawn up which identifies the student's learning needs for the placement and how these may be met and assessed. Also, each student has individualized practice learning experiences depending on the agency setting and the student's learning needs, but within a consistent framework of meeting SiSWE and the requirements of *Key Capabilities*.

Practice learning within university settings in earlier stages of degrees occurs by the use of simulation and videoing; in some cases, a panel of users and carers provide this simulated practice learning.

Because of the geographical location, in the North of Scotland practice learning has been organized in blocks (that is, the whole week on placement), rather than 'concurrent' where some time is spent on placement and some in the university. Where it is undertaken in urban conurbations, concurrent practice and academic learning may well facilitate an integrated approach to practice and theory. Distance-learning students have at least one block placement outside their own agency to experience other ways of practice and forms of organization and to ensure that the generic requirements of SiSWE are met.

Methods

The new model of practice learning identified by the LEEP projects (SIESWE, 2005) involves:

- interchangeable roles between university and agency staff in facilitating student learning
- the role of the practice facilitator/teacher as a manager of packages of learning opportunities as well as teaching and assessment of students
- developing service-specific and cross-sector packages of learning opportunities
- developing a team approach engaging a range of staff who coach/ supervise discrete pieces of work with students
- implementing group and individual student supervision
- ensuring user and carer involvement in student assessment.

The model involves a combination of teaching and learning experiences for the student such as case-based supervision with link workers responsible for coaching and assessing discrete pieces of work; group teaching and learning with the practice learning facilitator, agency and university staff using didactic input, case presentations, role plays and experiential learning exercises. The focus of these sessions is on values and ethics, skills, evidence for practice approaches and integration of theory, knowledge and practice. In addition there are individual sessions with the practice learning facilitator focused in particular on professional development and the students' individual learning needs and their progress in meeting assessed outcomes.

Assessment

Assessment, the content and structure of the student's learning and methods are inextricably interlinked (Boud, 1995). As has already been indicated, overall assessment is the responsibility of the practice teacher but discrete aspects of work are assessed by colleagues and link workers.

   Assessment methods typically include:

- critical incident accounts to assess the learning from key incidents in practice (linked to reflective learning)
- direct observations with an emphasis on evidence of ethics/values and skills development
- learning logs and reflective diaries which contribute to personal development plans and encourage critical, reflective analysis of practice
- work-based products including agency records, reports and letters
- case presentations where knowledge, for example, the legislation policy or research, is applied to a particular piece of ongoing practice
- skill rehearsal and role play which are used to prepare for practice but constitute part of the developing assessment and learning agenda
- searching the research base, for example, using a systematic review, to ensure that there is an evidence base for using a particular approach to practice (Lishman, 2007a; Morago, 2006)
- projects where a student carries out a piece of work on behalf of the agency, such as researching and presenting a topic of current relevance to the service user group drawing on current legislation, policy and research
- carrying out a small-scale evaluation of a specific project.

In terms of the process of assessment it is the practice teacher who has the overall responsibility to draw on evidence from the variety of sources described and to come to a judgement. In situations when a student is passing their practice assessment, a brief summary of the reasons for the recommendation is required. Where a student is marginal or failing, more detailed evidence of the reasons clearly linked to the SSSC Codes of Practice, SiSWE and the key capabilities is required, including when difficulties emerged and how. Here it is essential that the practice teacher presents a case which is not simply understandable to the practice assessment panel and Assessment Board (steeped in social work assessment practice) but clear to non-social work academics who will judge the appeal and ultimately, in Scotland, to the Public Services Ombudsman. The discipline of a legal court report is relevant here.

Full-time undergraduate and postgraduate students are required to undertake a readiness for practice assessment where social work academics, practice teachers and service users assess students' communication and engagement skills in order to ensure that they are ready to begin an initial practice learning experience.

Consideration and review remains ongoing about different levels of assessment in practice of SiSWE and key capabilities at different stages of the student's course and judgements and case law are currently being developed (often it is a Practice Assessment Panel) about requirements and standard at each stage, but this is complicated by the range of social work settings (local authority, voluntary and private) where not all settings offer equal learning opportunities; for example, a sophisticated group care setting may not provide adequate opportunities for assessment in law and statutory duties and responsibilities. Some courses take the view that, overall, SiSWE must be met to qualify, but that some requirements are essential at the first stage of practice learning, such as engagement, assessment and professional development. Where opportunities arise, other requirements (for example, teamwork and interdisciplinary work) are also assessed.

Continuing professional development

While professional social work does not have a probationary period, the SSSC has laid down a requirement that social workers in their first year of work undertake the equivalent of 24 days of continuing professional development. To re-register thereafter social workers have to show that they have undertaken 15 days over three years including five days of child protection/care training. Practice learning qualifications, mental health officer training, child protection training, criminal justice training and leadership training continue to be important elements of continuing professional development as does interprofessional training and education.

Essentially, these are the components of the social work CPD framework in Scotland, although working with vulnerable adults is also emerging as key. Although not required by the SSSC, in the North of Scotland in partnership with agencies, there is a graduate certificate in professional social work studies for entrants to the profession after at least one year's service.

Current debates

In the UK a major issue for social work education and training is how to review and evaluate the new degrees and when to do this. This is very important in Scotland given that most courses are, at the time of writing in 2008, only half-way through the final year of the first honours cohort, and evaluation of the effectiveness in practice of these students probably cannot take place until at least a year after they commence work.

A second issue in Scotland is the funding of higher education which did extremely badly in the Spending Review and does not have the option of charging top-up fees. Social work education is expensive in terms of staff time if the principles of practice learning, integrating theory, knowledge and practice learning, and ensuring good outcomes for service users and carers are to be addressed. There is a debate as to whether it is affordable.

Social work education needs to undertake high-quality research which *both* meets the university requirements (for example, the research assessment exercise (RAE) where additional funding is allocated to departments who meet pre-defined research criteria) *and* ensures high-quality practice and service delivery for service users. In Scotland, a research and development strategy for social services is being developed. The investment from a university in developing and supporting practice learning competes in staff resource terms with the requirements for RAEs and other research necessary for the development of the profession. The question is can these be reconciled and, if so, how?

A final tension is around the implications of disability legislation which questions the legality of the health requirement for registration and raises complex questions about suitability for social work and fitness to practise. For example, when do issues in relation to mental health raise questions about suitability for social work and how can we evidence these in competence terms? A student or worker with a bipolar illness can engage in entirely safe practice as long as they take appropriate medications and maintain contact with a psychiatrist (see GMC website, rules and requirements). Another student who denies any mental health issue but in practice appears to exhibit problematic behaviour is rather more complex; judgements about suitability for professional social work need to demonstrate a focus on behaviours and required competences.

Future developments

The future is always a matter of speculation, but the following issues are linked with those raised throughout the chapter.

1. How will social work in the UK be shaped over the next few years and what impact will this have on social work education? In England, criminal justice, children's services and adult services/community care have separated. This is not so in Scotland, but the organization of social services delivery has implications for social work education.
2. How can social work education retain a focus that is specific within a multi-disciplinary context, in particular with health, education and, in Scotland, the police and prison service?
3. How will we increase social work education's commitment to an evidence-based approach to ensure that research and evaluation is routine in social service delivery?
4. How will we manage potential tensions between equal opportunity of access to social work education and professional suitability and fitness-to-practise issues?
5. Will social work education play its part in creating a cultural change in social services delivery, where users and carers do feel they are receiving a personalized service? How will social work which involves the use of authority and control (such as child protection social work and, in Scotland, criminal justice social work) ensure the care and protection of vulnerable children and adults and remain part of an integrated social work policy agenda?

Core text recommendations

Doel, M., and Shardlow, S.M. (2005), *Modern Social Work Practice: Teaching and learning in practice settings*, Aldershot: Ashgate.

Acknowledgement

I would like to express my appreciation to Linda Bruce, The Robert Gordon University, for sharing helpful background reading.

11 The speech and language therapist

Shelagh Brumfitt and Cheryl Gray

Overview

Speech and language therapists work with children and adults who have difficulties with communication or with eating, drinking or swallowing. They work closely with parents and carers and other professionals such as teachers, psychologists, nurses, physiotherapists, occupational therapists and doctors. Approximately 10,000 speech and language therapists practise in the UK and the majority are employed by the National Health Service (NHS). Other therapists work for education services or charities and some work independently and treat patients privately. The contexts in which they work are varied, and include community health centres, hospital wards and outpatient departments, mainstream and special schools, day centres and clients' homes. Some speech and language therapists work in prisons and young offenders' institutions.

The professional qualification was originally at diploma level and then in the late 1970s transferred to undergraduate degree level. In the late 1980s the profession saw the development of master's level degrees at some of the universities. There are now 18 universities in the UK offering recognized undergraduate and postgraduate qualifying courses. The approximate number of students in training in the UK for the session 2005–06 is 2,600. In general the model for education is that of daily attendance at the university with placements running throughout all years of the programme. Some institutions focus more heavily on the block placement pattern than others. The Royal College of Speech and Language Therapists (RCSLT) with the Health Professions Council (HPC) require that students must complete 150 sessions of work-based learning, 100 of which need to be under direct supervision of a speech and language therapist. Each session is approximately 3½ hours long. Frameworks for guiding course development have included (initially) *Guidelines for the Accreditation of Courses* (RCSLT, 2001) and (subsequently) *National Standards for Practice-Based Learning* (RCSLT, 2006b); plus the RCSLT competency frameworks, QAA subject benchmark statements for speech and language therapy, the Health Professions Council standards of proficiency, HPC standards of conduct, performance and ethics, and HPC standards of education and training guidance for education providers.

Recent developments

The Royal College of Speech and Language Therapists is the professional body and recently celebrated its diamond jubilee (1945–2005). During this time the number of speech and language therapists has risen to approximately 10,000. The speech and language therapy (SLT) profession first came under state regulation on 1 October 2000 and the state regulator was the Council for Professions Supplementary to Medicine. However, the Health Act 1999 paved the way for the Health Professions Council, as independent regulator, and in 2001 the Health Professions Order established the rules by which the Health Professions Council would operate. The principle now is that of a speech and language therapist being registered with the Health Professions Council but this now serves as an autonomous body, not a government body, so the concept of state regulation no longer applies. The title of the profession is now protected.

The Royal College is also an autonomous organization with links to the Health Professions Council but not under its jurisdiction. It deals with representing members, promoting the profession and continuing professional education and development.

In addition to the professional becoming regulated by the HPC, the funding for student education has moved from the Higher Education Funding Council to the Department of Health. This occurred in the financial year 1998–99 and has made a huge impact on speech and language therapy education. The number of students in training increased during the period 2002 to 2005 and university departments were encouraged to expand but subsequently numbers have decreased slightly due to the financial situation in the NHS. Students receive a means-tested bursary and their fees are paid. Speech and language therapy was already a highly popular course but since the Department of Health funding, the number of applications has increased further.

Models of teaching and learning

Teaching and learning in the SLT profession has seen many developments over the last two decades. These developments are a response to two main drivers: firstly the ever-expanding and evolving knowledge base within the profession; and secondly the complex changing environments where speech and language therapists work. New graduates need to be competent in their practice – that is, they need to have the knowledge and skills to manage clients effectively, and the ability to be professional in their interactions with clients, their carers and colleagues. In addition to these core competencies, they are also expected to have the tools for reflection and self-development and have the capability to work in uncertain and changing environments. Schön (1987) describes these as the 'indeterminate zones of practice'. The goal of teaching and learning in practice settings is to produce speech and language therapists who are competent in their practice, have the skills to engage in lifelong learning and the abilities to interact with and respond to changing contexts and the people within them. These challenges facing new graduates are not unique to SLT; the world is demanding a new type of 'beginning practitioner' and a new form of education to meet the changing needs of global and local societies (Higgs and Edwards, 1999).

In order to acquire the knowledge and skills required for professional practice we need to apply adult learning philosophy to the clinical education setting. The importance of education in the clinical setting has always been recognized in SLT; however, the goals have changed from training and instruction to the development of professional competence and lifelong learning. Previously there was no epistemology to drive methods of education but this is beginning to change. McAllister et al. (1997) state that 'clinical education is the ideal context in which to adopt an adult learning approach'.

The literature on adult learning has been influential in changing approaches to the education of speech and language therapists. Schön's (1983, 1987) work on the development of the reflective practitioner, that of Boud and Walker (1990) on experiential learning and Eraut's (1994) description of the types of knowledge required for professional education have been particularly influential in the practice setting. These influences can be seen in Bines's model (1992) of professional education, which has been directly applied to SLT education (Stansfield, 2004). In order to meet the challenges of educating 'beginning practitioners' prepared to practise in complex and changing environments, speech and language therapy educators have recognized the need to move away from the more traditional, technocratic model of professional education towards a post-technocratic model (Bines, 1992). In the technocratic model, the curriculum is controlled and delivered by academics at universities and practice is supervised in a 'sitting by Nellie' model. The student has a fairly passive role as a learner of facts and clinical skills are learnt through direct observation of an expert and supervised practice. In a post-technocratic model, knowledge for practice is developed and there is a focus on the acquisition of professional competencies where learners have an active role in systematic reflection on practice. This operates within a partnership framework between universities and employers, where both contribute to curriculum development and the delivery of education. The latter has been a particularly true reflection since funding has moved to the Department of Health and courses are managed through contracts and partnership agreements between universities, strategic health authorities and practice learning providers. When reviewing course documentation for all courses in the UK, Stansfield (2004) states: 'speech and language therapy education appears, at least as shown in course documentation to be approaching Bines' post-technocratic model.'

Evidence for this evolution in professional education can be seen in models described in the literature. Baxter and Gray (2001) and Baxter (2004) look at the application of adult learning approaches in the practice setting; they recognize the need for a pedagogic shift in the role of the supervisor/ educator from that of didactic teacher to that of a facilitator of learning. They also stress the importance of the student-centred approaches of active and reflective learning to produce graduates with the skills of lifelong learning and the abilities to adapt to ever-changing contexts.

To try and meet the requirements of practice learning outlined above, educators, particularly in medicine but also other areas of health sciences including SLT, have turned to the method and philosophy of problem-based learning.

The educational methods used involve students working in small groups with a tutor identifying issues raised by certain written problems. The students work together on the problem to develop an understanding about underlying concepts and principles, acquiring new knowledge as part of the process. The philosophy and methods certainly attempt to apply all the principles of adult learning, thus fostering self-directed and deep approaches to learning with the aim that this becomes a lifelong process. However, some educationalists have begun to question whether problem-based learning is the only way forward. Some of the criticisms of this approach are that it is costly, it places additional demands on staff time and there is reduced acquisition of knowledge of basic sciences. Therefore, in order to meet the requirements of student-centred active learning approaches but also to overcome the disadvantages of problem-based learning, Whitworth et al. (2004) describe a hybrid PBL approach to an SLT curriculum. This moves away from the separation of theory and practice. Our knowledge needs include applied science and research-based techniques, but we also need the skills of 'professional artistry' to become competent in the 'grey areas' of practice in those situations which require critical thinking and problem-solving (Schön, 1987). An example of how students would approach a new client is given below.

Billy is the 3½-year-old son of **Zoë Benner**, a single parent, and they have been living in Green Hill flats for two years. Zoë has been concerned about Billy's speech because he cannot make himself understood to people. Zoë can understand him but she feels she has 'tuned' in to what he is trying to say. His development has been normal other than speech, for which his first word was only noticed at the age of 18 months. The health visitor has been monitoring his progress and he has now been referred to the speech and language therapy service.

Student **Jill**, who is in her final year of the degree programme, has been asked to assess Billy and make some recommendations to her practice educator for intervention strategies. (Typically Jill might have three to four cases associated with this placement.) Jill arranges an appointment with Billy and his mother and goes through a detailed case history with Zoë, discussing developmental milestones, and listening to Zoë's observations about Billy's behaviour and speech. Jill also plays informally with Billy, enabling him to feel comfortable with her and using the time to observe his communicative behaviours. Based on the information from this Jill selects a series of communicative assessments which she will complete with Billy and which will give her an indication of what level of communicative ability he has and a possible working diagnosis. Part of Jill's learning involves taking study time. The proportion of study time varies from placement to placement depending on client group, stage of training of student and whether it is a half-day ongoing placement or block placement, but it is used to learn about the method for carrying out the assessments, the interpretation of the test scores and what the key purpose of each assessment is. She will also prepare and carry out a phonetic inventory of the sounds which have emerged in Billy's speech so far.

Based on the assessment results, Jill will discuss ideas with her practice educator, having first prepared the ideas by further study. She may, for example, suggest that Billy needs an audiological assessment to rule out the effect of any hearing difficulties.

Jill will bring to this case her knowledge and understanding of developmental communication difficulties in children, intervention methods and knowledge of the evidence base in this area. She will be making use of a reflective log to facilitate her understanding. She will have knowledge and use of basic listening and counselling skills in order to work with Zoë, and have prepared material and a structure for how she will provide Zoë with support and information about Billy's difficulties and the potential effects of his difficulties on his capacity for literacy and education. Jill will use her experience on other placements to complete good record-keeping and ensure that the baseline assessments are recorded in a way that can be interpreted by another speech and language therapist. When the intervention strategies are agreed with the practice educator, Jill will commence a programme of therapy. This may involve Zoë, who would have to be able to continue with the material at home (Jill will have provided Zoë with help in how to communicate with Billy and how to implement the activities). Jill would also liaise with the health visitor and the nursery which Billy attends in order to facilitate Billy's communication in the latter environment. Jill may use Billy as a case study for one of the university assessments.

The teacher in the practice setting

The changes in SLT education in the practice setting have been referred to above; there has been movement from an apprenticeship or technocratic model to the structured learning or post-technocratic approach. The role of the 'teacher' in the practice setting has also changed and with these changes the terminology to describe the 'teacher' has changed from 'supervisor' to 'clinical educator', and more recently the term 'practice educator' is emerging as the favoured label. This is in recognition of both the changes in role from supervisor to educator and the changing contexts and approaches within the profession, moving away from a medical model towards a social model.

In general, speech and language therapists may take students on placement after two years of post-qualification experience, but there is some variation. 'After two years of post-qualification experience a speech and language therapist should commit to taking students. In situations where ongoing support is available from either their own service or the HEI, speech and language therapists may take students after one year' (RCSLT, 2006a, p. 177).

Currently there is no mandatory requirement, either from the professional body (the RCSLT) or from the regulatory body (the HPC), for practice educators to undergo any training to prepare them for their role as educators in the practice setting. However, there are guidelines and standards which make recommendations regarding levels of training. The Quality Assurance Agency (2004) on behalf of the HPC produced generic standards of education and training guidance for education providers, and a section of these relate specifically to the practice setting. These standards state that there is an expectation that practice educators will have relevant qualifications and experience and, unless otherwise agreed, must undertake practice educator training.

More recently the RCSLT (2006b) published profession-specific standards and an audit tool, *National Standards for Practice-Based Learning*. This document contains standards for practice educators, for the university and for students. These standards reflect the guidance from the HPC and state that the university, in partnership with the placement provider, will provide training for practice educators in practice-based learning; this will consist of initial training followed by ongoing training opportunities. The standards also require that practice educators will engage with the training arranged by the university. There is therefore an expectation that initial and ongoing training will be provided and that practice educators will engage with this.

Courses to prepare practice educators for their role have traditionally been provided and financed by the universities and have varied in both length and depth. In the past, practice educators with a specific interest in student education would attend an annual workshop or study day hosted by the local university. The main aims of these events were information-sharing, informing the attendees of any developments and changes in course content or assessment methods, and including discussion around supervision and feedback methods.

With the development of practice education to the structured learning or post-technocratic approach there have been changes in the focus and content of practice educator preparation. There has been a move away from the information-sharing events to structured preparation courses, the content of which now includes theories and approaches from the adult learning literature. The courses aim to extend practice educators' knowledge of adult learning and teaching, to increase their skills in teaching and assessment and to encourage them to reflect on their own teaching practice.

Alongside the changes in focus and content in preparation courses, there has been expansion in length and depth of some courses from the one-day workshop to four-day courses or modules of post-registration master's programmes. However, attendance at the longer courses has been limited, with problems with geographical or time access, lack of workplace support for attendance and lack of motivation having been cited as reasons for this. McAllister and Lincoln (2004) have noted similar findings in Australia. One response to this has been the development of a distance-learning package (Baxter and Gray, 2006). Individual educators can use this for self-study or it can be used as a training package which can be delivered locally within each practice provider environment. The professional body (the RCSLT) has no accreditation scheme for these types of courses currently, although some are recognized as credits towards postgraduate qualifications. The present situation, therefore, in the preparation of practice educators, is the provision by universities of some one-day courses, some longer courses and more recently the development of a distance-learning package. Funding of the initial training courses is within the context of the contract between universities and strategic health authorities. An example of the content and aims of a typical course are outlined in Table 11.1.

Table 11.1   Content of a typical clinical educator course for speech and language therapists

Aim:
To enable participants to:
- Extend their awareness of learning and the learning needs of their students.
- Develop and increase their skills in teaching, assessment and evaluation.
- Review and continue to improve their teaching practices.

Learning objectives:
- Produce aims and learning objectives for own teaching.
- Use a structured approach when planning teaching and learning activities.
- Select a small group method or approach and plan its use for a chosen topic.
- Employ strategies to involve individual students actively in their learning.
- Manage student learning problems constructively.
- Link assessment strategies to learning objectives.
- Give and receive constructive feedback.
- Use reflection as a basis for developing teaching practices.

The content would include:
- Exploring concepts of learning, learning approaches, and the implications for practice learning.
- Differentiating aims from objectives; levels and domains of objectives; writing objectives for teaching; competency outcomes for clinical skills.
- Strategies for working with individual students to enable learning: providing a structure for students' observations; using small group methods to involve students actively in their learning.
- Structuring learning the role of the tutor.
- Managing students; looking at ways of supporting students, developing their potential, addressing problems (such as poor performance, lack of interest or motivation).
- Characteristics of effective feedback, using constructive criticism, responding positively to feedback.
- Assessing learning and evaluating teaching.

The university is also responsible for maintaining and enhancing the quality of practice-based learning; this is partly addressed through the provision of suitable training courses and ongoing support to practice educators from the university. Quality monitoring is done through post-placement feedback, from the student to the university and from the placement provider to the university. The standards documents already cited (RCSLT, 2006b) set out guidelines for audit and monitoring activities to ensure and facilitate the quality of practice-based learning. Quality is monitored through the usual systems in place within universities but also through the contract review process between the university and the Department of Health.

In terms of enhancement of standards, the individual educator may be influenced by both internal and external factors. External motivators are expectations from the professional body, the regulatory body and the individual strategic health authorities. The RCSLT explicitly states the importance of the provision of practice education for the development and future of the profession and it recognizes this in the professional standards document, *Communicating Quality, 3* (RCSLT, 2006a). The RCSLT also recognizes that practice learning is beneficial to the educators in terms of developing reflective practice. This can also be recorded in each individual's CPD log. There are no additional honoraria, since remuneration for the supervision of students has been incorporated into salary scales for speech and language therapists for many years and this is still the case with the introduction of *Agenda for Change* within the NHS (DoH, 2001f). There is also an expectation from strategic health authorities that practice learning providers will have adequate placement capacity to meet the requirements of local workforce plans although this is not monitored formally. Motivating factors are not profession-specific and include such factors as continued learning, professional and personal development and the enjoyment of interacting with students.

The content and structure of the students' learning

The core subject areas in speech and language therapy require the integration of information from a broad interdisciplinary knowledge base and include typical and atypical communication, specific communication impairments (adult and paediatric), linguistics, phonetics, biomedical sciences, psychology, dysphagia and clinical method. All of these areas address the assessment, management and intervention approaches across all types of communication impairment.

Each university providing pre-registration courses develops and designs the content and structure of SLT students' practice education in partnership with the local strategic health authority. The RCSLT and HPC set out requirements that each course must meet, but in terms of practice education the requirements are fairly general and state the number of learning hours under the supervision of a qualified practitioner rather than the specific content of the hours. The learning hours must include a diversity of clients and contexts. Therefore each pre-registration course in the UK has different models of practice learning in place. Some courses exclusively use a block placement model, where students may be placed for up to 19 weeks in an NHS setting; others have regular weekly placements where students are based in the university but visit a practice setting once a week. There are advantages and disadvantages to each model and most courses now use a combination of both.

Despite the diverse content of practice learning for the various courses in the UK it is possible to pull out some commonalities. Every course has a clinical curriculum, which focuses on the development of clinical competencies and fitness to practise: there is recognition that this is a developmental process and practice learning is designed accordingly.

A useful framework is provided by McAllister and Lincoln (2004) who describe the developmental journey SLT students undertake on their path towards entry-level competency. This involves the transition from novice to intermediate and finally to entry-level student. These requirements are recognized in the design and delivery of clinical curricula. The typical pattern of learning involves students being taught about the definitions and theory of a communication impairment before entering a placement to apply this knowledge. The following example illustrates the way this works.

Frank Sunderland lives in Number 7, Green Hill flats, with his wife, **Edith**. They are both 75 years old. Frank suffered a stroke a month ago and he has been in acute care in a stroke unit having speech and language therapy as an inpatient from the speech and language therapy department based on the stroke unit. He will return home and continue with speech and language therapy, provided by the community speech and language therapy team. His difficulties include dysphagia and aphasia.

Frank and Edith have campaigned in order to keep their local shop open and Frank has been the chair of his local neighbourhood watch scheme. For these activities Frank has needed to have good communication skills, talking and negotiating with people outside his immediate community. Edith has developed diabetes in the last year and also has to wear a hearing aid.

Students will learn about dysphagia (swallowing difficulties) and aphasia (acquired language communication impairment) in the university setting. The teaching will include signs and symptoms of stroke, classification of swallowing disorders, and definition and classification of aphasic difficulties. Understanding aphasia will require specific teaching about linguistics, how the different components of language can break down in aphasia, cognitive psychology to explain how language is processed in the brain, and social psychology to discuss the personal impact of losing communication ability. The teaching about dysphagia will include specific understanding of the structures involved in the swallowing process and how these may be disordered. Students will learn about methods of assessing both the aphasic difficulty and the dysphagic problems. They will then learn about management of these conditions. Their learning will be ordered through various routes, including lecture formats, inquiry-based learning, case-based thinking, interactive work between students and use of video demonstrations for sample patients.

Frank will probably have had help with swallowing while on the ward and this will include being given specific types of pre-prepared foods to eat. He will have been encouraged to practise communication tasks and his wife will have been advised about ways to facilitate his communication. Frank may have been lent a computer to practise language exercises, such as matching up written words to pictures.

A student who has been placed on Frank's ward will have been able to observe the assessment of his difficulties and learn about the early stages of stroke in terms of both symptomology and the patient's personal experience of it. Case-based work may include the student following up methods for assessing language in the early stages of stroke, investigating approaches for helping carers to understand the nature of communication difficulties and writing a reflective log during this placement. The student will also have been able to see the effect the stroke has on Frank's wife, Edith. Edith may have been given leaflets to take home and read to help her understanding of stroke and communication impairments. Possibly both Frank and Edith have been able to attend a group meeting while on the ward so that they can meet other people in the same situation. The student would observe this meeting.

Another student may be placed in the community speech and language therapy team and this might enable the student to go and see Frank and Edith on Frank's return home to Green Hill flats. The student may be involved in the therapy management of Frank and be able to monitor the progress he is able to make over the next few months. The learning outcomes would include the following: understanding change over time in a person with aphasia and dysphagia; understanding the impact on a family when there is a stroke; understanding how aphasia and dysphagia present in a real patient; achieving a range of assessment and diagnostic skills and planning of intervention strategies; understanding how speech and language therapy services work; and understanding more about professional methods of working with people.

Methods

Students have different needs at each level and will therefore require varying intensities and types of support from their practice educators. Practice-based workshops are a typical approach to preparation for the placement. Often initial practice experiences are highly controlled and protected. These may take place in university clinical settings where group teaching of clinical methods is easier to arrange. Students often work in groups, planning and preparing assessment and therapy materials together with direct support and advice from their practice educator. Intervention is delivered under direct supervision; that is, the practice educator would be present in the therapy room with the students. It is common for pairs of students to work with the client; client contact is limited, allowing time for discussion, reflection and planning after each contact.

At the intermediate level students may work in pairs or individually with one practice educator and at this level supervision may be off-site with intensive pre-placement workshops and the practice educator working collaboratively with the student. An example of this is the innovative work reported by Baxter (2004) where pairs of students are provided with a mainstream school placement. Typically, speech and language therapists visit schools and assess and suggest therapy approaches for children identified by teachers and then work collaboratively with the teachers to manage a programme of remediation. Initially, the whole cohort of students are given a series of workshops on the university site to prepare them for the school placement. The pairs of students are taken to the school by the practice educator for the first session and then the two students visit the school on two afternoons each week for eight weeks. The students receive support visits from the university tutor and supervision is via a reflective log and meetings with the university tutor. While on the placement the students spend time in the classroom observing the children who have been identified as of concern regarding their communication. The students are given opportunities to assess and develop some therapy materials with specific children under the guidance of the teacher and the practice educator. Feedback from students, schools and practice educators is that this method provides real-life opportunities for students to work safely in the context of the school structure but still take responsibility for working with children on their communication. In addition the schools are appreciative of the additional speech and language therapy time available to these children.

Students who are approaching graduation would be expected to perform most of their clinical work independently and work consultatively with the practice educator. Typically, a student might be placed in a hospital environment where there might be a caseload of mainly clients with voice problems who would usually be referred through the Ear, Nose and Throat Department. The student would be given responsibility for three or four clients and be expected to assess and plan their therapy and management, independently but with consultation with the practice educator. The student session may be video-recorded with permission from the client and this may be played back to the practice educator for discussion and feedback.

All placements will have stated learning outcomes, which will have been provided for the practice educator and student at the start of the placement. Common practice is to provide a level or year handbook with details of outcomes for that year, along with detailed descriptions about other placements, the assessment outlines, information about reflective logs, self-evaluation forms, health and safety and risk assessment.

Assessment

The variability and commonalities in the content of students' practice learning has been described above, and this is reflected in assessment methods. Each university has its own particular model of assessment but again there are significant similarities which can be highlighted. All degree programmes have the same aim, which is to produce competent speech and language therapists who are fit for award, purpose and practice. Therefore the learning outcomes for practice learning and the evaluation of these reflect this.

In recognition of the philosophy of partnership working and that practice education is the joint responsibility of both the universities and practitioners, assessment of students is usually done collaboratively by the practice educators and visiting tutors from the universities. This may not be the case for each practice learning experience but certainly nearing the end of a pre-registration course this would be common. There are two main methods of assessment used: the first is the assessment of competence, where a practice educator will measure a student's strengths and weaknesses by completing a competency-based evaluation form at the end of a practice learning experience; this is an end-point assessment after a period of continuous assessment. The second method is the assessment of performance, where a university tutor will visit the student at the site of practice learning and observe their performance with a particular client and rate this in terms of competencies. This may be a client with whom the student is familiar or a client new to the student – the latter is often referred to as an unseen exam and is employed by most universities as a final practice assessment to measure fitness for purpose before graduation. A student would usually have several performance assessments during a pre-registration course.

Progression through the practice curriculum of a pre-registration course is dependent on successful completion of each level; therefore a student has to be judged to be competent at each level before progression to the next. The majority of students progress through each level of the course with no difficulties.

The procedures invoked for situations where students are not successful include provision of additional practice learning with enhanced support and specific learning objectives.

If we return to the student **Jill** who was working with **Billy Benner**, we note that Jill's practice educator began to have concerns about Jill's knowledge, skills and approach to learning at the start of her period of practice education. Jill arrived at her induction session with very little evidence of pre-placement planning; she had no personal learning objectives and demonstrated very limited knowledge of the client group she was going to be working with. During the first session Jill had the opportunity to observe her practice educator carrying out an initial assessment of a child and taking a case history. The practice educator provided Jill with the referral information for Billy and they began to prepare for Billy's initial appointment, which was scheduled for the following week. Jill was asked to arrive prepared for the next session with a detailed session plan, taking into account how to use the time available to achieve the session objectives. Jill did arrive with a plan for Billy and had considered what activities and tasks she might use to obtain the information she needed; however, during the actual session Jill struggled to gain Billy's cooperation and demonstrated very little empathy with **Zoë**. The practice educator had to intervene and continue the session whilst Jill observed.

Following the session, Jill was given the opportunity to reflect on her performance. She felt that her performance had been fine and did not understand why the practice educator had needed to intervene. The practice educator gave Jill explicit feedback about her strengths and weaknesses and they agreed to take the session with Billy jointly the following week. Despite detailed feedback and the use of video recording to facilitate the feedback process, and discussion with tutors at the university, Jill made little progress during her placement. She showed specific difficulties applying her theoretical knowledge to the practice setting; she did not demonstrate the skills to manage a session in terms of flow of activities and timing; she also struggled to interact appropriately with both Billy and Zoë and struggled to reflect on her performance in any meaningful way. Given these weaknesses, Jill did not meet the required level of competence on the end-point assessment from her practice educator or on the performance assessment completed by a university tutor.

Jill was very distressed by her assessment results, and she was given very detailed and specific feedback from her practice educator, the university tutor and her course director. She was given the opportunity to have an additional period of practice learning with specific learning objectives developed from her areas of identified weakness. If Jill's performance does not reach the required level of competence then she would fail this module of the course and, as with all other modules, would need to retake this during the next academic year before she could proceed with the rest of the course. During Jill's time out from the course she would be encouraged to get involved in activities which would facilitate her progress, for example, voluntary work in a nursery. If after a further re-sit Jill was still unsuccessful then she would be required to leave the course.

Continuing professional development

Both the RCSLT and the HPC require members to undertake continuing professional development. The HPC is proposing that this will be linked to the re-registration process in the future and a recent consultation process with registrants has taken place. The HPC have defined CPD as covering work-based learning, professional activity such as being a member of a specialist interest group, any sort of formal or informal courses, higher degrees and self-directed learning through reading journal articles, updating knowledge and, also, public service for the profession.

In 2004 the RCSLT made changes to its existing CPD requirements so that future records could be based on outcomes. The new approach requires members to maintain records of the impact of their learning on day-to-day practice, as well as the record of the learning activity itself; thus it is a reflective log. It has also recently launched two new developments; these are a CPD toolkit (which will include guidance on different CPD activities) and an interactive CPD diary system (which will allow members to record all their CPD activities online).

Current debates

Methods for teaching SLT have been at the forefront of the debate in pre-registration education. The traditional model of acquisition of knowledge first, to be followed by a skills-based approach, has been replaced by a recognition of the student's need to learn from a case-based formula from the start of their training. The methodology for teaching students how to become reflective practitioners who can use problem-solving skills is a key area for discussion in this profession (Whitworth et al., 2004). New research into the way SLT students learn to reason clinically has shown that they experience difficulties in the same way as those observed in medicine or other health-related professions (Hoben et al., 2007). Based on evaluation of verbal comments made by pairs of SLT students while watching assessments of three 'virtual' patients on an electronic patient database, a range of competence was demonstrated across 34 participants. Further work into the clinical reasoning process of SLT students is ongoing.

Whatever the level of sophistication of understanding into student learning we reach, we are still dependent on the amount and quality of the placement opportunities. There are continued difficulties in obtaining the required number of work placements for each pre-registration course. Many universities have created their own clinics in order to create a work-based environment for additional student learning. The aim of all courses is to provide a work-based placement which reflects the subject area studied by the students at each developmental point in the degree. However, that creates substantial difficulties in location of the placements as the educational need is for placements which reflect the subject area but also provide a common experience to the student cohort. As SLT is a specialized subject area, this is an additional difficulty. With the increase in student numbers the student placement issue remains an ongoing problem and this is widely recognized both in SLT research (Gascoigne and Parker, 2001) and

Department of Health guidance papers (*Meeting the Challenge,* DoH, 2000c; *Preparation of Mentors and Teachers,* DoH, 2001c).

Gascoigne and Parker (2001) is one of the few evidence-based papers to have considered these issues. The authors found that, in the early 1990s, there was great variation in how many placements were offered to universities. Evidence from the RCSLT working party on clinical experience (RCSLT, 1995) established that some SLT services offered no placement opportunities to students, whereas four services offered more than 30 sessions of placement per WTE member of staff in one year. The reasons for this have been reported as the lack of appropriately trained staff, general staffing matters such as unfilled posts, and increased student numbers. Gascoigne and Parker argued that these commonly cited reasons could obscure the real reasons which are related to the model of education adopted in the UK for health care professionals. Since this paper, changes to methods in clinical teaching have been established, although there remains a difficulty in finding enough placements.

The use of IT in the learning process has been well documented and represents a move forward in NHS policy (Milburn, 2001; DoH, 2001b). However, it is in the area of specifically designed computer-assisted learning packages for SLT students where there has been the most development and discussion (Freeman, 2004). Web-based learning is one method by which students can move from the traditional face-to-face teaching to more student-centred approaches. Hooper's (2002) course website on voice disorder and voice therapy is a key example of how students can interact with the website and gain increased insight and understanding into this area of communication impairments. Similarly, PATSy (www.patsy.ac.uk), which is a web-based multimedia database shell designed to make 'virtual patients' available to students (and professionals) has been used successfully on many of the pre-registration courses. Where the debate must now go is into providing evidence that IT approaches work; whether they work as a substitute for face-to-face teaching or as an enhancement of live work-based learning.

As with all other health care courses SLT has been encouraged to make use of more patient-centred learning and to engage patients in the development of the curriculum. SLT has had a long history of inviting patients into lecture classes for demonstration purposes. This has worked well in some contexts. For example, an adult with a stammer who has been having therapy will be pleased to take the opportunity to come into a lecture and use the situation to develop their speaking skills in a public setting. Where there remains a level of uncertainty is in the area of inviting patients to form part of the curriculum process. Many types of communication impairments leave patients with severe reading difficulties (aphasic speakers will have associated reading problems) or difficulties with expressing an informed opinion (traumatic brain-injured speakers may have pragmatic problems, autistic spectrum speakers may also have expressive difficulties) and so it is difficult to obtain a representative sample of the patient population who can contribute easily to debates about curriculum. This is not to imply that the educators do not try, but we are aware that there are specific issues associated with our patient groups which make this difficult. Work is ongoing in this area (Young et al., 2006).

Interprofessional education is another area where government health care policy is driving change. Interprofessional education is stated as a key feature of NHS education (DoH, 2000c). We note the lack of clarity on what constitutes interprofessional learning and also what impact interprofessional education has on working practice. Although there are many initiatives to use this form of learning in allied health courses across the UK, there remains a limited literature on evidence to show the effects of interprofessional learning in the post-qualification work-based setting. SLT students have frequently been taught alongside other students of allied health professions, medicine, dentistry or psychology. The methods for integrating real interprofessional awareness, however, have developed in different ways in different universities. For example, in Sheffield we provide interprofessional workshops at a clinic site where a range of professionals learn about how to evaluate a person with an acquired communication impairment and discuss their professional views.

There has been some flexibility in the design of qualifying courses in SLT as each one has developed. The types of courses now range from a 3½-year undergraduate degree, a four-year undergraduate degree, a postgraduate diploma and a master's level route. All of these lead to a recognized qualification in SLT. The future may require some modification of this, but to date the range of qualifying routes remains well received within the professional community.

Future developments

At the time of writing the NHS debt may influence the future of speech and language therapy, both in terms of the number of posts available in the UK and the subsequent number of student places funded in universities.

The education of a speech and language therapist is a responsive and proactive process. The profession and the universities will need to remain vigilant in order to respond to changes in the broad political environment, changes in the evidence base for clinical practice and teaching and learning methodology. For a relatively small profession we believe we have made some exciting progress in the latter part of the twentieth century. The educational process has the infrastructure to support and maintain new developments and we anticipate a time of interesting and stimulating further growth.

Core text recommendations

Brumfitt, S.M. (ed.) (2004), *Innovations in Professional Education for Speech and Language Therapy*, London and Philadelphia, PA: Whurr.

McAllister, L., and Lincoln, M. (2004), *Clinical Education in Speech and Language Pathology*, London: Whurr.

McAllister, L., Lincoln, M., McLeod, S., and Maloney, D. (1997), *Facilitating Learning in Clinical Settings*, Cheltenham: Stanley Thornes.

Part III

Interprofessional education

12 Interprofessional practice education and learning

Kate Leonard and Jenny Weinstein

Introduction

When asked to evaluate the experience of their professional courses, most health and care professionals value practice learning experiences above theoretical input because actually working with service users was their reason for doing the course. 'Practice learning essentially takes the specific practice event as the central source of learning. It also includes the cognitive and feeling aspects of that work as well as the behavioural' (Evans, 1999, p. 4). These findings are supported in studies such as Glen and Leiba (2004) who review the research in this area which, although not conclusive, points us towards the likelihood that the learning opportunities with most positive outcomes take place in the practice setting. Active learning can be put into practice with students from different professions enabled to work with the same users in a community such as the Green Hill estate (see examples below). This approach enables them to address key aspects identified by Barr et al. (2005): self, team, group and organizational change as well as service user perspectives which, in our view, must be at the heart of any interprofessional learning.

The weak but developing evidence base about the effectiveness of interprofessional education (IPE) in practice is supported by Zwarenstein et al. (2005) and Freeth et al. (2006) who undertook widespread studies of evaluations of IPE and found that, while there was little evidence for the effectiveness of college-based IPE at pre-registration level, there was a growing body of research indicating that IPE was effective once people were out in practice. The evaluation study of four pilot common learning sites (Miller et al., 2006) also found that while HEI-based initiatives were less popular with students, student groups involved in practice-based initiatives were cohesive, irrespective of professional membership. 'The role of the client in IPE helped illuminate what was congruent and what was diverse amongst professional roles and responsibilities' (Miller et al., 2006, p. xv). By working together with a real patient or client, it was much easier for student professionals to understand how their roles overlapped or differed and to realize why working collaboratively would make a real difference to the human being who was being helped.

Because of the changes in the way health and care services are delivered (Whittington, 2003a), IPE can no longer be seen as an 'add-on' to the curriculum nor can it be usefully delivered as a 'stand-alone' unit of learning – it has to move into the mainstream (Barr and Ross, 2006). 'The emphasis on multi-professional teams and clinical networks as the means of delivering a clear service driven *Agenda for Change* has implications for education ...' This means 'moving from the current predominance of uni-professional education programmes to those that are primarily interprofessional' (Hughes, 2006). 'The complexity of interprofessional and inter-agency work requires that the gaps and conflicts between different professional perspectives and practices should not only be bridged but creatively exploited' (Low and Weinstein, 2000, p. 216).

Three layers of interprofessional learning will be considered in this chapter: teaching professionally qualifying students, teaching practice educators to prepare students from their own profession, and teaching practice educators to provide learning and to contribute to the assessment of different professions. In order to contribute to a more explicit knowledge base for IPE (Whittington, 2003b) we aim to bring together information and recommendations from a range of evaluation/research studies with examples from our own experience of interprofessional education in practice. The term 'practice educator' will be used generically to describe colleagues from any profession who teach and assess students in practice (sometimes referred to as 'mentor', 'practice teacher' or 'practice assessor').

The nature and function of interprofessional learning

'Interprofessional education is an initiative to secure interprofessional learning and promote gains through interprofessional collaboration in professional practice' (Freeth et al., 2005, p. 11). IPE is not simply about students from different professions attending lectures together; in order to develop skills for interprofessional working students must actively learn together by, for example, considering issues or case examples and discussing them or, most effectively, working on them together 'live' in practice. In our experience, many students, especially those studying at pre-registration levels, can feel quite resistant to IPE. They resent time being taken away from their 'real' course of studies and do not see the relevance of learning with students from different professions. On those occasions when the IPE is delivered simply to 'tick a curriculum box' and has not been appropriately planned and delivered, students may feel that their concerns were justified and that the time was wasted. Unless the necessary time and planning are invested, IPE can be counterproductive. However, positive IPE experiences as described in some of the examples in this chapter, although resource-intensive and challenging to organize, are, in our experience, highly valued by the students.

The Brambleton Mental Health Trust and Northtown University have agreed to provide their mental health students with an interprofessional practice learning opportunity in their second year of practice. The students involved are mental health nursing students, medical students, student social workers and student occupational therapists, all of whom are on placement in the Trust.

All the students meet together for half a day with a facilitator to share their views and experiences of interprofessional working and to learn more about each other's roles. They are then divided into mixed groups to undertake visits to service users. **Mike**, a student doctor, **Bola**, a student mental health nurse, **Mina**, a student social worker, and **Giles**, a student occupational therapist, are allocated to visit **Jason Dean** and **Sam Weiner** at Number 2, Derby Street.

Jason and Sam have given their prior agreement to meeting the students as a group and supporting their interprofessional learning, even though, at the moment, Sam is quite unwell. Jason and Sam have often complained that the different services do not work together; they have to tell the same story over and over again; and one department does not know what the other is doing – so they are keen to help.

Prior to the visit, the group of students meet to look at the case notes. They then discuss their respective roles and how they each think they might work with the service users. They also identify areas of potential overlap and areas where they may need to collaborate to provide a holistic assessment of need.

They agree that Mike and Bola will jointly consider Sam's mental health difficulties, the treatment he is receiving and his views about how this is working. Mina will focus on Jason from the perspectives of how he feels he is progressing and on his needs as a carer for Sam. She will also explore the social needs of Sam. Giles will think about the needs of both service users and talk to them about whether there are any other activities that they could engage in together to improve their well-being.

In discussion, the students realize how much their roles overlap and how hard it is to draw clear lines between their different responsibilities. For example, Mike (student doctor) and Bola (student nurse) have different ideas about the treatment plan and the student social worker and student occupational therapist feel that their roles overlap in relation to helping the carer to access some support and leisure activities. Each professional views him/herself as providing a holistic model of assessment and therefore does not want to be confined to one aspect. It is interesting for the group to resolve differences and explore what emphasis they place on different aspects of the assessment such as diagnosis, treatment, care planning, social and medical needs of the user and needs of the carer

Following their visit, they have a further opportunity to have a meeting with their fellow students and each group provides a presentation of the work they have done together and there is time for critical reflection and identification of learning outcomes.

Interprofessional learning in practice combines the three main elements of professional education (Eraut, 1994) – propositional knowledge, personal knowledge and process knowledge. Propositional knowledge specific to each profession can be shared to offer a greater understanding of each other's role and knowledge base. Process knowledge is particularly relevant here – 'knowing how to conduct the various processes that contribute to professional action' (Eraut, 1994, p. 107) – and the 'value added' elements of IPE mean that this will be in relation to the processes involved in the work of *other* professions as well as their own. As in the example above, an effective interprofessional practice learning experience will offer the participants the opportunity to reflect on their learning and enhance their ability to give and receive feedback, utilizing both experiential learning and Schön's (1987) reflection-in-action paradigm.

Undergraduate education

Enthusiasm for and commitment to the development of IPE at undergraduate level has to be tempered with a health warning. In spite of the agreement between the NHS Executive and the Committee of Vice Chancellors and Principals (NHSE/CVCP, 2000) to provide a long-term, stable basis for the relationship between the NHS and higher education, including a shared commitment to the development of interprofessional education, the delivery of effective IPE for pre-registration students still involves overcoming barriers such as those identified by Low and Weinstein in 2000:

- structural barriers
- communication problems and cultural differences
- funding arrangements for both teachers and students
- different lengths of programmes
- timetable problems
- curricula issues and assessment processes
- different requirements of statutory bodies.

Six years later Freeth et al. (2006) found:

- ongoing scepticism because of the lack of tangible evidence about the effectiveness of interprofessional education
- vulnerability of trainers and facilitators when working with other professional groups and concern about being criticized for not meeting needs of particular groups
- continued dependence on a skilled and enthusiastic champion to enable initiatives to succeed and survive.

It is interesting that these barriers continue to exist despite the commonality of so many learning outcomes for students of different professions. Thus, for example, the common curriculum content of nine health and care professions was analysed in order to develop a shared curriculum for a government-funded study of IPE known as the 'New Generation Project' (O'Halloran et al., 2006) and the QAA benchmark statements for a range of professions were mapped into an *Interprofessional Capability Framework* by Gordon and Walsh (2005).

An exemplar set of collaborative competences adapted from Barr (1998) and Weinstein (1998) to be assessed in the training of all health and care professionals are the ability to:

- describe one's roles and responsibilities clearly to other professions and carry out own professional role competently
- keep other professionals closely informed about work with people whom they have referred or with whom they are working
- communicate and negotiate clearly and without jargon, orally and in writing, within small interprofessional groups, allied agencies and other organizations

- recognize and respect the roles, responsibilities and competence of other professions in relation to one's own, knowing when, where and how to involve those others through agreed channels
- work with other professions to review services, effect change, solve problems and improve standards
- work with other professions to assess, plan, provide and review care for service users and carers
- acknowledge and resolve interprofessional/inter-agency conflict or differences, openly and constructively
- encourage and facilitate the active involvement of users, carers, care workers or fellow professionals who, by reason of status, gender, race or other structural disadvantage, may feel less confident about their role or contribution
- facilitate or constructively contribute to interprofessional case conferences, meetings, team working and networking.

The interprofessional practice example presented above would offer the participating students the opportunity to demonstrate all these competences, which are, to a greater or lesser extent, part of the assessed curriculum for most health and care professionals. Unfortunately, the degree to which these competences are actually used, how or if they are assessed, what criteria/methods are employed, or whether students are ever failed for not demonstrating competence in interprofessional working, has not been thoroughly researched, although Miller et al. (2006) have undertaken some useful investigations discussed below.

Both authors of this chapter have been involved in developing IPE over many years and have come to the conclusion that barriers to effective interprofessional education will remain until there is a significant shift in the way professional education is delivered – in particular radical change would be required in the current regulatory approach of statutory and professional bodies. It seems contradictory that the impetus for IPE was driven by service user need for seamless care delivery and yet the emphasis of education statutory bodies remains on the *profession* rather than the needs of clients/patients/service users.

Maria is a student paediatric nurse who wanted an interprofessional placement in the community where she would gain enormously from working with families such as **Zoë Benner**'s at Number 1, Green Hill flats. A local children's centre would have offered an ideal placement for Maria to gain this opportunity but she was unable to go there because the qualified nurse who used to work there left and was replaced in post by a qualified social work practice educator. The fact that the social worker was doing exactly the same job as the nurse had been doing was not acceptable to the Nursing and Midwifery Council who insist that only a qualified nurse mentor can sign off a nursing student. The only way the placement could be facilitated was if an off-site practice educator with relevant qualifications was employed by the trust to work closely with the on-site supervisor who was the social work practice educator. It is interesting to note that statutory bodies such as the GSCC and the NMC now expect to see IPE built into the structure of programmes and evidence of students demonstrating IP competence in practice – and yet the inflexibility of their rules and regulations, especially with regard to teaching and assessment in practice, can stifle creative opportunities for delivery.

In spite of the significant amount of time and resources required to facilitate interprofessional practice learning for pre-registration students (Glen and Reeves, 2004; Dyer and Mathews, 2005), such opportunities are considered to be worthwhile according to criteria of effectiveness suggested by Freeth et al. (2006, p. 34) because they will:

- make participants more positive about learning with and from other professions
- enable participants to gain knowledge to improve their direct practice with/care for service users
- offer a stimulating learning experience because of its interactive nature and the diversity of participants.

Nevertheless, while there may be some impact on students' attitudes, knowledge and skills, there is, at the time of writing, no evidence to substantiate improved organizational practice or outcomes for patients from these college-led undergraduate initiatives (Barr et al., 2005).

A model of interprofessional education in practice

Adapting Kolb's (1984) cycle, a model is provided at Figure 12.1 for IPE in practice at pre-registration level. It is essential that this learning is facilitated by a professional who has been trained to deliver IPE (see section on IPE facilitation below).

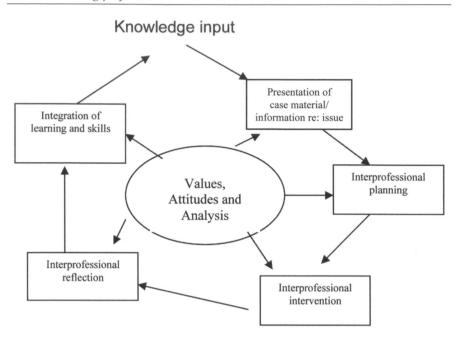

Figure 12.1   Interprofessional practice learning cycle
Source: Leonard and Weinstein, 2007.

Ideally, during their programme of study, students would be given the opportunity to travel through this cycle in each of their three years, thus integrating and deepening their knowledge as described by Areskog (1994) in a Swedish university. The reality in the UK is that many faculties can only manage to deliver a 'one-off' interprofessional learning opportunity during the three years and, where this is not part of the mainstream curriculum and does not attract credits, students can be sceptical about its value (Barr et al., 2005).

Range of interprofessional practice learning opportunities

The literature now offers information about a plethora of IPE projects that describe different approaches to delivering practice-based IPE. These include:

- college courses jointly facilitated with service users (for example, Mohr et al., 2006)
- interprofessional interventions on in-patient units (for example, Guest et al., 2002; Lamb and Lewandowski, 2005; Anderson et al., 2006)
- the use of problem/enquiry-based learning (Miller et al., 2001; Reynolds, 2003)
- home/community visits and interviews by interprofessional groups of students of patients/clients/service users (Anderson and Lennox, 2005; Van der Horst et al., 1995)
- the use of realistic scenarios and cases (Kilminster et al., 2003)
- the use of 'Sim Man' patient simulators (Huish and McMorran, 2005)
- e-learning applications such as the 'Virtual Family' (Pearce, 2005)
- development of 'collaborative learning sites' with an IPL capability framework as a learning and assessment tool, a model for interprofessional mentorship and some meaningful IP learning opportunities (Miller et al., 2006).

East Town University has a large health and social care faculty with strong links to the local teaching hospital. In each of their three years all medical, health and social work students are mixed in interprofessional groups for two weeks of interprofessional learning. All sessions are co-facilitated by academics from different professions and the emphasis is on students learning from each other during the first week and focusing on case studies requiring interprofessional input in the second week. On placement, students are encouraged to collaborate with other students from different professions as described below.

Frank Sunderland, from Number 7, Green Hill flats, was in the stroke unit at the City hospital. As part of their interprofessional practice experience, a medical student, nursing student, occupational therapy student, physiotherapy student and social work student met to discuss his rehabilitation plan. Very valuable learning was gained because **Edith**, Frank's carer, was very keen for him to come home immediately and the social work student advocated on her behalf as well as assessing the risks and needs of Frank and balancing these to help make decisions. The health care students were much more cautious, identifying many risks to Edith's health if she took on the care of Frank when she herself was unwell, and they were able to provide detailed information on the medical diagnosis and needs of Frank. The medical student was under pressure to encourage the social worker to make a discharge plan and was keen to release the bed. Resolving the conflict and negotiating a discharge plan that took on board the needs of both the user and carer offered a challenging interprofessional learning opportunity for this group of students.

Each student was expected to write up the experience as part of an assessed piece of work for their course so as to demonstrate both an understanding of the theory of interprofessional working and to evidence their own competence in team working and communication with different professionals.

Training the interprofessional education trainers

The complexities of delivering IPE mean that any initiative will take longer to plan and implement than a uni-professional learning initiative. Bray and Howkins (2006) found that collaboration is difficult at all levels and requires institutions to make explicit the value base from which they are engaging in IPE. One of the most essential but most time-consuming elements is ensuring that the trainers or facilitators of IPE are themselves well prepared to deliver the training. According to Miller et al. (2006), some staff in practice areas asked to deliver IPE expressed concerns about workloads although there was no evidence of negative effects on service caused by participation in the projects. It appeared that those practitioners who expressed these concerns were less convinced about the benefits of IPE. This study also noted that practitioners often expressed anxiety and a lack of confidence about taking on the role of practice facilitator. However, once they had actually experienced facilitating a group, they were able to own the skills and knowledge that they could offer and became more confident; they valued the additional opportunities for their own development that facilitation of IPE offered.

The facilitator of the group of students described in the practice example immediately above was a social work practice educator. She had done a two-day interprofessional facilitators course but she was very anxious because the majority of students were from health care professions. However, once the discussions commenced, she found that her skills in managing group dynamics, helping students to express their views, and reflecting her observations back to the group were generic skills and it was these generic skills that would enable the students to learn. She also helped them to involve and empower the service user and carer and to critically reflect on the process in preparation for writing their assignments.

Research indicates that the professional background of a facilitator is less important to students than their facilitation skills (Miller et al., 2006) and according to Bray and Howkins (2006) the actual skills required for IPE facilitation are not really different from the skills required by any competent facilitator:

- awareness and use of self
- dealing with difference and conflict
- group process and relationships
- power dimensions – facilitator and group
- context, planning, authenticity of process.

We would add:

- addressing prejudices, stereotypes and projections
- dealing with diversity and modelling cultural competence
- being learner-centred
- creating an interprofessional culture
- setting ground rules for interprofessional participation
- challenging participants to take risks by interacting with people from a different profession
- using examples from the range of professions present and encouraging participants to bring examples from their professional perspective
- providing a 'jargon sheet' to interpret each other's professional acronyms
- modelling open-mindedness and willingness to learn from other professions.

The Preparation for Interprofessional Learning and Teaching Project (PIPE, 2006) recommends that prospective IPE facilitators from different professions need to explore together:

- the notion of IPE as a philosophy or approach
- the centrality of context power and hierarchy
- perceived, intended and expected outcomes of IPE
- the need for students to experience good models of interprofessional collaboration in educational and clinical settings.

The role of the practice educator and designing interprofessional learning opportunities

Developing interprofessional learning opportunities in practice

The ability to provide a stimulating environment that models and teaches critically reflective and evidence-based interprofessional practice is essential in preparing people for the changing working environment where professionals from a range of agencies are now working together in either virtual or actual teams. On the other hand, poor interprofessional practice can reflect values and attitudes that are discriminatory and unprofessional and do not keep the user at the heart of the service provided.

Although interprofessional practice is now a competence on which most professionals have to be assessed in the workplace, some practice educators do not always identify interprofessional working as central to students' learning. There are a number of learning opportunities that can be made available across settings in health and social care, such as receiving and making referrals, attending planning meetings, child protection conferences, ward rounds and team meetings.

The user perspective must be included as an aspect on which students should focus regardless of their professional background. In order to learn and reflect, the learner needs clear guidelines from the educator with some questions to consider. Examples of relevant questions in relation to a critical incident analysis are provided by Barrett et al. (2005) for students to 'analyse and evaluate interprofessional working' (p. 195). This can be used in groups, teams or by an individual student practice educator or qualifying student and can be applied to work with a user, an event or a meeting observed or attended.

Ravee, a student mental health nurse, is asked to go and see **Avis Jenkins** (Number 3, Green Hill flats) while Avis is attending the Memory Joggers group. In supervision with his mentor, Ravee is asked to reflect on the perspective of the service user, the role of the different professions involved in the group and the way in which the professionals work together to run the service.

Another exercise might be to ask the student to:

- think about your working week, look in your diary and identify how many meetings, visits and tasks undertaken involved other professionals
- then review this list and identify whether the user or carer was involved or present in the discussions and decision-making that took place.

Assessment of interprofessional education

More challenging than the creation of interprofessional learning opportunities is the assessment of interprofessional competence. Although there is general agreement about the importance of interprofessional competence, Miller et al. (2006) found no consensus among academics and practitioners about the degree to which interprofessional competences should be assessed. Within the common learning pilots, approaches included portfolios, uni-professional coursework assignments, formative assessments, and assessments of group performance or projects. The study indicated that students' learning within the academic setting could be motivated by summative assessment while within the practice setting the crucial element was being able to understand the relevance of interprofessional working to improving the delivery of care. However, few interprofessional learning initiatives are summatively assessed and, for those that are, IPE does not appear to be a factor in exam pass rates.

Strategies for assessment of interprofessional competence within the practice context need to address some core principles identified by Race (1998). These are that the assessment method is transparent, valid and tests what it is meant to test and that the weighting given to interprofessional working is made explicit as part of the marking criteria. The strategy must include proof of authenticity not just that interprofessional work was undertaken but how this was done. Ideally the student should be assessed by someone who has observed the interaction; otherwise verification must be confirmed with professionals and service users that work was undertaken in an acceptable interprofessional manner. Assessment must be reliable across assessors and over time, not just a one-off snapshot, otherwise it is hard to assess whether the worker/student is consistent in their practice.

Sufficiency of evidence of good practice of interprofessional working is an ongoing debate. Examples of specific interprofessional projects have been provided above but where these are not available to students, most assessment schedules require evidence of interprofessional working in academic and practice-based assessments. The competences identified by

Weinstein (1998) and Barr (1998) earlier in this chapter could be used more systematically as explicit measurement tools.

Evidence of interprofessional working can be provided in portfolios of evidence for pre-qualifying students. This could include an integrated approach over time based on the competences of interprofessional and inter-agency working. The practice teacher could facilitate the collection of this practice evidence and enable the critical refection the student needs to undertake to identify the values and theoretical knowledge base in this area. Formative and summative assessments of practice might then include:

- evidence of attendance and participation in interprofessional and inter-agency meetings
- evidence of coordination to reduce need for service users to repeat their story numerous times
- working competently in an integrated team
- feedback from other professionals within and external to the team
- feedback from service users the student is working with
- the involvement of service user trainers experienced in assessing students who could observe the students' practice using a clear assessment schedule.

The assessment of practice educators also needs to engage with the IPE agenda through a portfolio containing formative and summative evidence. Examples using the principles for measuring competency outlined above could be:

- providing an explicit plan for including interprofessional learning opportunities over the duration of the learning episode
- evidence of teaching the student about the practice, knowledge and values of interprofessional and inter-agency working over time, which could be assessed by direct observation from an experienced teacher and feedback from the student
- including other professionals' views in the assessment of the student
- a critically reflective piece focusing on learning about their own role in facilitating and assessing competence in interprofessional and inter-agency working.

Interprofessional training of practice educators

The focus of any practice educator programme has to be the training of competent qualified professionals to assess students from their own profession. However, the knowledge, skills and values required to do this are shared by most caring professions (Emerson, 2004) and only partly profession-specific.

It is useful to recap the aspects that are common learning requirements for a trainee from any profession preparing to take students:

- induction to the placement area
- practice teacher's role in ensuring the student's well-being and safety
- agreement about learning opportunities to enable the student to meet the outcomes/competencies
- identifying tasks and timescales for work with service users
- protecting service users and providing them with a service of a standard expected by the organization
- providing feedback on an ongoing basis on strengths and gaps in the student's professional development
- formal assessment process, report writing, and so on
- linking of theory and practice
- linking professional values and anti-discriminatory practice to the student's work with clients, patients, service users, policy, legislation and the organization and team that they work in
- identifying teaching topics
- assisting the student to reflect on new learning and personal development (adapted from Shardlow and Doel, 1996)
- developing competence in interprofessional working.

Recognition of these commonalities facilitated the development of interprofessional practice teaching programmes discussed interestingly by Watkins and Redding (2000) and by Leiba and Leonard (2003) but which are closing, following the introduction of a new Post-Qualifying Social Work Framework. In their place, many universities now offer post-qualifying interprofessional teaching and learning modules that more or less cover the material that was jointly validated by participating statutory bodies in the Joint Practice Teaching Initiative (JPTI) (Weinstein, 1997). In addition, a number of deaneries (health care training areas) have opened up their general practitioner trainer programmes to other professionals who work in primary care. The advantage of the new arrangements is that they offer pathways in practice education from postgraduate diploma through to master's level for those committed to practice education long term. The value-added aspect of an interprofessional programme is the provision of interprofessional learning opportunities by using exercises such as the following example:

Concerns are raised about **Zoë Benner's** younger son **Billy**, aged 3½, which result in the holding of a child protection conference. A trainee social work practice educator, **Sandra**, invites a 'buddy', **Utah**, who is a trainee practice educator from community nursing, to attend the conference with her. After the conference they report back to colleagues about their respective reflections on the interprofessional process of the conference and the learning opportunities that they might identify for students from both professions. In addition to the interprofessional aspect studied, the trainees experience working collaboratively with someone from a different profession and offer, as part of the presentation, an interactive learning experience to their colleagues.

Conclusion

The reorganization of services into trusts or other organizations that focus on a particular service user group rather than the agencies who deliver a service – for example, mental health trusts, children's trusts (incorporating social services, health and education), older people's trusts, primary health care trusts – means that interprofessional working and professional integration are now part and parcel of the delivery of not just health and care but voluntary sector, housing, police, youth justice and many other services. This is not to say that these structural changes guarantee that there is no more duplication or that no one falls through the net (for example, transfers from children's to adults' services or ongoing conflicts about who pays for dementia care) but there are no longer any destinations for our qualifying students where interprofessional working is not high on the policy agenda. Preparation for working in this context is therefore crucial for all trainee professionals. Furthermore, there are identified interprofessional teaching and learning strategies and generic interprofessional competences that are now common to most health and care professions. Although this has been recognized in the assessment requirements by a number of statutory bodies, in practice interprofessionality often receives scant attention; the relevant learning opportunities are not provided, or, where they are, this may be in a haphazard, project-based manner delivered temporarily by local champions.

In this chapter, we have identified numerous successful interprofessional learning models currently in use but the literature suggests that many are still 'pilots' and few have been genuinely integrated within professional training. Most are offered in practice settings because this is found to be more effective but the interprofessional competences of participating students are not systematically assessed.

In order to ensure that qualified professionals are 'fit for purpose', interprofessional practice learning must be integrated into the mainstream of professional education. This will only happen if all the statutory bodies collaborate and modify their regulations to encourage this approach. One key step forward would be to ensure that all practice educators are prepared and assessed interprofessionally.

Core text recommendations

Eraut, M. (1994), *Developing Professional Knowledge and Competence*, London: Falmer Press.

Freeth, D., Hammick, M., Reeves, S., Koppel, I., and Barr, H. (2005), *Effective Interprofessional Education Development, Delivery and Evaluation*, Oxford: CAIPE and Blackwell.

Preparation for Interprofessional Learning and Teaching Project (PIPE) (2006), 'The PIPE Project'. Available at www.PIPE.ac.uk.

Part IV

Appendices

Appendix 1

Comparative information about the education of health and social care professionals

The community mental health nurse (see 'The nurse' below)

The doctor

Name of professional award	MBChB or MBBS.
Length and level of study	The majority of courses are 5 years. Some offer opportunities for graduates (from related health science courses mostly) to complete in 4 years. A number of students extend their courses to 6 years by additionally undertaking a BSc additional year.
Validating body	All are inspected by the GMC, in addition to being required to comply with university/HE requirements.
Typical placement settings	A full variety from the first year of the course, within academic, hospital, community, charitable and voluntary organizations.
Kinds of specialisms, if appropriate	Generic degree; specialism comes after graduation in the UK.
Placement finances	Students may claim travel expenses for clinical placements; no other financial arrangements.
Number of placements, with total days	Extremely variable, from visits of a few hours' duration to attachments of many months.
How the placement is found	Collaboration between HEI and NHS/health care provider.
What 'governs' the placement?	Contract between SHA and universities, and an agreement between the SHA and providers, and an agreement between the providers and the universities.
Title of person supervising students' practice	Entirely dependent on the placement – ranges from members of public through to academic professors. There will be a lead supervisor in each placement.

Training for purpose of supervising students' practice?	This is not mandatory, although it is viewed as good practice for all university courses to provide teaching on clinical education methods.
How the students' competence is assessed	Combination of continuous assessment, observed practice, formal written examinations using a variety of methods, and a range of clinical assessments from structured (often simulated) encounters through to observation and assessment in practice settings.
Approx. number of UK students graduating each year	6,400.

The health visitor

Name of professional award	BSc (Hons) or BA (Hons) or PGDip in Specialist Community Public Health Nursing.
Length and level of study	At least 52-week course – at HEI (approval of prior learning). Entry requirements are specific re. nursing registration on Part 1 or 2 (NMC) and 1 year post-registration experience.
Validating body	Joint validation by the Nursing and Midwifery Council (NMC) and the university. Registration to the third part of the Register – Specialist Community Public Health Nursing.
Typical placement settings	Community health care settings (clinics, medical centres). Community-based public health settings re. collaborative working. Students work with individuals, families, groups and communities.
Kinds of specialisms, if appropriate	
Placement finances	In many areas there is funding through the MPET Levy, with partnerships for delivery of the course with the SHA and PCTs, and the placements supported by the employing PCT. Without this funding placements must be negotiated, with possible financial requirements to be met by a PCT or the student themselves.
Number of placements, with total days	50% of the learning is practice in the first two semesters – third semester is 10 weeks supervised practice.
How the placement is found	Partnership with PCTs.
What 'governs' the placement?	Practice placement standards determined by the NMC. Contract with SHA – partnership agreement between SHA, PCT and HEI. Audited placements. Live register of practice teachers maintained by PCT.
Title of person supervising students' practice	Practice teacher.

Training for purpose of supervising students' practice?	Postgraduate study to meet the standards for practice teachers (NMC, 2006b). Programmes are jointly validated by the universities and the NMC. Annual update and ongoing demonstration of meeting standards.
How the students' competence is assessed	Students must demonstrate competence to NMC Standards for Specialist Community Public Health Nurses and the 2002 Standards for Health Visitor Preparation. Well-established portfolio and practice assessment schedules, with a final sign-off recommendation for registration.
Approx. number of UK students graduating each year	500 at 43 institutions (2006).

The midwife

Name of professional award	BSc (Hons) Midwifery.
Length and level of study	The programmes are either 3 years (direct entry) or 18 months (for Registered Nurses) in length. From September 2008 all programmes must be at degree level.
Validating body	Conjoint validation between the NMC and university.
Typical placement settings	Maternity units and other hospital settings, midwifery-led units, community clinics, community midwifery service, teams/caseload midwifery service, independent midwifery practice.
Kinds of specialisms, if appropriate	
Placement finances	No specific financial arrangements, except that students can claim travel expenses to and from placement settings.
Number of placements, with total days	Approximately 50% of the programme in practice (NMC requires at least 40% theory). A variety and range of placements allocated.
How the placement is found	SHA requires NHS trusts to provide student placements (expressed within the education contract).
What 'governs' the placement?	Three-way agreement – contract between SHA and universities. Three-way agreement – between the SHA and provider trusts, the providers and the universities, and the SHA and university.
Title of person supervising students' practice	Midwifery mentors/supervisors.
Training for purpose of supervising students' practice?	NMC-approved mentorship programme. Regular mentor update courses are mandatory.

| How the students' competence is assessed | Continuous assessment of practice based on direct client/patient contact and demonstrating achievement of NMC proficiency standards. OSCEs and some simulated learning in skills laboratories sometimes used for formative and summative assessments. Portfolio of evidence of achievement of EU Directives. Assessments include professional conduct criteria. |
| Approx. number of UK students graduating each year | Approx. 1,700 from 49 programmes. |

The nurse

Name of professional award	Registered Nurse on a named part of the register; for example, mental health.
Length and level of study	Length of study = 4,600 hours over 3 years at degree or diploma in higher education level. A small number of courses offered at postgraduate level for students holding a relevant degree. In England most nurses are prepared for registration to diploma level, whereas in the other countries of the UK it is at degree level.
Validating body	NMC in collaboration with HEIs.
Typical placement settings	Hospitals, community care, GP practices, clinics, walk-in centres, independent sector hospitals, nursing homes, nurseries, voluntary sector, other government agencies such as prisons and schools.
Kinds of specialisms, if appropriate	*Adult nursing students* must experience medical and surgical nursing, community care, care of older people, child and mental health. This is an EU directive. *Mental health students* experience care of people with acute and long-term conditions in hospitals, clinics and the community. They often have placements in areas specializing in child and adolescent mental health. *Learning disability students* experience care and support of people across the life continuum, in a range of settings. *Children's nursing students* experience child health needs in the community, educational settings, nurseries and acute care settings. They often have placements in maternity units and child and adolescent centres.
Placement finances	No funding is available to pay placement providers for students' experiences or to pay for mentors.
Number of placements, with total days	2,300 hours in total. Practice placements must constitute 50% of the programme at each stage in the programme. Students are expected to experience care delivery at different times over the 24-hour and 7-day-a-week cycle as supernumerary members of the clinical team.

How the placement is found	Placement providers are identified by the HEI in collaboration with different agencies (that is, SHAs, NHS trusts, independent, voluntary and charitable health and social care agencies) engaged as partners in student preparation. Each placement is audited against criteria recommended by the professional statutory regulatory body as a partnership activity. These include indemnity insurance and being treated as employees for the purposes of their placement experience. Some criteria relate to those of the Commission for Health Improvement as they relate to clinical practice.
What 'governs' the placement?	With the introduction of the National Benchmark price (2006) for pre-qualification health programmes, a Learning Agreement between SHAs and NHS placement providers, and between all placement providers and individual HEIs, will be drawn up and agreed. Other placement providers engage in a service level agreement with the HEI programme provider. Both agreements define the relationship specifying mutual expectations and obligations.
Title of person supervising students' practice	Each student must be supervised by a suitably qualified practitioner, known as a 'mentor', for a minimum of 40% of their placement, and by a registered practitioner for the remaining time.
Training for purpose of supervising students' practice?	Mentors must be registered with the NMC and demonstrate professional knowledge beyond that of the level of students to be mentored prior to successfully completing an NMC approved diploma or degree programme (Teaching and Assessing in Practice) and undertake a yearly update course. A live register of mentors is held by the HEI and the placement provider. Mentors supervising final-year students are required to have additional preparation as well as dedicated time each week to supervise and support their student. These mentors are required to verify whether the student has demonstrated achievement of the NMC Proficiencies required for completion of the placement aspect of their programme and professional registration.
How the students' competence is assessed	Students are assessed in placements against pre-specified learning outcomes. Transition from the Common Foundation Year of their programme is on successful completion of practice outcomes relating to skills clusters and competencies. Transition from the final year to registration is only on demonstration of achievement of professionally identified practice proficiencies and certification of satisfactory conduct and health by a 'sign-off' mentor. Students are required to carry a passport of capability between placements so their progress and history can be noted by each placement supervisor.
Approx. number of students registering with the NMC who were prepared in the UK each year	21,000 new registrants from 85 HEIs in the UK. (Note: not all students who successfully complete their pre-registration nursing programme (diploma, undergraduate or postgraduate degree in nursing) register with the NMC.)

The occupational therapist

Name of professional award	BSc (Hons) Occupational Therapy; Postgraduate Diploma in Occupational Therapy; MSc Occupational Therapy (pre-registration).
Length and level of study	Minimum 90 weeks duration over varying periods of 2 to 4½ years depending on whether the course is full- or part-time, traditional or accelerated. All within HEIs.
Validating body	Validated by the HEI; approved by the regulatory body – the UK HPC. Accredited by the professional body, the College of Occupational Therapists.
Typical placement settings	Occupational therapy services across health and social care in primary, secondary and tertiary services; voluntary services, social services, independent and private practice such as medico-legal work, in education, industry and vocational rehabilitation services.
Kinds of specialisms, if appropriate	Students gain experience in a range of situations including mental health and forensic services, physical disability services, intermediate care, learning disability services, hospice settings, schools, vocational services and across the age range of children, adolescents, young adults, adults and older adults.
Placement finances	No financial provision for paying for placements. Contributing to practice education is an expectation specified in the profession's Code of Ethics and Professional Conduct and in job descriptions of those working in health services. No placement fee is paid to the placement agency.
Number of placements, with total days	The number of practice experiences varies from course to course but commonly there will be 3 to 5 different experiences that must total 1,000 hours of assessed experience altogether.
How the placement is found	A database of known placements is held by the HEI but new placements must be sought all the time to meet the growing demand. This relies on excellent communication between tutors in the HEI and local practitioners. HEI tutors also purposely seek out organizations and services where occupational therapy is not yet, but could be, developed and use these as role-emerging practice experiences.
What 'governs' the placement?	Honorary contracts are normally in place with the regular practice providers.
Title of person supervising students' practice	Practice educator.
Training for purpose of supervising students' practice?	The minimum is an introductory course (2–3 days) on adult learning and teaching methods and assessment processes. Some longer CATS-accredited courses are available; some of these are interprofessional.

How the students' competence is assessed	Assessment criteria are approved in the validation process and are provided by the HEI to practice educators on a form that has to be completed at the end of the practice experience. In some HEIs, forms are also completed at the half-way stage. There is no national assessment form but the range of criteria is fairly common across courses nationally. Students and educators add comments and sign the form, which is returned to the HEI for external examination purposes.
Approx. number of UK students graduating each year	1,650+ from 31 providers.

The physiotherapist

Name of professional award	BSc (Hons) Physiotherapy; MSc Physiotherapy (pre-registration)
Length and level of study	BSc (Hons) 3 years (full-time equivalent) in HEI (4 years Scotland); 4 years' part-time study for BSc (Hons) in England. MSc pre-registration course – 2 years full-time.
Validating body	HPC in association with the professional body (CSP).
Typical placement settings	Primary care community settings, secondary care in hospital or specialist units, schools, independent health sector organizations.
Kinds of specialisms, if appropriate	The degree will offer students practice learning in a wide area of client groups and conditions, including respiratory conditions, neurology, orthopaedic/general surgery and musculoskeletal problems in a variety of health and social care settings under the supervision of HPC-registered physiotherapists.
Placement finances	Placements in England are commissioned via the SHA. Some students may be eligible for NHS bursaries to cover tuition fees and placement expenses. Student grants are means-tested.
Number of placements, with total days	1,000 hours of placement experience, distributed through the 3 years in ways determined by each programme. Placements are currently sourced by HEIs.
How the placement is found	A database of known placements is held by the HEI but new placements must be sought all the time to meet the growing demand. This relies on excellent communication between tutors in the HEI and local practitioners. Elective placements are sourced and arranged by the individual student.
What 'governs' the placement?	HEIs have local honorary contracts with NHS trusts, PCTs and private/voluntary sector providers who offer student placements.
Title of person supervising students' practice	Placement educator/supervisor.

Training for purpose of supervising students' practice?	It is recommended that placement educators have 2 years' post-qualification experience and have attended educator training at the relevant HEI before supervising students. Some educators who are CSP members are registered with the CSP as accredited educators.
How the students' competence is assessed	Students must demonstrate competence by passing each assessed placement and the academic assignments linked to placement activity; students may not progress from one level until all areas are passed.
Approx. number of UK students graduating each year	2,600 students from 36 programmes (2007).

The social worker (Scotland)

Name of professional award	BA (Hons) Social Work. MSc/PG Dip Social Work.
Length and level of study	Four years honours. Two years MSc.
Validating body	University/Scottish Social Services Council
Typical placement settings	Local authority (including criminal justice), voluntary organization and private sector.
Kinds of specialisms, if appropriate	
Placement finances	Paid in Scotland by a daily rate from Scottish government funding to universities.
Number of placements, with total days	200 days of which 160 must be in an agency setting.
How the placement is found	By university placements coordinators and agency coordinators.
What 'governs' the placement?	University governs award.
Title of person supervising students' practice	Practice teacher/practice learning coordinator.
Training for purpose of supervising students' practice?	Practice learning qualifications.
How the students' competence is assessed	Via SIESWE.
Approx. number of UK students graduating each year	500 in Scotland.

The speech and language therapist

Name of professional award	Speech and language therapy (degree title varies across university courses).
Length and level of study	The programmes are a variety of lengths from 3 years (undergraduate) to 4 years (undergraduate), 2 years (master's level), 1-year postgraduate diploma. These are all qualifying courses.
Validating body	HPC in association with professional body (Royal College of Speech and Language Therapists).
Typical placement settings	Speech and language therapy departments in educational settings, hospital settings, community clinics, community rehabilitation settings.
Kinds of specialisms, if appropriate	Generic degree. Students are expected to learn about all types of communication impairment and gain experience in observation, assessment, management and the practice of therapeutic intervention.
Placement finances	Students may claim travel expenses for clinical placements; no other financial arrangements.
Number of placements, with total days	150 sessions (1 session = 3½ hours).
How the placement is found	Usually via placement provider group in the workforce confederation.
What 'governs' the placement?	Contract between SHA and universities, and an agreement between the SHA and providers, and an agreement between the providers and the universities.
Title of person supervising students' practice	Clinical educators or practice educators.
Training for purpose of supervising students' practice?	This is not mandatory, although it is viewed as good practice for all university courses to provide teaching on clinical education methods.
How the students' competence is assessed	Combination of continuous assessment and performance assessment. Students must have successfully completed an HPC/RCSLT accredited degree. Students will have met HPC competencies and newly qualified practitioner competencies (RCSLT).
Approx. number of UK students graduating each year	750 per year.

Appendix 2
Student supervision and teaching models

Growth and development	Apprenticeship ('Sitting by Nellie')
Largely individualized teaching Focus on student's feelings Development of self-awareness Reflective style of supervision Premium on confidentiality Assessment linked with personal growth *Philosophy:* '**Being**' *Therapeutic models* *Professional performance depends on personal growth* *Psycho-social theories* *Emphasis on process*	Primary relationship with supervisor Work with available cases Global, ad hoc approach Supervision as discussion, use of process records Rate of progress measured against competencies *Philosophy:* '**Doing**' *Learning by doing* *Good practice means replicating existing work practices* *Behavioural theories* *Process and outcome in relative balance*
Structured learning	**Managerial**
Team teaching common A planned curriculum, perhaps in a modular form Systematic and varied teaching methods Use of simulations Pre-defined standards for assessment *Philosophy:* '**Learning**' *Educational models* *Direct observation important* *Adult learning theories* *Outcome and process in relative balance*	Planned workload Skills-based Problem-solving approach in supervision Emphasis on agency policy as arbiter of good practice Assessment measured by ability to follow procedures accurately *Philosophy:* '**Managing**' *Learning by doing* *Protection of clients paramount* *Rule-directed behaviour* *Emphasis on outcome*

There have been many changes in the way students are expected to learn professional practice. It is important for people who teach students their professional craft to become acquainted with these changes, because expectations might be different from the way in which they experienced their own learning.

The change of terminology from 'student supervision' to 'practice teaching' or 'practice educator' reflects a real change in emphasis and style. Whereas student supervision has generally drawn more from theories of therapeutic involvement, practice education is developing more from theories of learning, with an emphasis on curriculum development. The 'structured learning' model has gained currency, with an emphasis on students as adult learners.

Appendix 3
Teaching and learning techniques

Below are some of the many possible 'action techniques' which can be used to help students learn about professional practice. These techniques are grouped into four categories. There is an additional note about the various possible arrangements (one-to-one, small group, and so on) for deploying the techniques. This approach is adapted from Catherine Sawdon's 'Action Techniques' (unpublished handout).

1 Experiential

Role-play	Drama
Rehearsal	Simulation
Exercises	Activities
Guided fantasy	Sculpting
Games	'Quick-think'
Discussions	Meetings
Ward rounds	Tribunals
Court appearances	

2 Written word

Practice folder   Minutes   Logs
Reports   Summaries   Day books
Case records   Resource files
Task analysis   Questionnaires   Letters
Critical incident analysis   Contracts
Evaluation sheets
E-mails
Individual care plans   Quizzes
Recorded, timed observations
Articles   Handouts   Books
Novels   Texts   Reports
Newspaper items   Journals
Policy documents
Procedure manuals   Statistics

3 Graphic

OHP	Flipcharts
Plans	Photographs
Diagrams	Drawings
Cartoons	Sketches
Charts	Posters
Artwork	Mapping
Cards	Calendars
Family trees	Montages
Guided imagery	Metaphors

4 Hardware

Audio   Video   Tape
Slides   OHP   Film
Computer   One-way screens
Internet
CD-TV Interactional video
Video-conferencing

In addition to the various techniques suggested above, there is a wide range of structural arrangements which can shape the way in which these methods are used. Examples of different structural arrangements are:

One-to-one   Pairs   Tandem   Peer group   Co-work
Joint work   Tag   Outreach   Periodic on-site   Long-arm/off-site
Direct observation   Live teaching in the same room   Team-linking

Bibliography

Readers are advised to use the List of Acronyms in the preliminary pages to check the full names of authoring bodies.

Accredited Clinical Educator (2006). Available at: http://www.csp.org.uk/director/careersandlearning/continuingprofessionaldevelopment/postqualifyingprogrammes (accessed 7 December 2006).

Adams, T. (ed.) (2007), *Dementia Care Nursing: Promoting well-being in people with dementia and their families*, Basingstoke: Palgrave Macmillan.

Aggarwal, N., Vass, A., Minardi, H., Ward, R., Garfield, C., and Cybyk, B. (2003), 'People with Dementia and their Relatives: Personal experiences of Alzheimer's and of the provision of care', *Journal of Psychiatric and Mental Health Nursing*, 10 (2): 187–97.

Aldgate, J. (2007), 'The Place of Attachment Theory in Social Work with Children and Families', in J. Lishman (ed.), *Handbook for Practice Learning in Social Work and Social Care: Knowledge and theory*, London: Jessica Kingsley (pp. 57–73).

Allan, P. (ed.) (1982), *Nursing, Midwifery and Health Visiting since 1900*, London: Faber & Faber.

Allen, S., Strong, J., and Polatajko, H.J. (2001), 'Graduate Entry Master's Degrees: Launchpad for occupational therapy this millennium', *British Journal of Occupational Therapy*, 64 (11): 572–6.

Alsop, A. (2006), 'Qualifying as an Occupational Therapist: An educational journey from ward-based to workplace learning', *British Journal of Occupational Therapy*, 69 (10): 442–9.

Alsop, A. (2007), 'Service Learning: The challenge of civic responsibility' (Editorial), *British Journal of Occupational Therapy*, 70 (4): 139.

Alsop, A., and Cooper, A. (2005), 'Partnership and Participation in the Workplace: Developing the occupational potential of assistants', Abstracts, College of Occupational Therapists 29th Annual Conference at Eastbourne, London: COT.

Alsop, A., and Ryan, S. (1996), *Making the Most of Fieldwork Education: A practical approach*, Cheltenham: Stanley Thornes.

Alzheimer's Society (2007), 'Dementia UK: A report into the prevalence and cost of dementia prepared by the Personal Social Services Research Unit (PSSRU) at the London School of Economics and the Institute of Psychiatry at King's College London, for the Alzheimer's Society', London: Alzheimer's Society. Available at: www.alzheimers.org.uk/news_and_

campaigns/Campaigning/PDF/Dementia_UK_Full_Report.pdf (accessed 20 March 2008).

Anderson, E., and Lennox, A. (2005), 'Learning Together in Disadvantaged Communities: Evaluating the impact of undergraduate interprofessional learning', paper presented to Interprofessional Learning Conference, 20 June, Bradford.

Anderson, E., Manek, N., and Davidson, A. (2006), 'Evaluation of a Model for Maximizing Interprofessional Education in an Acute Hospital', *Journal of Interprofessional Care*, 20 (2): 182–94.

Areskog, N.H. (1994), 'Multi-Professional Education at the Undergraduate Level – the Linkoping model', *Journal of Interprofessional Care*, 8 (3): 279–82.

Ashworth, P.M., and Castledine, G. (1980), 'Joint Service-Education Appointments in Nursing', *Medical Teacher*, 12 (6): 295–9.

Association for Medical Education in Europe (AMEE). Available at: http://www.amee.org.

Association for the Study of Medical Education (ASME). Available at: http://www.asme.org.uk.

Atkins, S., and Williams, A. (1995), 'Registered Nurses' Experiences of Mentoring Undergraduate Nursing Students', *Journal of Advanced Nursing*, 21 (5): 1006–15.

Aveyard, B. (2001), 'Education and Person-Centred Approaches to Dementia Care', *Nursing Older People*, 12 (10): 17–19.

Banerjee, S., and Chan, J. (2008), 'Organization of Old Age Psychiatric Services', *Psychiatry*, 7 (2): 49–54.

Barnett, R. (ed.) (1997), *The End of Knowledge in Higher Education*, Cassell: London.

Barr, H. (1998), 'Competent to Collaborate: Towards a competency-based model for interprofessional education', *Journal of Interprofessional Care*, 12 (2): 181–8.

Barr, H. (1999), 'New NHS, New Collaboration, New Agenda for Interprofessional Education', inaugural lecture, 13 April, London Greenwich University.

Barr, H. (2002), *Interprofessional Education Today, Yesterday and Tomorrow: A review commissioned by The Learning and Teaching Support Network for Health Sciences and Practice*, London: The UK Centre for the Advancement of Interprofessional Education (CAIPE). Available at: www.swap.ac.uk.

Barr, H., and Ross, F. (2006), 'Mainstreaming Interprofessional Education in the United Kingdom: A position paper', *Journal of Interprofessional Care*, 20 (2): 96–104.

Barr, H., Koppel, I., Reeves, S., Hammick, M., and Freeth, D. (2005), *Effective Interprofessional Education: Argument, assumption and evidence*, Oxford: Blackwell.

Barrett, G., Sellman, D., and Thomas, J. (2005), *Interprofessional Working in Health and Social Care: Professional perspectives*, Basingstoke: Palgrave Macmillan.

Bartholomew, A., Davis, J., and Weinstein, J. (1995), *Interprofessional Education and Training – Developing new models: Report of JPTI*, London: CCETSW.

Baxter, S. (2004), 'Fit for Practice: New models for clinical placements', in S.M. Brumfitt (ed.), *Innovations in Professional Education for Speech and Language Therapy*, London and Philadelphia, PA: Whurr (pp. 116–41).

Baxter, S., and Gray, C. (2001), 'The Application of Student-Centred Learning Approaches to Clinical Education', *International Journal of Language and Communication Disorders*, 36 (supplement): 396–400.

Baxter, S.K., and Gray, C. (2006), 'Teaching and Learning in the Clinical Setting: Learning resources', Sheffield: University of Sheffield.

Beale, H. (2001), 'Teaching, Supervision and Learning in the Workplace' (Anglia University). Available at: www.swap.ac.uk/learning (accessed June 2006).

Begley, C. (1999), 'Student Midwives' Views of "Learning to be a Midwife" in Ireland', *Midwifery*, 15 (4): 264–73.

Ben-David, M.F. (1999), 'AMEE Guide No. 14: Outcome-Based Education: Part 3 – Assessment in outcome-based education', *Medical Teacher*, 21 (1): 23–5.

Ben-David, M.F., Davis, M.H., Harden, R.M., Howie, P.W., Ker, J., and Pippard, M.J. (2006), 'AMEE Medical Education Guide No. 24: Portfolios as a method of student assessment', *Medical Teacher*, 23 (6): 535–51.

Benner, P.E. (2001), *From Novice to Expert: Excellence and power in clinical nursing practice* (commemorative edn), Upper Saddle River, NJ: Prentice Hall.

Berenbaum, R. (2005), 'Learning about the Lived Experience of Dementia', *Journal of Dementia Care*, 13 (1): 20–21.

Beresford, P., and Croft, S. (2001), 'Service Users' Knowledge and the Social Construction of Social Work', *British Journal of Social Work*, 1 (3): 295–316.

Berliner, D.D. (2001), 'Learning about and Learning from Expert Teachers', *International Journal of Educational Research*, 35 (5): 463–82.

Bharj, K. (2006), 'Fit for Practice: Preparing student midwives', *Practising Midwife*, 9 (8): 20–24.

Bines, H. (1992), 'Issues in Course Design', in H. Bines and D. Watson (eds), *Developing Professional Education*, Buckingham: SRHE/Open University.

Blaka, G. (2006), 'Newcomers' Learning of Midwifery Practice in a Labour Ward: A socio-cultural perspective', *Learning in Health and Social Care*, 5 (1): 35–44.

Bloom, B.S. (1954), *Taxonomy of Educational Objectives Handbook I: Cognitive Domain*, New York: D. McKay & Co. Inc.

Bloom, B.S. (1956), *Taxonomy of Educational Objectives Handbook II: Affective Domain*, New York: D. McKay & Co. Inc.

Borger, R., and Seabourne, A. (1966), *The Psychology of Learning*, Harmondsworth: Penguin.

Borton, T. (1970), *Reach, Touch and Teach*, London: Hutchinson.

Bossers, A., Cook, J., Polatajko, H., and Laine, C. (1997), 'Understanding the Role-Emerging Fieldwork Placement', *Canadian Journal of Occupational Therapy*, 64 (1): 70–81.

Boud, D. (1995), 'Assessment and Learning: Contradictory or complementary?', in P. Knight, *Assessment for Learning in Higher Education*, London: Kogan Page (pp. 35–48).

Boud, D., Keogh, R., and Walker, D. (1993), *Using Experience for Learning*, Bristol: Open University Press.

Boud, D., and Walker, D. (1990), 'Making the Most of Experience', *Studies in Continuing Education*, 12 (2): 61–80.

Bourdieu, P. (1985), 'The Forms of Capital', in J.G. Richardson (ed.), *Handbook of Theory and Research for the Sociology of Education*, New York: Greenwood (pp. 241–58).

Boursicot, K.A., Roberts, T.E., and Pell, G. (2006), 'Standard Setting for Clinical Competence at Graduation from Medical School: A comparison of passing scores across five medical schools', *Advances in Health Sciences Education Theory and Practice*, 11 (2): 173–83.

Bradley, P., and Postlethwaite, K. (2003), 'Setting up a Clinical Skills Learning Facility', *Medical Education*, 37 (1): 6–13.

Bray, J., and Howkins, E. (2006), 'Facilitating Interprofessional Work-Based Learning: A research project using the Delphi technique', *Work-Based Learning in Primary Care*, 4 (3): 223–5.

Brennan, J., and Little, B. (1996), *A Review of Work-Based Learning in Higher Education*, London: Department of Education and Employment.

Brooker, D. (2006), *Person-Centred Dementia Care: Making services better*, London: Jessica Kingsley.

Brumfitt, S.M. (ed.), (2004), *Innovations in Professional Education for Speech and Language Therapy*, London and Philadelphia, PA: Whurr.

Bruner, J.S. (1960), *The Process of Education*, Cambridge, MA: Harvard University Press.

Brunt, C. (2003), 'Learning Not to Teach: Part one', *British Journal of Midwifery*, 11 (6): 376–9.

Bryans, M., Keady, J., Turner, S., Wilcock, J., Downs, M., and Iliffe, S. (2003), 'An Exploratory Survey into Primary Care Nurses and Dementia Care', *British Journal of Nursing*, 12 (17): 1029–37.

Buckley, E.R., and Dunn, N.J. (2000), 'Delivering Quality in Midwifery Practice and Education', in D. Fraser (ed.), *Professional Studies for Midwifery Practice*, Edinburgh: Churchill Livingstone.

Burton, J., and Jackson, N. (2003), *Work-Based Learning in Primary Care*, Abingdon: Radcliffe Medical Press.

Butler, A. (2005), 'A Strengths Approach to Building Futures: UK students and refugees together', *Community Development Journal*, 40 (2): 147–57.

Callaghan, P., Light, I., Morris, M., and Campbell, P. (2005), 'Mental Health Nurse Academics (UK) Draft Position Paper 4: The role of users and carers in mental health nursing education and research'. Available at: http://mnhauk.swan.ac.uk/PositionPapers/PositionPaper4.Users&Carers. pdf.

Canham, J., and Bennett, J. (2002), *Mentoring in Community Nursing: Challenges and opportunities*, Oxford: Blackwell Science.

Cantley, C., Woodhouse, J., and Smith, M. (2005), 'Listen to Us: Involving people with dementia in planning and delivering services', Dementia North, University of Northumbria: Newcastle-upon-Tyne. Available at: http://www.dementianorth.org.uk/PDFs/IPWD%20report.pdf (accessed 20 March 2008).

Carr, W., and Kemmis, S. (1986), *Becoming Critical: Education, knowledge and action research*, London: Falmer Press.

Chambers, N. (1999), 'Close Encounters: The use of critical reflective analysis as an evaluation tool in teaching and learning', *Journal of Advanced Nursing*, 29 (4): 950–57.

Chartered Society of Physiotherapy (CSP) (2002), *Curriculum Framework for Qualifying Programmes in Physiotherapy*, London: CSP.

Chartered Society of Physiotherapy (CSP) (2003), *Clinical Education Placement Guidelines*, London: CSP.

Chartered Society of Physiotherapy (CSP) (2005), *Workplace Learning, Information Paper 31, CPD Learning and Development*, London: CSP.

Chartered Society of Physiotherapy (CSP) (2006a), *Competences and Competence Frameworks, Guidance Paper MOS/COMP/V1, Learning and Development*, London: CSP.

Chartered Society of Physiotherapy (CSP) (2006b), website at: http://www. csp.org.uk/director/careersandlearning/ukqualifyingprogrammes.cfm (accessed 4 December 2006).

Cheston, R., Bender, M., and Byatt, S. (2000), 'Involving People who Have Dementia in the Evaluation of Services: A review', *Journal of Mental Health*, 9 (5): 471–80.

Clapton, G., and Daly, M. (2007), 'Bridging the Theory–Practice Gap: Student placement groups co-facilitated by lecturers and practice teachers', *Groupwork*, 17 (3): 60–75.

Clarke, C.L., Keady, J., and Adams, T. (2003), 'Integrating Practice and Knowledge in a Clinical Context', in J. Keady, C.L. Clarke and T. Adams (eds), *Community Mental Health Nursing and Dementia Care: Practice perspectives*, Maidenhead: Open University Press (pp. 17–32).

Coleman, J.S. (1988), 'Social Capital in the Creation of Human Capital', *American Journal of Sociology*, 94 (Supplement), S95–S120.

College of Occupational Therapists (COT) (2002), 'Position Statement on Lifelong Learning', *British Journal of Occupational Therapy*, 65 (5): 198–200.

College of Occupational Therapists (COT) (2005), *Code of Ethics and Professional Conduct*, London: COT.

College of Occupational Therapists (COT). Available at: www.cot.co.uk (accessed 24 August 2007).

Collington, V. (2005), *An Investigation into the Perceived Influence of Reflective Journal Writing in the Process of Pre-Registration Midwifery Students' Experiential Learning*, London: Kingston University.

Collington, V., and Hunt, S.C. (2006), 'Reflection in Midwifery Education and Practice: An exploratory analysis', *Evidence-Based Midwifery*, 4 (3): 76–82.

Colliver, J.A. (2000), 'Effectiveness of Problem-Based Learning Curricula Research and Theory', *Academic Medicine*, 75 (3): 259–66.

Community Practitioners' and Health Visitors' Association (CPHVA) (2007), 'Shaping the Future', *Community Practitioner*, 80 (8): 18–21.

Cook, A. (2006), 'The Value of Clinical Practice to Lecturers in Higher Education', *British Journal of Midwifery*, 14 (7): 396–400.

Council for the Education and Training of Health Visitors (CETHV) (1977), *An Investigation into the Principles of Health Visiting*, London: CETHV.

Council of Deans (CoD) (2006), *Workforce Planning, Education and Training in England* (Council paper), London: CoD for Nursing and Allied Health Professions.

Council of Deans (CoD) (2007), *Implications of National Policy Changes on Recruitment and Commissioning of Health Care Practitioners*, London: CoD.

Council of Deans (CoD) and Heads of UK University Faculties for Nursing and Health Professions (2007), Press release on workforce planning and the funding of education for nursing, midwifery and the allied health professions, London: CoD, 24 May.

Cowley, S., and Frost, M. (2006), *The Principles of Health Visiting: Opening the door to public health practice in the 21st century*, London: CPHVA.

Creek, J. (2003), *Occupational Therapy Defined as a Complex Intervention*, London: COT.

Crosling, G., and Webb, G. (2002), *Supporting Student Learning: Case studies, experience and practice*, London: Kogan Page.

Cruess, R.L., and Cruess, S.R. (2006), 'Teaching Professionalism: General principles', *Medical Teacher*, 28 (3): 205–8.

Cruess, S.R., Johnston, S., and Cruess, R.L. (2004), '"Profession": A working definition for medical educators', *Teaching and Learning in Medicine*, 16 (1): 74–6.

Dahlgreen, G., and Whitehead, M. (1991), *Policies and Strategies to Promote Social Enquiry in Health*, Stockholm: Institute of Future Studies.

Daniel, B. (2007), 'Assessment and Children', in J. Lishman (ed.), *Handbook for Practice Learning in Social Work and Social Care: Knowledge and theory*, London: Jessica Kingsley (pp. 115–27).

Darra, S., Hunter, B., McIvor, M., Webber, F., and Morse, N. (2003), 'Education: Developing a midwifery skills framework', *British Journal of Midwifery*, 11 (1): 43–7.

Davis, A. (2007), 'Structural Approaches to Social Work', in J. Lishman (ed.), *Handbook for Practice Learning in Social Work and Social Care: Knowledge and theory*, London: Jessica Kingsley (pp. 27–38).

Dent, J.A., and Harden, R.M. (2001), *A Practical Guide for Medical Teachers*, Oxford: Churchill Livingstone.

Dent, J.A., and Harden, R.M., (2005), *New Horizons in Medical Education* (2nd edn), Edinburgh: Churchill Livingstone.

Dent, T., and Tourville, A. (2002), 'University–Community Partnerships: Practicum learning for community revitalization', in S.M. Shardlow and M. Doel (eds), *Learning to Practise Social Work: International approaches*, London: Jessica Kingsley (pp. 25–42).

Department of Education and Skills (2006), 'Every Child Matters'. Available at http://www.Everychild matters.gov.uk.

Department of Health (DoH) (1993), *A Vision for the Future: The nursing, midwifery and health visiting contribution to health care*, London: HMSO.

Department of Health (DoH) (1997), *The New NHS, Modern and Dependable*, London: DoH.

Department of Health (DoH) (1998a), *A First-Class Service: Quality in the new NHS*, London: DoH/HMSO.

Department of Health (DoH) (1998b), *Working Together: Securing a quality workforce for the NHS*, London: DoH/HMSO.

Department of Health (DoH) (1999), *Making a Difference – Strengthening the nursing, midwifery and health visiting contribution*, London: DoH.

Department of Health (DoH) (2000a), *National Health Service Plan. A plan for investment; a plan for reform*, London: HMSO.

Department of Health (DoH) (2000b), *A Health Service of All the Talents*, London: HMSO.

Department of Health (DoH) (2000c), *Meeting the Challenge: A strategy for the allied health professions*, London: DoH.

Department of Health (DoH) (2001a), *Shifting the Balance of Power within the NHS*, London: DoH.

Department of Health (DoH) (2001b), *Building the Information Core: Implementing the NHS Plan*, London: DoH.

Department of Health (DoH) (2001c), *Preparation of Mentors and Teachers: A new framework of guidance*, London: DoH.

Department of Health (DoH) (2001d), *National Service Framework for Older People: Falls prevention*, London: HMSO.

Department of Health (DoH) (2001e), *Working Together, Learning Together: A framework for lifelong learning in the NHS*, London: HMSO.

Department of Health (DoH) (2001f), *Agenda for Change*, London: HMSO.

Department of Health (DoH) (2004a), *National Service Framework for Children, Young People and Maternity Services*, London: DoH.

Department of Health (DoH) (2004b), *The NHS Knowledge and Skills Framework (NHS KSF) and the Development Review Process (October 2004)*, London: DoH.

Department of Health (DoH) (2004c), *The Ten Essential Shared Capabilities: A framework for the whole of the mental health workforce*, London: HMSO.

Department of Health (DoH) (2004d), *Agenda for Change*. Available at: www.dh.gov/policyandguidance/humanresourcesandtraining/monitoringpay/agendaforchange (accessed 12 December 2006).

Department of Health (DoH) (2004e), *NHS Reference Costs and National Tariff*, London: HMSO.

Department of Health (DoH) (2004f), *NHS Improvement Plan: Putting people at the heart of public services*, London: HMSO.

Department of Health (DoH) (2004g), *Standards for Better Health*, London: HMSO.

Department of Health (DoH) (2004h), *Choose and Book – Patient's choice of hospital and booked appointment*, London: HMSO.

Department of Health (DoH) (2005), *Securing Better Mental Health for Older Adults*, London: HMSO.

Department of Health (DoH) (2006a), *Standards for Better Health*, London: HMSO.

Department of Health (DoH) (2006b), *Our Health, Our Say, Our Care: New directions for community services*, London: DoH.

Department of Health (DoH) (2006c), *From Values to Action: The Chief Nursing Officer's review of mental health nursing*, London: HMSO.

Department of Health (DoH) (2006d), *The Regulation of Non-Medical Healthcare Professions: A review by the Department of Health*, London: DoH.

Department of Health (DoH) (2006e), *Best Practice Competencies and Capabilities for Pre-Registration Mental Health Nurses in England*, London: HMSO.

Department of Health (DoH) (2006f), *Good Doctors, Safer Patients: Proposal to strengthen the system to assure and improve the performance of doctors and to protect the safety of patients. A report by the Chief Medical Officer*, London: DoH.

Department of Health (DoH) (2006g), *Modernising Nursing Careers*, London: HMSO.

Department of Health (DoH) (2006h), *A Stronger Local Voice: A framework for creating a stronger local voice in the development of health and social care services*, London: HMSO.

Department of Health (DoH) (2007a), *Facing the Future: A review of the role of health visitors* (Chair: R. Lowe). Available at: www.dh.gov.uk/cno (accessed August 2007).

Department of Health (DoH) (2007b), *Maternity Matters: Choice, access and continuity of care in a safe service*, London: DoH.

Department of Health (DoH) (2009), *Living Well with Dementia: A national dementia strategy*, London: HMSO.

Department of Health and Care Services Improvement Partnership (DoH/CSIP) (2005), *Everybody's Business: Integrated mental health services for older adults: a service development guide*, London: Care Services Improvement Partnership.

Department of Health and Social Security (DHSS) (1972), *Report of the Committee on Nursing* (Chair: Lord Briggs), Command 5115 (known as the Briggs Report), London: HMSO.

Department of Health and Social Security (DHSS) (1979), *Royal Commission on the National Health Service* (Chair: Lord Merrison), London: HMSO.

Department of Health and Social Security (DHSS) (1983), *NHS Management Inquiry* (Chair: Lord Griffiths), London: HMSO.

Dingwall, R., and Robinson, K. (1993), 'Policing the Family? Health visiting and the public surveillance of private behaviour', in A. Beattie, M. Gott, L. Jones and M. Sidell (eds), *Health and Wellbeing – A reader*, Basingstoke: Macmillan.

Doel, M. (2006), *Improving Practice Learning in Local Authorities 1: Developing effective strategies*, in the series 'Capturing the Learning', London: Skills for Care. Available at: www.practicelearning.org.uk.

Doel, M., Deacon, L., and Sawdon, C. (2007) 'Curtain Down: Practice learning in the first year of the new social work award', *Social Work Education*, 26 (3): 217–32.

Doel, M., and Shardlow, S.M. (2005), *Modern Social Work Practice: Teaching and learning in practice settings*, Aldershot: Ashgate.

Donaghy, M.E., and Morss, K.T.I. (2000), 'Guided Reflection: A framework to facilitate and assess reflective practice within the discipline of physiotherapy', *Physiotherapy Theory and Practice*, 16 (1): 3–14.

Dreyfus, H.L., and Dreyfus, S.E. (1986), *Mind over Machine: The power of human intuition and expertise in the era of the computer*, New York: Free Press.

Dreyfus, S.E., and Dreyfus, H.L. (1980), *A Five-Stage Model of Mental Activities Involved in Directed Skill Acquisition*. Unpublished report supported by the Air Force Office of Scientific Research (Contract F49620-79-C-0063), Berkeley, CA: University of California at Berkeley.

Durgahee, T. (1996), 'Promoting Reflection in Post-Graduate Nursing – A theoretical model', *Nurse Education Today*, 16 (6): 419–26.

Dyer, B., and Mathews, C. (2005), 'Know your Nuts: Developing IPE in undergraduate education', paper given at the Interprofessional Learning Conference, 20 June 2005, Bradford; sponsored by CAIPE, W. Yorkshire NHS WDC, Bradford City NHS Teaching PCT.

Edmond, C. (2001), 'A New Paradigm for Practice Education', *Nurse Education Today*, 21 (4): 251–9.

Emerson, T. (2004), 'Preparing Placement Supervisors for Primary Care: An interprofessional perspective from the UK', *Journal of Interprofessional Care*, 18 (2): 165–82.

English National Board for Nursing, Midwifery and Health Visiting (ENB) (1993a), *Education, Dialogue and Assessment: Creating partnerships for improving practice*, London: ENB. (Research project co-directors: T. Phillips., J. Schostak., H. Bedford and J. Robinson.)

English National Board for Nursing, Midwifery and Health Visiting (ENB) (1993b), *A Detailed Study of the Relationship between Teaching, Support, Supervision and Role Modelling for Students in Clinical Areas within the Context of Project 2000 Courses*, London: ENB. (Researchers: E. White, S. Davies, S. Twinn and E. Riley.)

English National Board for Nursing, Midwifery and Health Visiting (ENB) (1997), *Standards for the Approval of Higher Education Institutions and Programmes*, London: ENB.

English National Board for Nursing, Midwifery and Health Visiting (ENB) (1998), *Preparing Effective Midwives: An outcome evaluation of the effectiveness of pre-registration midwifery programmes of education*, London: ENB. (Project leaders: D. Fraser, R. Murphy and M. Worth-Butler.)

English National Board for Nursing, Midwifery and Health Visiting (ENB) (2000), *Practice and Assessment. An evaluation of the assessment of practice at diploma, degree and post-graduate level in pre- and post-registration nursing and midwifery education*, London: ENB. (Research project co-directors: J. Schostak, T. Phillips and J. Tyler.)

English National Board for Nursing, Midwifery and Health Visiting (ENB) (2001), *Preparation of Mentors and Teachers: A new framework of guidance*, London: ENB and DoH.

Epstein, R.M., and Hundert, E.M. (2002), 'Defining and Assessing Professional Competence', *Journal of the American Medical Association (JAMA)*, 287 (2): 226–35.

Eraut, M. (1994), *Developing Professional Knowledge and Competence*, London: Falmer Press.

Eraut, M. (2000), 'Non-Formal Learning and Tacit Knowledge in Professional Work', *British Journal of Educational Psychology*, 70 (1): 113–36.

Eraut, M., Alderton, J., Cole, G., and Senker, P. (2000), 'The Development of Knowledge and Skills at Work', in F. Coffield (ed.), *Differing Visions of a Learning Society*, vol. I, Bristol: Policy Press (pp. 231–62).

European Commission (2003), *The Social Situation in the European Union*, Luxembourg: Office for Official Publications of the European Communities.

Evans, D. (1999), *Practice Learning in the Caring Professions*, Aldershot: Ashgate.

Family and Parenting Institute (2007), *Health Visitors – An endangered species*, London: Family and Parenting Institute.

Ferguson, K., and Hope, K. (1999), 'From Novice to Competent Practitioner: Tracking the progress of undergraduate mental health nursing students', *Journal of Advanced Nursing*, 29 (3): 630–39.

Finnerty, G., Graham, L., Magnusson, C., and Pope, R. (2006), 'Empowering Midwife Mentors with Adequate Training and Support', *British Journal of Midwifery*, 14 (4): 187–90.

Finucane, P.M., Johnson, S.M., and Prideaux, D.S. (1998), 'Problem-Based Learning: Its rationale and efficiency', *Medical Journal of Australia*, 168: 445–8.

Fisher, M., and Moore, S. (2005), 'Enquiry-Based Learning Links Psychology Theory to Practice', *British Journal of Midwifery*, 13 (3): 148–52.

Fook, J. (2007), 'Reflective Practice and Critical Reflection', in J. Lishman (ed.), *Handbook for Practice Learning in Social Work and Social Care: Knowledge and theory*, London: Jessica Kingsley (pp. 363–75).

Forrest, S., Risk, I., Masters, H., and Brown, N. (2000), 'Mental Health Service User Involvement in Nurse Education', *Journal of Psychiatric and Mental Health Nursing*, 7: 51–7.

Fraser, D.M. (2000), 'Action Research to Improve the Pre-Registration Curriculum, Part 3: Can fitness for practice be guaranteed? The challenges of designing and implementing an effective assessment in practice scheme', *Midwifery*, 16 (4): 287–94.

Fraser, D.M., Murphy, R., and Worth-Butler, M. (1997), *An Outcome Evaluation of the Effectiveness of Pre-Registration Midwifery Programmes of Education*, London: English National Board for Nursing, Midwifery and Health Visiting.

Freeman, M. (2001), *ViSuAL Voice Version 2 Sheffield*, Sheffield: Learning Media Unit, University of Sheffield.

Freeman, M. (2004), 'Getting Professional Education Online', in S.M. Brumfitt (ed.), *Innovations in Professional Education for Speech and Language Therapy*, London and Philadelphia, PA: Whurr (pp. 145–69).

Freeth, D., Hammick, M., Reeves, S., Koppel, I., and Barr, H. (2005), *Effective Interprofessional Education Development, Delivery and Evaluation*, Oxford: CAIPE and Blackwell.

Freeth, D., Hammick, M., Reeves, S., Koppel, I., and Barr, H. (2006), 'Effective Interprofessional Education: Evidence and issues', presentation given to All Together Better Health III, Conference, 10–12 April, Imperial College, London.

Furber, C., Hickie, J., Lee, K., McLoughlin, A., Boggis, C., Sutton, A., Cooke, S., and Wakefield, A. (2004), 'Interprofessional Education in a Midwifery Curriculum: The "Learning Through the Exploration of the Professional Task" project (LEAPT)', *Midwifery*, 20 (4): 358–66.

Gascoigne, M., and Parker, A. (2001), 'All Placements Great and Small: An analysis of clinical placement offers made by SLT services', *International Journal of Language and Communication Disorders*, 36: 144–9.

General Medical Council (GMC) (1993), *Tomorrow's Doctors: Recommendations on undergraduate medical education*, London: GMC.

General Medical Council (GMC) (2003), *Tomorrow's Doctors: Recommendations on undergraduate medical education*, London: GMC.

General Medical Council (GMC) (2005a), 'Strategic Options for Undergraduate Medical Education Consultation',. Available at: http://www.gmc-uk.org/education/med_ed/index.asp (accessed December 2006).

General Medical Council (GMC) (2005b), *The New Doctor: Guidance on PRHO training*, London: GMC.

General Medical Council (GMC) (2005c), *What will Doctors be Doing by 2050?*, London: GMC.

General Medical Council (GMC) (2006), *Good Medical Practice*, London: GMC.

General Nursing Council (GNC) (1969), *Explanatory Memorandum on Proposed Changes in the Syllabus of Subjects for Examination and Record of Practical Instruction. 69/4/3. Paper A*, London: GNC.

General Nursing Council for England and Wales (1974), *Review of Four Specialised Periods of Experience (74/8/18)*, London: GNC.

General Nursing Council (GNC) (1977), *Education Policy Document. 77/19/B*, London: GNC.

General Nursing Council (GNC) (1983), *Education Policy. 83/13*, London: GNC.

General Social Care Council (GSCC) (2003), *Working Towards Full Participation*, London: GSCC.

Ghaye, T., and Lillyman, S. (1997), *Learning Journals and Critical Incidents: Reflective practice for healthcare professionals*, Salisbury (Wiltshire): Mark Allen Publishing Ltd.

Gibbs, G. (1988), *Learning by Doing: A guide to teaching and learning methods*, Oxford: Further Education Unit, Oxford Polytechnic.

Gillmore, A. (1999), *Report of the Analysis of the Literature Evaluating Pre-Registration Nursing and Midwifery Education in the UK*, London: UKCC.

Glen, S., and Leiba, T. (2004), *Interprofessional Post-Qualifying Education for Nurses*, Basingstoke: Macmillan.

Glen, S., and Reeves, S. (2004), 'Developing Interprofessional Education in the Pre-Registration Curricula: Mission impossible?', *Nurse Education in Practice*, 4: 45–52.

Glen, S., and Wilkie, K. (eds) (2000), *Problem-Based Learning in Nursing*, Basingstoke: Macmillan.

Goffman, E. (1959), *The Presentation of Self in Everyday Life*, Harmondsworth: Penguin Press/Anchor Books.

Goldsmith, M. (1996), *Hearing the Voice of People with Dementia: Opportunities and obstacles*, London: Jessica Kingsley.

Gonzalez, J., and Wagenaar, R. (2006), *Tuning Educational Structures in Europe – Universities' contribution to the Bologna process, An introduction*, Tuning Socrates-Tempus, Bilbao and Groningen: University of Deusto and University of Groningen.

Gordon, F., and Walsh, C. (2005), *The Interprofessional Capability Framework*, Sheffield Hallam University and Coventry University Centre for Interprofessional E-Learning. Available at: http://www.cipel.ac.uk/events/presentations/documents/Capability/Sheets.pdf (accessed August 2006).

Greene, J. (1968), 'The Psychiatric Nurse in the Community Nursing Service', *International Journal of Nursing Studies*, 5: 175–84.

Greenfield, P. (1984), 'A Theory of the Teacher in the Learning Activities of Everyday Life', in B. Rogoff and J. Lave (eds), *Everyday Cognition: Its development in the social context*, Cambridge, MA: Harvard University Press (pp. 117–38).

Greenwood, J. (1998), 'The Role of Reflection in Single and Double Loop Learning', *Journal of Advanced Nursing*, 27 (5): 1048–53.

Guest, C., Smith, L., Bradshaw, M., and Hardcastle, W. (2002), 'Facilitating Interprofessional Learning for Medical and Nursing Students in Clinical Practice', *Learning in Health and Social Care*, 1 (1): 132–8.

Gusfield, J.R. (1975), *The Community: A critical response*, New York: Harper Colophon.

Habermas, J. (1984), *The Theory of Communicative Action, vol. 1: Reason and the rationalization of society*, trans. T. McCarthy, Cambridge: Polity Press in association with Blackwell.

Hall, V., and Hart, A. (2004), 'The Use of Imagination in Professional Education to Enable Learning about Disadvantaged Clients', *Learning in Health and Social Care*, 3 (4): 190–202.

Hammick, M. (ed.) (2005), *Journal of Interprofessional Care, Special Issue: Interprofessional education for collaboration patient-centred care, Canada as a case study*, 19 (Suppl.), compiled by I. Oandasan and K. Barker.

Hannigan, B., and Coffey, M. (eds) (2003), *The Handbook of Community Mental Health Nursing*, London: Routledge.

Hansard (2007), Midwives' training, debate 24 July. Available at: www. publications.parliament.uk.

Harden, R.M. (1999), 'AMEE Guide No. 14: Outcome-based education: Part 1 – An introduction to outcome-based education', *Medical Teacher*, 21 (1): 7–14.

Harden, R.M., Crosby, J., Davis, M.H., Howie, P.W., and Struthers, A.D. (2000), 'Task-Based Learning: The answer to integration and problem-based learning in the clinical years', *Medical Education*, 34 (5): 391–7.

Harden, R.M., and Stamper, N. (1999), 'What is a Spiral Curriculum?', *Medical Teacher*, 21 (2): 141–3.

Harris, P.B. (2007), 'People with Early Stage Alzheimer's Disease as Mentors: Developing a truly collaborative research process', *Alzheimer's Care Quarterly*, 8 (1): 1–6.

Hastie, A., Hastie, I., and Jackson, N. (2005), *Postgraduate Medical Education and Training: A guide for primary and secondary care*, Abingdon: Radcliffe.

Hayes, N. (1994), *Foundations of Psychology: An introductory text*, London: Routledge.

Hays, R. (2006), *Teaching and Learning in Clinical Settings*, Oxford: Radcliffe Publishing.

Healthcare Commission (n.d.), website at: http://www.chai.org.uk/ homepage.cfm (accessed 4 December 2006).

Healthcare Commission (2006), *The Annual Health Check 2006/07: Assessing and rating the NHS*, London: Healthcare Commission.

Health Professions Council (HPC) (2004), *Standards of Education and Training*, London: HPC.

Health Professions Council (HPC) (2006), 'Approvals and Monitoring'. Available at: http://www.hpc.org/education&training/approvals&monit oring-introduction (accessed 12 December 2006).

Hector, W. (1973), *Mrs Bedford Fenwick: The work of Mrs Bedford Fenwick and the rise of professional nursing*, London: Royal College of Nursing.

Herbert, R., Jamtvedt, G., Mead, J., and Birger Hagen, K. (2005), *Practical Evidence-Based Physiotherapy*, Oxford: Elsevier.

Higgs, J., and Edwards, H. (1999), *Educating Beginning Practitioners: Challenges for health professional education*, Oxford: Butterworth Heinemann.

Higgs, J., and Jones, M. (1995), *Clinical Reasoning in the Health Professions*, Oxford: Butterworth Heinemann (2nd edn 2005).

Hills, J. (2004), *Inequality and the State*, Oxford: Oxford University Press.

Hoben, K., Varley, R.A., and Cox, R. (2007), 'Clinical Reasoning Skills of Speech and Language Therapy Students', *International Journal of Language and Communication Disorders*, 42 (Suppl. 1): 103–23.

Hocking, C., and Ness, E. (2002), *Revised Minimum Standards for the Education of Occupational Therapists*, Perth, Western Australia: World Federation of Occupational Therapists.

Hong, C.S., and Harrison, D. (eds) (2004), *Tools for Continuing Professional Development*, Salisbury (Wiltshire): Quay Books.

Hooper, C. (2002), 'Welcome to the Index Page of Web Therapy Teaching'. Available at: www.unc.edu/~chooper/classes/voice/webtherapy/index. html.

Hughes, L. (2006), 'The UK Government's Role in IPE', paper delivered to All Together Better Health III, Conference, 10–12 April, Imperial College, London.

Huish, E., and McMorran, P. (2005), 'Interprofessional Learning in Practice with Clinical Simulation', paper given at the Interprofessional Learning Conference, 20 June, Bradford.

Hunter, B. (2004), 'Conflicting Ideologies as a Source of Emotion Work in Midwifery', *Midwifery*, 20 (3): 261–72.

Hunter, L.P., and Hunter, L.A. (2006), 'Story-Telling as an Educational Strategy for Midwifery Students', *Journal of Midwifery and Women's Health*, 51 (4): 273–8.

International Association of Schools of Social Work/International Federation of Social Workers (2001), *International Definition of Social Work*, Addis Ababa: IASSSW. Available at: www.iasssw-aiefs.org.

International Confederation of Midwives (ICM) (1998), *International Code of Ethics for Midwives*, The Hague: ICM.

International Council of Nurses (n.d.), 'Definition of Nursing'. Available at: http://www.icn.ch/definition.htm (accessed July 2007).

International Federation of Social Workers (IFSW) (2000), 'Ethics in Social Work, Statement of Principles'. Available at: http://www.ifsw.org/en/ p38000324.html.

Jarvis, P., and Gibson, S. (1997), *The Teacher Practitioner and Mentor in Nursing, Midwifery and Health Visiting*, Cheltenham: Stanley Thornes.

Jasper, M. (1996), 'The Portfolio Workbook as a Strategy for Student-Centred Learning', in G. Rolfe, *Closing the Theory–Practice Gap: A new paradigm for nursing*, Oxford: Butterworth Heinemann.

Jasper, M. (2003), *Beginning Reflective Practice: Foundations in nursing and health care*, Cheltenham: Nelson Thornes.

Jensen, G.M., Shepard, K.F., Gwyer, J., and Hack, L.M. (1992), 'Attribute Dimensions that Distinguish Master and Novice Physical Therapy Clinicians in Orthopedic Settings', *Physical Therapy*, 72 (10): 711–22.

Johns, C. (1998), 'Opening the Doors of Perception', in C. Johns and D. Freshwater (eds), *Transforming Nursing through Reflective Practice*, Oxford: Blackwell Science (pp. 1–20).

Johns, C. (2004), *Becoming a Reflective Practitioner: A reflective and holistic approach to clinical nursing, practice development and clinical supervision* (1st edn 2000), Oxford: Blackwell Science.

Johns, C., and Freshwater, D. (1998), *Transforming Nursing through Reflective Practice*, Oxford: Blackwell Science.

Jordan, B. (1989), 'Cosmopolitical Obstetrics: Some insights from the training of traditional midwives', *Social Science and Medicine*, 28 (9): 925–44.

Keady, J., and Adams, T. (2001), 'Community Mental Health Nursing and Dementia Care, Article 1', *Journal of Dementia Care*, 9 (1): 35–8.

Keady, J., Clarke, C.L., and Adams, T. (eds) (2003), *Community Mental Health Nursing and Dementia Care: Practice perspectives*, Maidenhead: Open University Press.

Keady, J., Clarke, C.L., and Page, S. (eds) (2007), *Partnerships in Community Mental Health Nursing and Dementia Care: Practice perspectives*, Maidenhead: Open University Press/McGraw-Hill.

Kember, D. (ed.) (2001), *Reflective Teaching and Learning in the Health Professions*, Oxford: Blackwell Science.

Kent, J., MacKeith, N., and Maggs, C. (1994), *Direct but Different: An evaluation of the implementation of pre-registration midwifery education in England: A research project for the Department of Health*, Bath: Maggs Research Associates Ltd.

Kilminster, S.M., Delmotte, A., Frith, H., Jolly, B.C., Stark, P., and Howdle, P.D., (2001), 'Teaching in the New NHS: The specialised ward-based teacher', *Medical Education*, 35 (5): 437–43.

Kilminster, S.M., Hale, C., Lascelles, M., Morris, P., Roberts, T., Stark, P., Sowter, J., and Thistlewaite, J. (2003), 'Can Interprofessional Education Workshops Affect Interprofessional Communications?', *Journal of Interprofessional Care*, 17 (2): 199–200.

Kitwood, T. (1997), *Dementia Reconsidered: The person comes first*, Buckingham: Open University Press.

Kitzinger, S. (2000), *Rediscovering Birth*, London: Little, Brown.

Knowles, M. (1990), *The Adult Learner: A neglected species* (4th edn), Houston, TX: Gulf.

Knowles, M.S., Holton III, E.F., and Swanson, R.A. (1998), *The Adult Learner (5th edn), The definitive classic in adult education and human resource development*, Woburn, MA: Butterworth Heinemann.

Kolb, D.A. (1984), *Experiential Learning as the Source of Learning and Development*, Englewood Cliffs, NJ: Prentice-Hall.

Kurtz, S.M., Silverman, J., and Draper, J. (2005), *Teaching and Learning Communication Skills in Medicine* (2nd edn), Abingdon: Radcliffe.

Lamb, A., and Lewandowski, J. (2005), 'Patients at the Centre of Interprofessional Education', paper given at the Interprofessional Learning Conference, 20 June, Bradford.

Laming, Lord (2003), *The Victoria Climbié Inquiry*, Norwich: HMSO.

Lancet Commission (1932), *Commission on Nursing (Chair: The Earl of Crawford and Belcarres): Final Report*, London: The Lancet.

Lathlean, J. (1997), *The Lecturer Practitioner in Action*, Oxford: Butterworth Heinemann.

Lathlean, J., Burgess, A., Coldham, T., Gibson, C., Herbert, L., Levett-Jones, T., Simons, L., and Tee, S. (2006), 'Experiences of Service User and Carer Participation in Health Care Education', *Nurse Education Today*, 26 (8): 732–7.

Lave, J., and Wenger, E. (1991), *Situated Learning: Legitimate peripheral participation*, Cambridge: Cambridge University Press.

Leathard, A. (1994), *Going Interprofessional*, London: Routledge.

Leiba, T., and Leonard, K. (2003), 'Interprofessional Education: The reality of an interprofessional practice teacher course', *Journal of Practice Teaching*, 4 (3): 14–28.

Leitch, S. (Lord) (2006), *The Leitch Review of Skills: Prosperity for all in the global economy – world-class skills*, London: Department for Education and Schools.

Levy, M., Oates, T., Hunt, M., and Dobson, F. (1989), *Work-Based Learning, Information Sheet 2*, London: London University.

Lewin, K. (1936), *Principles of Topological Psychology*, trans. F. Heider and G.M. Heider, in W.F. Hill (1990), *Learning: A survey of psychological interpretations*, New York: Harper & Row (pp. 106–12).

Lindquist, I., Engardt, M., Garnham, L., Poland, F., and Richardson, B. (2006), 'Physiotherapy Students' Professional Identity on the Edge of Working Life', *Medical Teacher*, 28 (3): 270–76.

Lishman, J. (1994), *Communication in Social Work*, Basingstoke: Macmillan.

Lishman, J. (2002), 'Personal and Professional Development in Social Work', in R. Adams, L. Dominelli and M. Payne, *Themes, Issues and Critical Debates* (2nd edition), Basingstoke: Palgrave.

Lishman, J. (2007a), 'Research, Evaluation and Evidence-Based Practice', in J. Lishman (ed.), *Handbook for Practice Learning in Social Work and Social Care: Knowledge and theory*, London: Jessica Kingsley.

Lishman, J. (ed.) (2007b), *Handbook for Practice Learning in Social Work and Social Care: Knowledge and theory*, London: Jessica Kingsley.

Lorenzo, T., Duncan, M., Buchanan, H., and Alsop, A. (eds) (2006), *Practice and Service Learning in Occupational Therapy: Enhancing potential in context*, Chichester: John Wiley & Sons.

Low, H., and Weinstein, J. (2000), 'Interprofessional Education', in R. Pierce and J. Weinstein (eds), *Innovative Education and Training for Care Professionals: A providers' guide*, London, Jessica Kingsley (pp. 205–20).

Loxton, J., Lishman, J., Love, A., and Bruce, L. (2004), *Practice Audit: Agency-based practice learning opportunities*, Edinburgh: SIESWE.

McAllister, L., and Lincoln, M. (2004), *Clinical Education in Speech and Language Pathology*, London: Whurr.

McAllister, L., Lincoln, M., McLeod, S., and Maloney, D. (1997), *Facilitating Learning in Clinical Settings*, Cheltenham: Stanley Thornes.

MacDonald, G., and Sheldon, B. (1998), 'Changing One's Mind: The final frontier?', *Issues in Social Work Education*, 18 (1): 3–25.

Mackenzie, A., Craik, C., Tempest, S., Cordingley, K., Buckingham, I., and Hale, S. (2007), 'Interprofessional Learning in Practice: The student experience', *British Journal of Occupational Therapy*, 70 (8): 358–61.

Macleod Clark, J., Maben, J., and Jones, K. (1997), 'Project 2000: Perceptions of the philosophy and practice of nursing: preparation for practice', *Journal of Advanced Nursing*, 26 (2): 246–56.

Maggs, C.R. (1981), 'Control Mechanisms and the New Nurses, 1981–1914', *Nursing Times*, Occasional Paper, 77 (36): 97–100.

Maggs, C.R., and Rapport, F. (1996), 'Getting a Job and Growing in Confidence in the Dual Experience of Newly Qualified Midwives Prepared by the Pre-Registration Route', *Nursing Times Research*, 1 (1): 68–78.

Mandsley, G. (1999), 'Do We All Mean the Same Thing by Problem-Based Learning? A review of concepts and a formulation of ground rules', *Academic Medicine*, 74 (2): 178–85.

Manthorpe, J., Iliffe, S., and Eden, A. (2003), 'Early Recognition of Dementia by Nurses', *Journal of Advanced Nursing*, 44 (2): 183–91.

Maran, N.J., and Glavin, R.J. (2003), 'Low- to High-Fidelity Simulation – A continuum of medical education?', *Medical Education*, 37 (1): 22–8.

Marsh, P., and Triseliotis, J. (1996), *Ready to Practise? Social Workers and Probation Officers: Their training and first year in work*, Aldershot: Avebury.

Mattick, K., and Bligh, J. (2006), 'Undergraduate Ethics Teaching: Revisiting the consensus statement', *Medical Education*, 40 (5): 329–32.

Mattingly, C., and Fleming, M.H. (1994), *Clinical Reasoning: Forms of inquiry in a therapeutic practice*, Philadelphia, PA: F.A. Davis.

May, N., Veitch, L., McIntosh, J.B., and Alexander, M.F. (1997), *Preparation for Practice. Evaluation of nurse and midwife education in Scotland, 1992 programmes*, Glasgow: Department of Nursing and Community Health, Glasgow Caledonian University. (Research funded by the National Board for Nursing, Midwifery and Health Visiting for Scotland.)

Mead, G.H. (1934), *Mind, Self and Society*, Chicago: University of Chicago Press.

Melia, K.M. (1984), 'Student Nurses' Construction of Occupational Socialisation', *Sociology of Health and Illness*, 6 (2): 132–51.

Melia, K.M. (1987), *Learning and Working. The occupational socialization of nurses*, London: Tavistock.

Meyler, E., and Trenoweth, S. (2007), *Succeeding in Nursing and Midwifery Education*, Chichester: John Wiley & Sons.

Mezirow, J. (1991), *Transformative Dimensions in Adult Learning*, San Francisco: Jossey-Bass.

Milburn, A. (2001), 'Foreword', in *Building the Information Core: Implementing the NHS Plan*, London: DoH.

Miller, C., Freeman, M., and Ross, N. (2001), *Interprofessional Practice in Health and Social Care*, London: Arnold.

Miller, C., Woolf, C., and Mackintosh, N. (2006), *Evaluation of Common Learning Pilots and Allied Health Professions First Wave Sites*. Research commissioned by DoH. Available from: Prof. C Miller, University of Brighton, Centre for Nursing and Midwifery Research, Mayfield House, Village Way, Brighton, East Sussex, BN1 9PH.

Miller, G.E. (1990), 'The Assessment of Clinical Skills/Competence/ Performance', *Academic Medicine* (Suppl.), 65: S63–S67.

Modernising Medical Careers (MMC), website at: http://www.mmc.com.

Mohr, P., Bass, G., and Schill, M.J. (2006), 'Model for the Development and Evaluation of a Family-Centred Multi-Disciplinary Course in Paediatric Intervention for Children with Disabilities', paper presented at All Together Better Health III, Conference, 10–12 April 2006, Imperial College, London.

Moon, J. (2000), *Reflection in Learning and Professional Development: Theory and practice*, London: Kogan Page.

Morago, P. (2006), 'Evidence-Based Practice: From medicine to social work', *European Journal of Social Work*, 9 (4): 461–77.

Morgan, R. (2000), 'Lifelong Learning', in D. Fraser (ed.), *Professional Studies for Midwifery Practice*, Edinburgh: Churchill Livingstone.

Morley, M. (2007), 'Developing a Preceptorship Programme for Newly Qualified Occupational Therapists: Action research', *British Journal of Occupational Therapy*, 70 (8): 330–38.

Morris, J. (2002), 'Current Issues of Accountability in Physiotherapy and Higher Education: Implications for physiotherapy educators', *Physiotherapy*, 88 (6): 354–63.

Morton-Cooper, A., and Palmer, A. (2000), *Mentorship, Preceptorship and Clinical Supervision: A guide to professional roles in clinical practice*, Oxford: Blackwell Science.

Murdoch-Eaton, D., Ellershaw, J., Garden, A., Newble, D., Perry, M., Robinson, L., Smith, J., Stark, P., and Whittle, S. (2004), 'Student-Selected Components in the Undergraduate Medical Curriculum: A multi-institutional consensus on purpose', *Medical Teacher*, 26 (1): 33–8.

Muzumdar, K., and Atthar, R. (2002), 'Social Work Placements in Police Stations: A force for change', in S.M. Shardlow and M. Doel (eds), *Learning to Practise Social Work: International approaches*, London: Jessica Kingsley (pp. 43–58).

National Audit Office (NAO) (1992), *Nursing Education: Implementation of Project 2000 in England*, London: HMSO.

National Audit Office (NAO) (2001), *Educating and Training the Future Health Professional Workforce for England (HC277)* (NAO's report to Parliament), London: Stationery Office.

National Audit Office (NAO) (2007), *Improving Services and Support for People with Dementia*, London: Stationery Office.

National Health Service Education for Scotland (n.d.), *The Development of Quality Standards for Practice Placements: Final report*, Edinburgh: NHS Scotland.

National Health Service Executive/Committee of Vice Chancellors and Principals (NHSE/CVCP) (2000), *NHS Executive/Committee of Vice Chancellors and Principals – A partnership statement*, London: NHS and CVCP.

National Institute for Health and Clinical Excellence (NICE), website at: http://www.nice.org.uk/ (accessed 4 December 2006).

National Institute for Health and Clinical Excellence/Social Care Institute for Excellence (NICE/SCIE) (2007), *Dementia: Supporting people with dementia and their carers in health and social care. NICE clinical practice guideline 42*, London: NICE.

Newble, D., and Cannon, R. (2001), *A Handbook for Medical Teachers* (4th edn), Lancaster: Kluwer Academic Publishers.

Newman, M. (2003), *A Pilot Systematic Review and Meta-Analysis on the Effectiveness of Problem-Based Learning*, Newcastle-upon-Tyne: Higher Education Academy Subject Centre for Medicine, Dentistry and Veterinary Medicine (Medev).

Nicol, M., and Glen, S. (eds) (1999), *Learning Clinical Skills: Return of the practical room*, Basingstoke: Palgrave Press.

Nixon, I., Penn, D., and Shewell, J. (2006), *Workplace Learning in the North East: Report to HEFCE by the KSA Partnership*, Wolsingham, County Durham: KSA Partnership.

Nolan, P. (2003), 'Voices from the Past: The historical alignment of dementia care to nursing', in J. Keady, C.L. Clarke and T. Adams (eds), *Community Mental Health Nursing and Dementia Care: Practice perspectives*, Maidenhead: Open University Press.

Norman, G.R., and Brooks, L.R. (1997), 'The Non-Analytical Basis of Clinical Reasoning', *Advances in Health Sciences Education*, 2 (2): 173–84.

Nursing and Midwifery Council (NMC) (n.d.), *Updates on Consultations, Fitness for Practice and Registration*. Available at: www.nmc-org.uk (accessed 8 August 2007).

Nursing and Midwifery Council (NMC) (2001), *Education and Training: Article 15 of the Statutory Instrument, of the Nursing and Midwifery Council Order*, London: NMC.

Nursing and Midwifery Council (NMC) (2004a), *Standards of Proficiency for Pre-Registration Midwifery Education*, London: NMC. *(Replaced with*

Standards for Pre-Registration Midwifery Education *(2009) – information used here remains the same.)*

Nursing and Midwifery Council (NMC) (2004b), *Midwives Rules and Standards*, London: NMC.

Nursing and Midwifery Council (NMC) (2004c), *Code of Professional Conduct: Standards for conduct, performance and ethics*, London: NMC.

Nursing and Midwifery Council (NMC) (2004d), *Standards of Proficiency for Specialist Community Public Health Nurses*, London: NMC.

Nursing and Midwifery Council (NMC) (2004e), *Standards for Proficiency for Pre-Registration Nurse Education*, London: NMC.

Nursing and Midwifery Council (2004f), *Standards of Proficiency for Pre-Registration Nursing Education. Standards 02.04.* Available at: http://www.nmc-uk.org/aFrameDisplay.aspx?DocumentID=328.

Nursing and Midwifery Council (NMC) (2005), *Statutory Instrument 2005: No. 3354. Health Care and Associated Professions. The Nursing and Midwifery Council (Education, Registration and Registration Appeals) (Amendment) Rules Order of Council*, London: NMC.

Nursing and Midwifery Council (NMC) (2006a), *Standards for the Preparation and Practice of Supervisors of Midwives*, London: NMC.

Nursing and Midwifery Council (NMC) (2006b), *Standards to Support Learning and Assessment in Practice: NMC standards for mentors, practice teachers and teachers*, London: NMC.

Nursing and Midwifery Council (NMC) (2006c), *The PREP Handbook*, London: NMC.

Nursing and Midwifery Council (NMC) (2006d), *Preceptorship Advice Sheet.* Available at: www.nmc-uk.org (accessed August 2007).

Nursing and Midwifery Council (NMC) (2006e), *Statistical Analysis of the Register, 1st April 2005–31st March 2006*, London: NMC.

Nursing and Midwifery Council (NMC) (2007a), *The Code: Standards of conduct, performance and ethics for nurses and midwives*, London: NMC. Available at: http://www.nmc-uk.org/aArticle.aspx?ArticleID=3056 (accessed 7 April 2007).

Nursing and Midwifery Council (NMC) (2007b), *Statistical Analysis of the Register, 1stApril 2006–31st March 2007.* Available at: http://www.nmc-uk.org/aFrameDisplay.aspx?DocumentID=3600.

Nursing and Midwifery Council (NMC) (2007c), *Annual Report*, London: NMC.

Nursing and Midwifery Council (NMC) (2008a), website at: www.nmc.uk.org (accessed 2 August 2008).

Nursing and Midwifery Council (NMC) (2008b), *Standards to Support Learning and Assessment in Practice: NMC standards for mentors, practice teachers and teachers*, London: NMC.

O'Brien, S. (2003), *Report of the Caleb Ness Enquiry*, Edinburgh: Edinburgh and the Hollmans Child Protection Committee.

O'Halloran, C., Hean, S., Humphris, D., and Macleod Clark, J. (2006), 'Developing Common Learning: The New Generation Project: undergraduate curriculum model', *Journal of Interprofessional Care*, 20 (1): 12–28.

O'Neill, P.A., Metcalfe, D., and David, T.J. (1999), 'The Core Content of the Undergraduate Curriculum in Manchester', *Medical Education*, 33 (2): 121–9.

O'Neill, P.A., Willis, S.C., and Jones, A. (2002), 'A Model of How Students Link Problem-Based Learning with Clinical Experience through "Elaboration"', *Academic Medicine*, 77 (6): 552–61.

Osler, W. (1932), *Aequanimitas: With other addresses to medical students, nurses and practitioners of medicine* (3rd rev. edn), New York: McGraw-Hill. Orig. publ. 1905.

Owen, S., Ferguson, K., and Baguely, I. (2005), 'The Clinical Activity of Mental Health Lecturers in Higher Education Institutions', *Mental Health Practice*, 8 (9): 40–45.

Parker, J., Doel, M., and Whitfield, J. (2006), 'Does Practice Learning Assist the Recruitment and Retention of Staff?', *Research, Policy and Planning*, 24 (3): 179–96.

PATSy (2003), 'Welcome to the PATSy Website: Data base for teaching and research'. Available at: www.patsy.ac.uk/main.html.

Pavlov, I.P. (1927), *Conditioned Reflexes*, Oxford: Oxford University Press.

Pearce, P. (2005), 'The Interprofessional Learning Project', paper presented to the Interprofessional Learning Conference, Bradford 2005. Available at: www.virtualfamily.leeds.ac.uk.

Polanyi, M., and Prosch, H. (1973), *Meaning*, Chicago: University of Chicago Press.

Pollard, N., Alsop, A., and Kronenberg, F. (2005), 'Reconceptualising Occupational Therapy', *British Journal of Occupational Therapy*, 68 (11): 524–6.

Pollard, N., and Sakellariou, D. (2007), 'Occupation, Education and Community-Based Rehabilitation', *British Journal of Occupational Therapy*, 70 (4): 171–4.

Portes, A. (1998), 'Social Capital: Its origins and applications in modern sociology', *Annual Review of Sociology*, 24 (1): 24.

Postgraduate Medical Education and Training Board (PMETB), website at: http://www.pmetb.org.uk.

Preparation for Interprofessional Education Project (PIPE) (2006), 'The PIPE Project'. Available at: www.PIPE.ac.uk.

Pugh, R. (2000), *Rural Social Work*, Lyme Regis: Russell House.

Pulsford, D., Hope, K., and Thompson, R. (2007), 'Higher Education Provision for Professionals Working with People with Dementia: A scoping exercise', *Nurse Education Today*, 27 (1): 5–13.

Putnam, R.D. (1993), 'The Prosperous Community. Social capital and public life', *The American Prospect*, 4 (13): 35–42.

Putnam, R.D. (2000), *Bowling Alone: The collapse and revival of the American community*, New York: Simon & Schuster.

Quality Assurance Agency for Higher Education (QAA) (n.d.), 'Quality Assurance of Healthcare Education'. Available at: www.qaa.ac.uk (accessed 8 August 2007).

Quality Assurance Agency for Higher Education (QAA) (2001a), *Benchmark Statements for Midwifery*, Cheltenham: QAA.

Quality Assurance Agency for Higher Education (QAA) (2001b), *Framework for Higher Education Qualifications in England, Wales and Northern Ireland*, Cheltenham: QAA.

Quality Assurance Agency for Higher Education (QAA) (2003), *Code of Practice for Quality Assurance of Academic Quality and Standards in Higher Education. Programme approval, monitoring and review*. Available at: http://www.qaa.ac.uk/academicinfrastructure/codeOfPractice/default.asp.

Quality Assurance Agency for Higher Education (QAA) (2004), *The Partnership Quality Assurance Framework for Healthcare Education in England: A consultation*, Gloucester: Major Review Group, QAA.

Race, P. (1998), *The Lecturer's Toolkit* (2nd edn), London: Kogan Page.

Repper, J., and Breeze, J. (2004), 'A Review of the Literature on User and Carer Involvement in the Training and Education of Health Professionals', on the website of the University of Sheffield, at: http://www.shef.ac.uk/content/1/c6/01/34/62/Finalreport.pdf (accessed 20 March 2008).

Reynolds, B.C. (1942), *Learning and Teaching in the Practice of Social Work*, New York: Rinehart & Company.

Reynolds, B.C. (1965), *Learning and Teaching in the Practice of Social Work* (2nd edn), New York: Russell & Russell.

Reynolds, F. (2003), 'Initial Experiences of Interprofessional Problem-Based Learning: A comparison of male and female students' views', *Journal of Interprofessional Care*, 17 (1): 35–44.

Richardson, B. (1999), 'Professional Development 2. Professional knowledge and situated learning in the workplace', *Physiotherapy*, 85 (9): 467–74.

Richardson, B., Higgs, J., and Arbrant Dahlgren, M. (2004), 'Recognizing Practice Epistemology in the Health Professions', in J. Higgs, B. Richardson and M. Arbrant Dahlgren (eds), *Developing Practice Knowledge for Health Professionals*, Oxford: Butterworth Heinemann (pp. 127–46).

Ritchie, J.H. (chair) (1994), *Report of the Inquiry into the Care and Treatment of Christopher Clunis*, London: HMSO.

Robotham, A., and Sheldrake, D. (2000), 'Reflective Practice in Health Visiting', in A. Robotham and D. Sheldrake (eds), *Health Visiting: Specialist and higher level practice*, London: Churchill Livingstone (pp. 129–48).

Rogers, A. (1996), *Teaching Adults* (2nd edn), Buckingham: Open University Press.

Rogers, C. (1969), *Freedom to Learn*, Columbus, OH: Merrill.

Rogoff, B. (1990), 'Shared Thinking and Guided Participation: Conclusions and speculations', in B. Rogoff, *Apprenticeship in Thinking: Cognitive development in social context*, New York: Oxford University Press (Ch. 10, pp. 189–210).

Rogoff, B. (1995), 'Observing Socio-Cultural Activity on Three Planes: Participatory appropriation, guided participation, and apprenticeship', in J.V. Wertsch, P. Del Rio and A. Alvarez (eds), *Sociocultural Studies of the Mind*, Cambridge: Cambridge University Press (pp. 139–63).

Rosza, M., and Lincoln, M. (2005), 'Collaboration in Clinical Education', in M. Rose and D. Best (eds), *Transforming Practice through Clinical Education, Professional Supervision and Mentoring*, London: Elsevier Churchill Livingstone (pp. 229–47).

Rounce, K., and Workman, B. (eds) (2005), *Work-Based Learning in Health Care*, Chichester: Kingsham Press.

Royal College of Midwives (RCM) (n.d.), 'Midwifery Practice, Standards and Audit'. Available at: www.rcm.org.uk (accessed 8 August 2007).

Royal College of Midwives (RCM) (2003), *Valuing Practice: A springboard for midwifery education*, London: RCM.

Royal College of Midwives (RCM) (2008), website at: www.rcm.org.uk (accessed 2 August 2008).

Royal College of Nursing (RCN) (1964), *A Reform of Nursing Education: First report of a special committee on nurse education* (Chair: Lord Platt), London: RCN.

Royal College of Nursing (RCN) (1971), *Evidence to the Committee on Nursing*, London: RCN.

Royal College of Nursing (RCN) (1984), *The Education of Nurses: A dispensation. The Report of the Commission on Nursing Education* (Chair: Sir Harry Judge), London: RCN.

Royal College of Nursing (RCN) (2003), 'Defining Nursing'. Available at: http://www.rcn.org.uk/downloads/definingnursing/definingnursing-a4.pdf (accessed July 2007).

Royal College of Nursing/Age Concern (2008), *An Ageing Population: Education and practice preparation for nursing students learning to work with older people*, London: RCN.

Royal College of Physicians (RCP) (1981), *Organic Mental Impairment in the Elderly: A report of the Royal College of Physicians by the College Committee on Geriatrics*, London: Royal College of Physicians.

Royal College of Physicians (RCP) (2005), 'Doctors in Society: Medical professionalism in a changing world: Report of a Working Party of the RCP of London'. Available at: www.rcplondon.ac.uk/pubs/brochure. aspx?e=75 (accessed January 2006).

Royal College of Physicians (RCP), website, education section, at: http:// www.rcplondon.ac.uk/education.asp (accessed January 2006).

Royal College of Speech and Language Therapists (RCSLT) (1995), *Forums on Tutoring for Experiential Learning: Clinical experience*, London: RCSLT.

Royal College of Speech and Language Therapists (RCSLT) (2001), *Guidelines on the Accreditation of Courses leading to a Qualification in Speech and Language Therapy*, London: RCSLT.

Royal College of Speech and Language Therapists (RCSLT) (2006a), *Communicating Quality, 3*, London: RCSLT.

Royal College of Speech and Language Therapists (RCSLT) (2006b), *National Standards for Practice-Based Learning*, London: RCSLT.

Ruiz, J.G., Mintzer, M.J., and Leipzig, R.M. (2006), 'The Impact of E-Learning in Medical Education', *Academic Medicine*, 81 (3): 207–12.

Ryan, S. (1995), 'Teaching Clinical Reasoning to Occupational Therapists in Clinical Education', in J. Higgs and M. Jones (eds), *Clinical Reasoning in the Health Professions*, Oxford: Butterworth Heinemann (pp. 246–57).

Ryan, S. (2001), 'Perspectives on Widening University Access: Critical voices of newly qualified occupational therapists', *British Journal of Occupational Therapy*, 64 (11): 534–40.

Sackett, D.L., Straus, S.E., Richardson, W.S., Rosenberg, W., and Haynes, R.B. (2002), *Evidence-Based Medicine; How to practice and teach EBM* (2nd edn) Edinburgh: Churchill Livingstone (1st edn 1997).

Sajiwandani, J. (1993), 'Exploring the Process of Learning in Human Ecology', *Nurse Education Today*, 13 (5): 349–61.

Sandars, J. (2006), *e-Learning for GP Educators*, Abingdon: Radcliffe Publishing.

Savin-Baden, M. (2000), *Problem-Based Learning in Higher Education: Untold stories*, Buckingham: SRHE/Open University Press.

Schmidt, H.G., Norman, G.R., and Boshuizen, H.P. (1990), 'A Cognitive Perspective on Medical Expertise: Theory and implication', *Academic Medicine*, 65 (10): 611–21.

Schön, D. (1983), *The Reflective Practitioner: How professionals think in action*, New York: Basic Books (reissued Aldershot: Arena, 1994).

Schön, D. (1987), *Educating the Reflective Practitioner. Toward a new design for teaching and learning in the professions*, San Francisco, CA: Jossey-Bass (2nd edn 1991).

School of Allied Health Professions (2006–07), *BSc. Physiotherapy Placement Educators' Handbook*, Norwich: University of East Anglia.

Schutz, A. (1970), 'On Phenomenology and Social Relations', in H.R. Wagner (ed.), *Selected Writings*, Chicago: University of Chicago Press.

Scottish Executive (2003), *The Framework for Social Work Education in Scotland (SIESWE)*, Edinburgh: COSLA, QAA, SSSC and Scottish Executive. Also available at: http://www.scotland.gov.uk.

Scottish Executive (2004), *Report of the Inspection of Scottish Borders Council Social Work Services for People Affected by Learning Disabilities*, Edinburgh: Scottish Executive.

Scottish Executive (2006a), *Changing Lives: The report of the 21st Century Social Work Review*, Edinburgh: Scottish Executive.

Scottish Executive (2006b), *Rights, Relationships and Recovery: The report of the National Review of Mental Health Nursing in Scotland*, Edinburgh: Scottish Executive.

Scottish Institute for Excellence in Social Work Education (SIESWE) (2005), *Learning for Effective and Ethical Practice (LEEP): Comprehensive knowledge review*, Dundee: SIESWE.

Scottish Social Services Council (SSSC) (2003), *Codes of Practice for Social Service Workers and Employers*, Dundee: SSSC.

Scottish Social Services Council (SSSC) (2006), *Key Capabilities in Child Care and Protection*, Dundee: SSSC.

Scottish Social Services Council and Scottish Institute for Excellence in Social Work Education (SSSC/SIESWE) (2004), *Confidence in Practice Learning*, Edinburgh: Scottish Executive.

Seagraves, L., Osborne, N., Neal, P., Dockrell, R., Hartshorn, C., and Boyd, A. (1996), *Learning in Smaller Companies* (final report), Stirling: University of Stirling Educational Policy and Development.

Shardlow, S.M., and Doel, M. (1996), *Practice Learning and Teaching*, Basingstoke: Macmillan.

Shribman, S. (2007), *Making it Better: For mother and baby – Clinical case for change* (report), London: HMSO.

Shulman, L.S. (1986), 'Those who Understand: Knowledge growth in teaching', *Educational Researcher*, 15 (1): 4–14.

Sim, J., and Richardson, B. (2004), 'The Use and Generation of Practice Knowledge in the Context of Regulating Systems and Moral Frameworks', in J. Higgs, B. Richardson and M. Arbrant Dahlgren (eds), *Developing Practice Knowledge for Health Professionals*, Oxford: Butterworth Heinemann.

Simmons, S., and Brooker, C. (1986), *Community Psychiatric Nursing: A social perspective*, London: William Heinemann.

Skills for Health (2006), 'Assuring and Enhancing the Quality of Healthcare Education. Interim Standards'. Available at: www.skillsforhealth.org.uk.

Skills for Health (2007), 'Public Health Career Framework – Ongoing consultation'. Available at: www.skillsforhealth.org.uk (accessed October 2007).

Smith, S.R. (1999), 'AMEE Guide No, 14: Outcome-based education: Part 2 – Planning, implementation and evaluating a competency-based curriculum', *Medical Teacher*, 21 (1): 15–22.

Social Care Workforce Research Unit (2003), *Social Care Workforce Research: Needs and priorities*, London: Social Care Workforce Research Unit, Kings College.

Sookhoo, M.L., and Biott, C. (2002), 'Learning at Work: Midwives judging progress in labour', *Learning in Health and Social Care*, 1 (2): 75–85.

Spector, N. (2006), 'Systematic Review of Studies of Nursing Education Outcomes: An evolving review'. Available at: https://www.ncsbn.org/Final_Sys_Review_04_06.pdf (accessed 20 May 2008).

Spouse, J. (1990), *An Ethos for Learning*, London: Scutari Press.

Spouse, J. (1996), 'The Effective Mentor: A model for student-centred learning in clinical practice', *Nursing Times Research*, 1 (2): 120–33.

Spouse, J. (1998a), 'Scaffolding Student Learning in Clinical Practice', *Nurse Education Today*, 18 (4): 259–66.

Spouse, J. (1998b), 'Learning to Nurse through Legitimate Peripheral Participation', *Nurse Education Today*, 18 (5): 345–51.

Spouse, J. (2002), 'Bridging Theory and Practice in the Supervisory Relationship: A sociocultural perspective', *Journal of Advanced Nursing*, 33 (4): 512–22.

Spouse, J. (2003), *Professional Learning in Nursing*, Oxford: Blackwell.

Stansfield, J. (2004), 'Education for Competent Speech and Language Therapy Practice', in S.M. Brumfitt (ed.), *Innovations in Professional Education for Speech and Language Therapy*, London and Philadelphia, PA: Whurr (pp. 3–28).

Stephenson, R. (1998), 'Can Clinical Reasoning be an Effective Tool for CPD?', *British Journal of Therapy and Rehabilitation*, 5 (6): 325–9.

Stern, D. (2006), *Measuring Medical Professionalism*, Oxford: Oxford University Press.

Symonds, R., and Hunt, S. (1996), *The Midwife and Society: Perspectives, policies and practice*, Basingstoke: Macmillan.

Taylor, I. (1997), *Developing Learning in Professional Education: Partnerships for practice (Society for Research into Higher Education)*, Buckingham: SRHE and Open University Press.

Tew, J., Gell, C., and Foster, S. (2004), 'Learning from Experience: Involving service users and carers in mental health education and training', Higher Education Academy/NIMHE/Trent Workforce Development Confederation. Available at: http://www.mhhe.heacademy.ac.uk/docs/lfeguide/learningfromexperience.pdf (accessed 11 April 2006).

Thomas, S., Cross, J., Harden, B., and ten Hove, R. (2003), 'Competence in On-Call Physiotherapy, 1. Designing a framework', *International Journal of Therapy and Rehabilitation*, 10 (7): 321–7.

Thompson, R., Capstick, A., Heyward, T., Pulsford, D., and Hope, K. (2007), 'Involving People with Dementia and their Carers in Professional Education', *Journal of Dementia Care*, 15 (4): 26–8.

Thompson, R., and Devenney, D. (2007), 'Training in Dementia for Primary Care Professionals: The role of the Admiral Nurse', *Primary Care*, 17 (3): 36–40.

Totten, C., and Pratt, J. (2001), 'Innovation in Fieldwork Education: Working with members of the homeless population in Glasgow', *British Journal of Occupational Therapy*, 64 (11): 559–63.

Towell, D. (1975), *Understanding Psychiatric Nursing*, London: RCN.

Trevithick, P. (2005), *Social Work Skills: A practice handbook*, Maidenhead: Open University Press.

Tuning Occupational Therapy Project Group (2008), *Reference Points for the Design and Delivery of Degree Programmes in Occupational Therapy*, Bilbao and Groningen: University of Deusto and University of Groningen.

Twinn, S., and Cowley, S. (1992), *The Principles of Health Visiting: A re-examination*, London: UKSC/CPHVA.

Underhill, D., with Betteridge, C., Harvey, B., and Patient, K. (2002), 'Learning Opportunities and Placements with Asylum Seekers', in S.M. Shardlow and M. Doel (eds), *Learning to Practise Social Work: International approaches*, London: Jessica Kingsley (pp. 77–90).

United Kingdom Central Council for Nursing, Midwifery and Health Visiting (UKCC) (1986), *Project 2000: A new preparation for practice*, London: UKCC.

United Kingdom Central Council for Nursing, Midwifery and Health Visiting (UKCC) (1989), *Project 2000: A new preparation for practice*, London: UKCC.

United Kingdom Central Council for Nursing, Midwifery and Health Visiting (UKCC) (1999a), *Commission for Nursing and Midwifery Education. Fitness for practice: Full report*, London: NMC.

United Kingdom Central Council for Nursing, Midwifery and Health Visiting (UKCC) (1999b), *Fitness for Practice* (Chair: Sir Leonard Peach) (known as the Peach Report), London: UKCC Commission for Nursing and Midwifery Education.

United Kingdom Central Council for Nursing, Midwifery and Health Visiting (UKCC) (2001), *Fitness for Practice and Purpose. The report of the UKCC's Post-Commission Development Group* (Chair: Valerie Morrison), London: The UKCC Commission for Nursing and Midwifery Education.

Van der Horst, M., Turpie, I., Nelson, W., Cole, B., Sammon, S., Sniderman, P., and Tremblay, M. (1995), 'St. Joseph's Community Health Centre

Model of Community-Based Interdisciplinary Health Care Team', *Health and Social Care in the Community*, 3: 33–42.

Vernon, D.T.A., and Blake, R.L. (1993), 'Does Problem-Based Learning Work? A meta-analysis of evaluative research', *Academic Medicine*, 68 (7): 550–63.

von Glasersfeld, E. (1995), *Radical Constructivism: A way of knowing and learning*, London: Falmer Press.

Vygotsky, L.S. (1978), *Mind in Society: The development of higher psychological processes*, eds M. Cole, V. John-Steiner, S. Scribner and E. Souberman, Cambridge, MA: Harvard University Press.

Wallace, M. (1999), *Lifelong Learning: PREP in action*, Edinburgh: Churchill Livingstone.

Watkins, M., and Redding, M. (2000), 'The Practice Teaching Award and Community Practice Teacher Programme' (Oxford Brookes University). Available at: www.swap.ac.uk/learning (accessed June 2006).

Watson, H., and Harris, B. (1999), *Supporting Students in Practice Placements in Scotland*. Research commissioned by the National Board for Nursing, Midwifery and Health Visiting for Scotland. Publ. Glasgow: Department of Nursing and Community Health, Glasgow Caledonian University.

Watson, R., Hogston, O., Norman, I., Simpson, A., Sanderson, D., O'Reilly, J., and Baulcomb, S. (2005), 'Quality Assurance in UK Nursing Education: Public protection in an era of streamlined assessment', *Nurse Education Today*, 25 (1): 49–55.

Weinstein, J. (1997), 'The Development of Shared Learning: Conspiracy or constructive development?', in J. Øvretveit, P. Mathias and T. Thompson (eds), *Interprofessional Working for Health and Social Care*, Basingstoke: Macmillan (pp. 131–56).

Weinstein, J. (1998), 'The Professions and their Interrelationships', in P. Mathias and T. Thompson (eds), *Standards and Learning Disability*, London: Ballière Tindall (pp. 323–42).

Wenger, E. (1998), *Communities of Practice, Learning, Meaning and Identity*, Cambridge: Cambridge University Press.

Wenger, E., McDermott, R., and Snyder, W. (2002), *Cultivating Communities of Practice*, Cambridge, MA: Harvard Business School Press.

Wertsch, J. (1991), *Voices of the Mind: A sociocultural approach to mediated action*, London: Harvester Wheatsheaf.

Wertsch, J., and Stone, C.H. (1979), 'A Social Interactional Analysis of Learning Disabilities Remediation', in B. Rogoff and J. Lave (eds), *Everyday Cognition: Its development in the social context*, Cambridge, MA: Harvard University Press. (Originally a paper presented at the International Conference of the Association for Children with Learning Disabilities, San Francisco.)

Westcott, L., and Rugg, S. (2001), 'The Computation of Fieldwork Achievement in Occupational Therapy Degrees: Measuring a minefield?', *British Journal of Occupational Therapy*, 64 (11): 541–7.

White, E. (1999a), 'Community Mental Health Nursing: An interpretation of history as a context for contemporary research', in J. McIntosh (ed.), *Research Issues in Community Nursing*, London: Macmillan (pp. 105–25).

White, E. (1999b), 'The 4th Quinquennial National Community Mental Health Nursing Census of England and Wales', *Australian and New Zealand Journal of Mental Health Nursing*, 8 (3): 86–92.

White, R. (1978), *Social Change and the Development of the Nursing Profession*, London: Kimpton.

White, R. (1984), 'Nursing: Past trends, future policies', *Journal of Advanced Nursing*, 9: 505–12.

Whittington, C. (2003a), 'Collaboration and Partnership in Context', in J. Weinstein, C. Whittington and T. Leiba (eds), *Collaboration in Social Work Practice*, London: Jessica Kingsley (pp. 13–38).

Whittington, C. (2003b), *Learning for Collaborative Practice with Other Professions and Agencies. A study to inform development of the Degree in Social Work*, London: DoH.

Whitworth, A., Franklin, S., and Dodd, B. (2004), 'Case-Based Problem Solving for Speech and Language Therapy Students', in S.M. Brumfitt (ed.), *Innovations in Professional Education for Speech and Language Therapy*, London and Philadelphia, PA: Whurr (pp. 29–50).

Wilby, H. (n.d.), *Perceptions of the Role Emerging Model of Fieldwork Education*, Cheshire & Merseyside Workforce Development Confederation.

Wilson-Barnett, J., Butterworth, T., White, E., Twinn, S., Davies, S., and Riley, L. (1995), 'Clinical Support and the Project 2000 Nursing Student: Factors influencing this process', *Journal of Advanced Nursing*, 21: 1152–8.

Wolf, F.R. (1993), 'Problem-Based Learning and Meta-Analysis: Can we see the forest through the trees?', *Academic Medicine*, 66 (7), 542–4.

Wong, K.Y., Kember, D., Chung, L.Y.F., and Yan, L. (1995), 'Assessing the Level of Student Reflection from Reflective Journals', *Journal of Advanced Nursing*, 22 (1): 48–57.

Wood, D. (2003), 'ABC of Learning and Teaching in Medicine: Problem-based learning', *British Medical Journal*, 326 (8): 328–30.

Wood, D., Bruner, J., and Ross, G. (1976), 'The Role of Tutoring in Problem Solving', *Journal of Child Psychology*, 17(2): 89–100.

World Bank (1999), 'What is Social Capital?'. Available at: http://www.worldbank.org/poverty/scapital/whatsc.htm (accessed 10 November 2007).

World Health Organization (2001), *The International Classification of Functioning, Disability and Health*, Geneva: WHO.

Young, A., Pearl, G., and Bowen, A. (2006), 'Challenges in Maximising Recruitment to an RCT through Working with a Service User Group', paper presented at 12th International Aphasia Rehabilitation Conference, Sheffield, UK.

Zwarenstein, M., Reeves, S., and Perrier, L. (2005), 'Effectiveness of Pre-Licensure Interprofessional Education and Post-Licensure Collaborative Interventions', *Journal of Interprofessional Care*, 19 (May), suppl. 1, 148–65.

Index